DEERING PLANTATION

DEERING PLANTATION

*Sixty Thousand Acres
in the Bootheel of Missouri*

Ophelia R. Wade

Ophelia R. Wade

Ophelia R. Wade
911 Osborn Ave.
Kennett, MO 63857-2154

Copyright © 1999 by Ophelia R. Wade.

Library of Congress Number: 99-091071
ISBN #: Hardcover 0-7388-0618-8
         Softcover 0-7388-0619-6

All rights reserved. No part of this book may be reproduced or transmitted in any form or by any means, electronic or mechanical, including photocopying, recording, or by any information storage and retrieval system, without permission in writing from the copyright owner.

This is a work of fiction. Names, characters, places and incidents either are the product of the author's imagination or are used fictitiously, and any resemblance to any actual persons, living or dead, events, or locales is entirely coincidental.

This book was printed in the United States of America.

To order additional copies of this book, contact:
Xlibris Corporation
1-888-7-XLIBRIS
www.Xlibris.com
Orders@Xlibris.com

CONTENTS

Introduction 11

SECTION ONE
DEERING—A LUMBER TOWN

Chapter One
    William Deering 17
Chapter Two
    The Deering Harvester Company 21
Chapter Three
    Pemiscot County Land 26
Chapter Four
    The History of Deering, Missouri 31
Chapter Five
    Dogskin and Vicksburg 41
Chapter Six
    My Life in Deering and Pondertown 43
Chapter Seven
    Deering: My Hometown 53
Chapter Eight
    Draining the Swamps 61
Chapter Nine
    COME TO "THE HEEL OF MISSOURI" 77
Chapter Ten
    Doctor Asier Jacob Speer 87
Chapter Eleven
    My Recollections of Deering 99

SECTION TWO
DEERING—AN AGRICULTURAL METROPOLIS

Chapter Twelve
    Charles B. Baker 107
Chapter Thirteen
    The Plantation of Deering 111
Chapter Fourteen
    The Farm Managers 117
Chapter Fifteen
    Mildred Callis Farr - School Teacher 127
Chapter Sixteen
    Sentimental Journey 133
Chapter Seventeen
    Dunklin County Land 148
Chapter Eighteen
    Villages on Highway 84 153
Chapter Nineteen
    "AUNT PAUL" 163
Chapter Twenty
    Gobler on the County Line Road 167
Chapter Twenty One
    Settlements in Dunklin County 180

SECTION THREE
DEERING—INDIVIDUAL OWNERSHIP

Chapter Twenty Two
    Alvin Thomas Earls 191
Chapter Twenty Three
    Deering Consolidated C-6 School 194
Chapter Twenty Four
    Deering Post Office 204
Chapter Twenty Five
    Deering Methodist Church 206

Chapter Twenty Six
  Eating Establishments in Deering 222
Chapter Twenty Seven
  Delta Ruritan Club 225
Chapter Twenty Eight
  My, How Deering Has Changed! 230

APPENDIX

1900 Federal Census Deering, Missouri 238
1910 Federal Census Deering, Missouri 242
1920 Federal Census Deering, Missouri 256

This book is dedicated to all the people who have ever been, or who now are, associated with the town of Deering, giving special emphasis to those people who assisted me in gathering this wealth of information for publication and prosperity.

INTRODUCTION

This book is entitled *Deering Plantation* as that is simply what the little place was. It does not adhere itself to hooped skirts, mint juleps and large white houses like we tend to associate with a southern plantation. It was a self-sufficent town, owned and maintained by the Wisconsin Lumber Company, a subsidiary of the International Harvester Company. William Deering was the man responsible for the beginning of the settlement, so it was named for him.

It began as a lumber town, built in the middle of swampy forest land with wild animals still in abundance. The little protrusion, which really belonged to Arkansas, was nicknamed the Heel of Missouri. As the story unfolds in the pages of this book, it is clearly seen it was a unique little village.

Very little history has been written about the town. My starting point was a mimeographed seventeen-page booklet found in the school library, and I am thankful to have that information. In the preface the sixth grade class thanked these local people for their useful local history: Mr. Joe Curry, Mr. Miles Miller, Mr. G. G. Goodman, Mr. Tom Turner, Mr. W. A. Hudson, Mr. W. M. Williams and Rev. Fred Woods. As I have continued research on this area, I found only one mistake in this booklet. The story says the black people came in when the farming started. According to the Federal census of 1910, approximately 90 black people lived in Deering. The 1920 Federal census shows about 180 black people in Deering. The story should have said that the Mexicans came in when the farming started.

In 1970, after I earned the name of a local historian, I began collecting essays from the older citizens, most of whom are now deceased. Every story would encourage me to try to learn more and more. When it became evident this centennial celebration was going to take place, I volunteered to compile this book. I dug deeper and deeper into the rich history of this town that offered a livelihood to the people of the twentieth century. My husband assisted me in this diligent research.

In an attempt to cover all angles, I compiled a letter and mailed to all the present citizens of Deering (and also of Braggadocio only three miles away), asking for pictures, and any oral or written history they could add to my collection. The response was low-key, as basically, the ones living in Deering today are not direct descendants of the settlers of the town. I know this is not all the history of the village, but it is what was contributed plus what I researched. Wouldn't it have been wonderful if the letters of inquiry had uncovered some of the photographs taken by Clarence Mills back in 1910?

Originally I have edited the publication of two books about Deering. In 1976 I helped the senior class publish a bicentennial project and we named it *History of Delta C-7 School District*. It has been reprinted three or four times. The graduating classes of 1947 and 1948, under my editorship, printed *Legacy of the Forties*. Both books are out of print. The essays in these two books are reprinted in this book, as they are from the interviews I did at the beginning of my research. I did some ghost writing of those stories in both books, as I have in this book. Some of these stories are thirty years old, but I have left them in their original context. I will comment on them, when necessary, in this introduction to *Deering Plantation*.

The Superintendents in charge of the Wisconsin Lumber Company operations were Mr. Medca, then Mr. Shew followed by Henry Pingle who was serving in that capacity in June 1915. Oce O. Moore served from 1917-1923 when he had a heart attack. They replaced him with Raymond H. Collier, who up until then, had been the shipping clerk for Wisconsin Lumber Company. While serving in this capacity, each family lived in the tall two-story house on Main Street, just across the street and west of the company store. It was torn down in the 1950's and a new brick house built for Mrs. Opal Earls Atwill.

When Bryon C. Mobley took the 1900 census, he enumerated some men at the very end of his route who listed their employment as "mill hands." It is believed this was the settlement of Deering beginning to take shape. Their surnames were Adams, Albright, Enochs, Faris, Gleaves, Laborn, McCann, McMeans, McWorden, Noblin, Skinner, and Thompson. Almost all of these are "boarders" and not "head of households."

Willie (Garrett) Baxter told me her Uncle Jonah Garrett came here when he was seventeen years old. He was born ca 1882, so that means he came about 1899-1900. I found an article in a magazine published in 1956 that refers to Deering starting in 1899. William Deering filed his first land purchase in August 1899 and then filed more deeds in 1900. There is no doubt that work began immediately. This first land was in Pemiscot and Dunklin Counties and was purchased from Cottonwood Lumber Company.

People came to this area from about twenty-one different states with most of them from Arkansas, Illinois, Indiana, Kentucky, Mississippi, Tennessee and Virginia. These people came from many ethnic backgrounds, such as England, France, Germany, Ireland, Norway, Sweden and Switzerland. Can't you image how their jabbering sounded while working at the lumber mill or railroad? It was a melting pot of America and they lived harmoniously with each other.

There was an ex-slave named Pauline Rice and I have reprinted the newspaper account of her. Bettie Pillow was her same age, and it is believed she was also an ex-slave. Rose Stockton, younger than the other two, therefore not in slavery as long, also came to this town.

Over the years several landmarks in town have been destroyed by fire. The big two-story store building burned on Friday, April 27, 1962. The office building burned December 19, 1975. The records from both these establishments were saved, as they were daytime fires. The three-room white school building burned December 15, 1939 and all the children and teachers escaped without being hurt. They had just completed a fire drill earlier in the morning.

Everyone that has ever lived at Deering has a story to tell. Not all of them relate the facts alike. That is why I have chosen to leave each person's rendition as it was told. Some of the accounts disagree in facts but agree in context. They are all about a little isolated village out in the midst of swamps named *Deering Plantation*.

Nobody can deny that Deering is strictly an agricultural town, thriving on an area of ten miles of farms from the nearest town. Is this unique little village ready for the next one hundred years? Will it survive the destruction of nature and neglect? Whatever the outcome, it can never be said that it did not have an outstanding first hundred years.

SECTION ONE
DEERING— A LUMBER TOWN

In 1898, William Deering from Chicago, Illinois began purchasing tracts of land in this area. His interest was solely for the cypress, sycamore, gum, oak, ash, elm, hickory, cottonwood, hackberry and maple trees that grew on it. He needed the finest of wood for his harvesting machines and agricultural implements. A daily average of 44,000 feet of lumber was cut and 125 men were employed at the mill. It was the second largest lumber mill in the United States.

When they were mud boating the large boiler for the mill along the trail, it became stuck in the ground and would not budge. After checking their survey lines, it was found that the boiler was on property of Wisconsin Lumber Co., a subsidary of International Harvester. They decided to build the little town in this location and forget their original plans of having it five miles southwest of here.

This area was part of the Southeast Missouri undrained swampland. Deering was isolated from the outside world with only a pole road leading in from the east from Braggadocio. In 1912, the Deering South West Railroad connected Deering eastward to Caruthersville and westward to Hornersville. A large railroad station was on the south side near the lumber mill.

Main Street, west to east, had the doctor's house, school teacher's house, supervisor's house, barber shop, company store with bowling alley upstairs, main office building, hotel, and the Methodist church building. Also, the town had an amusement hall with player piano and ice cream parlor and electricity. In 1927, the two-story brick school building was completed. Large wooden walks connected all the houses and businesses. The entire town was fenced to keep out the wild animals. It was a company town while International Harvester owned it.

CHAPTER ONE

William Deering

April 25, 1826 - December 9, 1913

Manufacturer, the son of James and Eliza (Moore) Deering, both of Puritan descent, was born in South Paris, Maine, where his father was engaged in woolen cloth manufacturing. He was educated in the public schools and he attended Readfield Seminary, from which he graduated in 1844. He then began the study of medicine with Dr. Barrows of Fryeburg, Maine, but his father persuaded him to enter his manufacturing company in which for several years he acted as manager.

On October 31, 1849, he was married to Abby Reed Barbour, daughter of Charles and Joanna (Cobb) Barbour. During the next few years he was interested in western farming lands, but, on the death of his wife in 1856, he returned to South Paris, where he opened a dry-goods store. He was married to Clara Hamilton, on December 15, 1856.

After a number of years he organized a wholesale commission dry-goods house under the firm name of Deering, Milliken & Company in 1865 with headquarters at Portland, Maine, and offices in New York City. He continued as its directing head for five years acquiring in the interval the executive ability and foresight which enables him subsequently to take a leading part in the development of American's agricultural machinery business.

In the meantime one of his old Maine friends, a Methodist preacher named Elijah H. Gammon, who had been for many years in Illinois, became interested in the manufacture of agricultural machinery, particularly in the hand-binding harvester of the brothers of Charles W. and William W. Marsh. Gammon purchased the rights to manufacture the Marsh harvester and aroused Deering's interest in the project to such an extent that he gave up his wholesale business and went to Plano, Illinois to join Gammon as a partner.

Deering invested $40,000 in the company, and, owing to his persistent and tireless management, the harvester trade was pushed out into channels that it had hitherto been unable to reach. A year later the manufacture of the Gordon wire binder was undertaken much against the advice of his partner, but Deering seemed to see more clearly than any one else the demand for a harvesting machine with automatic binding.

Again, in 1879, when he became sole owner of the business, Deering made another bold move by beginning the manufacture of a twine binder after the invention of John F. Appleby, and with the jeers of his competitors ringing in his ears he built and moved to a new and larger establishment at Chicago. The venture almost failed, because of the difficulty of finding a twine adapted for use on the binder.

Deering at last persuaded Edwin H. Fitler, a large Philadelphia rope manufacturer, to undertake experiments for him, and Fitler eventually produced a single strand manila twine that made the binder successful. From 1880 the business progressed steadily. Year after year the shops were enlarged and new departments added until it became the largest agricultural-implement factory in the world, employing in the neighborhood of 9,000 operatives.

Deering had the business incorporated in 1883 under the name William Deering & Company, having taken into the organization in 1880 his two sons, Charles W. and James E., and subsequently, his son-in-law, Richard F. Howe. Later the name was changed to the Deering Manufacturing Company. In 1901 Deering retired and in 1902 the corporation was merged with the International Harvester Company of Chicago.

William Deering, 1826-1913
He established the little town of Deering when he set up the Wisconsin Lumber Company mill to cut and process the timber in the swamps which he needed for his harvesting equipment.

Although his knowledge of public affairs was recognized, Deering's only public service was in the councils of Governors Chamberlain and Perham of Maine in 1870-73. He was a director of the Metropolitan National Bank of Chicago and president of the board of trustees of Northwestern University at the time of his death. His gifts to educational and charitable institutions were many, especially to Northwestern University, the Garrett Biblical Institute, and Wesley Hospital, all of Chicago. He also built and endowed the Deering School at Lake Bluff, near Chicago, for the accommodation of the orphanage there. He died at his winter home at Coconut Grove, Florida, survived by his wife and two sons.

(William Deering (Chicago, privately printed, 1914); *William Deering* (n.d.); E. L. Barker, *Creeds of Great Business Men* (1913): Robert L. Ardrey, *American Agricultural Implements* (1894), *Chicago Evening Post, Chicago American,* and the *Portland Evening Express and Daily Advertiser,* all December 10, 1913; *Chicago Daily Tribune, Daily Inter Ocean* (Chicago), and *Farm Implement News* (Chicago), all December 11, 1913; *Implement Age* (Springfield, Ohio), December 20, 1913; *Custer County Chief* (Broken Bow, Nebraska), December 26, 1913) C.W.M.

CHAPTER TWO

The Deering Harvester Company

McCormick's greatest challenge came from the machines that carried the Deering trademark. While Cyrus McCormick was developing the reaper, William Deering was acquiring some wealth in the dry goods business. In 1870, Deering invested some of his fortune with E. H. Gammon, an old acquaintance that had recognized the significance of the Marsh harvester at an early date and by 1869 had become a leading producer of the hand binding machine. Deering soon became a full partner and compensated for his lack of farm machinery experience with keen business sense and raw courage.

The Gammon & Deering partnership, one of the first to exploit the Marsh harvester, would forge ahead again in 1874, with the production of wire binders. By 1879, when Gammon retired from the partnership, William Deering was sufficiently knowledgeable to capitalize on the greatest advance of the era—the Appleby twine binder. The very next year, while McCormick and others were still strongly advocating the benefits of wire binders, Deering had already experimented with, produced, and sold over 3,000 twine binders. As one associate later recalled, "The harvest of that year (1880) was a Waterloo defeat for the wire binders. Mr. Deering won a complete victory; he established twine binding machines as the grain harvesters of the time and of the future and himself as the acknowledged leader of the movement."

By 1880, Deering had taken another bold step. Having realized that the production facilities in Plano, Illinois, were growing increasingly inadequate, he ordered the construction of a huge new facility in Chicago. The threat to McCormick was all too clear. In just ten years, William Deering became a leader and pioneer in an industry which he so recently entered. This success continued—eventually his company's sales and profits nearly matched those of the McCormick Company.

By 1885, Deering advertisers could claim that their twine binder had been successful for six harvest seasons. Not even McCormick could match that claim.

While the popularity of the twine binder was the basis of William Deering's success, his company also offered a full line of grain and grass cutting machinery. Deering's mower and light reaper would rival similar McCormick machines for years to come.

Since the introduction of the first successful twine binder, William Deering's firm had been identified as an innovative leader in the farm equipment industry. Such aggressive research brought more success to Deering in 1892 when a machine that used roller and ball bearings was first put on the market. Incorporated into the Deering Ideal, the natural result of this technology was a quieter, lighter draft machine. Once again, William Deering was forcing the industry to adapt.

William Deering, with essentially no farming or engineering experience, nevertheless, emerged as a leading farm implement manufacturer in a matter of just ten years. Recalling the time just before he became a full partner with E. H. Cammon, Deering said, "At the time, I didn't know the appearance of our machine." It wasn't long, however, before his image became inseparable with the machines his company created.

Deering's original twine binder had evolved throughout the 1890's and emerged the next decade as the Deering "Ideal" binder. Many thousands were sold by the time production was discontinued in 1937—nearly forty years after it was first introduced!

The International Harvester Corporation was launched in the summer of 1902. Five companies, once fierce rivals, finally agreed to work together in cooperation. The consolidation included the following companies:

McCormick Harvesting Machine Company
Deering Harvester Company
Warder, Bushnell & Glessner Company
(Makers of Champion machines)
Plano Manufacturing Company
Milwaukee Harvester Company

Reaching this point was not easy, but by calling a truce to the harvester war, the manufacturers could increase production efficiencies that ultimately benefited not just the owners, but the farmers as well. The combination that first was the source of much suspicion later created the deepest loyalties for generations to come.

To the five companies that formed International Harvester, merging was simply a matter of survival. The competition of the harvester wars was devastating the industry, and the company executives knew it.

(The above article was taken from "Challenges in a New Era—The Search for Strength and Supremacy." It was given to me by Darrell Darst who is involved in the International Harvester Collectors Club and is presently editor of their publication, "Harvester Highlights." He also passed along the next article, taken from "The Farmer's Guide", published February 1905.)

Harvester Talks to Farmers - No. 3

The matter of lumber is of special importance, for this country is threatened with a lumber famine, the nature of which is appalling when we stop to consider it.

The consumption of lumber increases every year; the supply, according to the best authorities, decreases at the rate of 3 per cent per annum, and the price consequently jumps from 1 per cent to 5 per cent every year. No 3 pine, for instance, in June, 1896, sold for $6.75 per thousand feet; in June, 1904, only eight years later, it sold for $15.50, and other lumber has advanced accordingly.

The great harvester companies, realizing that it is only a question of time until the lumber problem will be one of the most serious confronting the manufacturer, inaugurated several years ago a policy in keeping with what they are doing in iron, steel, coal and coke—that is, to become entirely independent of the lumber markets by securing a source of supply of their own.

Their timber lands in the famous St. Francis Valley consist of 60,000 acres which the International Company owns in southeastern Missouri and 22,000 acres leased in northeastern Arkansas, both a portion of the reclaimed "sunken land districts."

The Missouri lands are near the new town of Deering, which the International Company is making a model lumber town, with all the advantages and comforts of modern life in the midst of the forests. The land is heavily timbered with oak, ash, elm, hickory, cottonwood, cypress, gum, hackberry and maple. At the principal mill a daily average of 44,000 feet of lumber is cut, and 125 men are employed at the mill and in the timber.

On the Arkansas lands the mill is at Truman, 85 men are employed and the average output is 35,000 feet per day.

On both tracts, tramways, canals, and every modern facility for the economical handling of logs and lumber are provided.

The entire output of both tracts, after it has been properly air-dried, is used by the plants of the International Harvester Company in manufacturing harvesting machines and agricultural implements.

But the most important feature of the company's lumber operations is this: *All timber is cut in strict accordance with the rules of forestry.* Instead of denuding the land, only ripe trees with well-matured, hardened wood are cut, and the greatest care is exercised to protect and preserve all young timber, so that by the time the best timber is once selected from this vast tract of 82,000 acres—even at the rate of 20,000,000 feet per year, the present consumption of the International factories—a new supply will be grown to a commercial size.

In other words, the company by this far-sighted policy has secured practically a perpetual supply of the lumber necessary for the manufacture of the harvesting machines used by the American farmer. It is in position for the next generation, at least, to secure lumber of the highest quality and is absolutely independent of fluctuating markets, and, at the same time, by conserving the forests is not only reaping a benefit for itself and its customers, but is serving the best interests of the country at large.

CHAPTER THREE

Pemiscot County Land

William Deering, of Evanston, Illinois, began purchasing land in Pemiscot County in August 1899 when he bought 1440 acres from Cottonwood Lumber Company in T16N R10E, listed in Book 18 page 46 in the Recorder's office at Caruthersville. In the months that followed, he purchased more land from them. In 1900, he also obtained real estate from M. E. Cunningham, J. H. McFarland and Ella his wife, John E. Franklin and his wife, Edwin H. Riley, Davis B. Riley and Katie his wife, J. E. Franklin, and Maria O. Gordon for a total of almost 5,000 acres. Undoubtedly there are many more transactions scattered in the deed books which I did not investigate. This sawmill operation that he was pursuing was big, and a large acreage of trees was required to make it a profitable venture.

In December 1904 and again in 1908, Deering family members deeded the land between kinfolks, and eventually it became known as Deering Harvester Company and then Wisconsin Lumber Company. These were affiliates of International Harvester who owned the entire business, but transacted business in Deering under the name of Wisconsin Lumber Company.

When the large equipment mired down in the mud just inside the border of the Pemiscot County land, Mr. Deering built the lumber mill and town at what later became the town of Deering. When this settlement applied for a post office, they sent their choice of names as "Deering Sawmill," but the post office department simply named it Deering around 1900.

On December 27, 1910 (book 47 pages 140-152), Wisconsin Lumber Company (grantee) purchased fourteen more large tracts of swamp land all in Range 11. They were S10 T 18, S12 T 18, S21 T18, S22 T 18, S24 T16, T32 T18, S9 T18, S15 T18, S3 T18, S3 T18 and S21 T18.

The lumber mill operation was successful during its infancy and up to around 1925 when the timber ran out. The little town of Deering had to cease being a lumber mill town and turn into an agricultural town. The land was not ready to farm, as it still had the "stumpies" on it. These were the tree trunks that were below the water when the tree was cut.

When International Harvester realized they were not successful as farmers, they put the land up for sale. In 1925, they issued a newsletter "Come to The Heel of Missouri Where Diversified Farming Pays Big," trying to sell the land with no down payment and payments so low that almost anyone could afford to buy. The depression came in 1929, and the land did not readily sell.

There have been misconceptions as to whom really owned the operation when it was doing business when the lumber mill was in operation. Deed Book 133 page 518 explains it in detail.

"This Indenture made this 31st day of December in the year of our Lord One Thousand Nine Hundred Thirty five (1935) between Wisconsin Lumber Company, a corporation created and existing under and by virtue of the laws of the State of Wisconsin and licensed to transact business in the State of Missouri, hereinafter designated as "Grantor," and International Harvester Company, a corporation created and existing under and by virtue of the laws of the State of New Jersey, having an office for the transaction of business at 606 South Michigan Avenue in the City of Chicago and State of Illinois, hereinafter designated as "Grantee,," witnesseth That:

"Whereas, the Grantee many years heretofore became the beneficial owner of all of the capital stock of the Grantor, consisting of twenty-five hundred (2500) shares authorized, issued and outstanding, and has ever since been the owner, and now own and controls the same through its nominees; and

"Whereas, the Directors of the Grantor in a Special Meeting heretofore duly held upon January 27, 1925, in the City of Chicago, Illinois, at which a quorum of the Directors was present, unanimously duly adopted the following resolution, to wit:

"Resolved, that all lands owned by the Wisconsin Lumber Company in Pemiscot and Dunklin Counties, Missouri, no longer needed in carrying on its business, shall be sold, and that the President, or any Vice President, shall have the right at any time to fix and determine the price that shall be charged for any single tract of land, and the terms upon which it shall be sold, and thereupon to enter into, execute and deliver for the consideration therein provided, a contract and/or a deed, and/or release, and/or any other necessary document, with or without covenants of general warranty, confirming said title in the purchaser thereof, his successors or assigns, and likewise each and every other tract of land until all thereof shall have been sold and conveyed. Said authority shall extend to any President or Vice President hereafter elected until all of the said lands shall have been sold and conveyed to the Purchasers thereof, and . . . "

When the land did not sell due to the depression, International Harvester began looking for an enterprise that would buy the town and outlying real estate in Pemiscot County. Mr. Charles B. Baker of Kennett, Missouri went to Chicago and made negotiations with them. In the Recorder's Office, Deed Book 133, page 515-517, dated 22 May 1936 records this acreage. Mr. Baker operated under the name of Deering Farms, Inc. until he sold it to Mr. A. T. Earls.

An investigation into the Caruthersville courthouse records shows that some of the deeds to the grantees were issued from Wisconsin Lumber Company and some showed International Harvester as the seller. Some were warranty deeds, others were quit claim deeds, and some were sheriffs deeds where the purchaser was paying the back taxes. Several of the people are listed more than once. All the people did not immediately file their deeds at the courthouse, and we found them scattered throughout the indexes. Therefore, this may not be an accurate listing, but it is what we found in the early books.

Henry F. Abbot & wife, T. W. Alexander, Alick Amick, W. L. Anchlin, Joe Armasky, G. R. Ash, L. Atterbury, W. W. Austin,

Harry Bailey, C. B. Baker, William M. Barksdale, Clyde Barnett, I. J. Barnett, J. C. Barton, L. L. Bearden, William Bennett, Robert L. Blair, Hal Bogle, Jesse Bond, H. A. Boswell, Lincoln M. Bowman, J. H. Brinn, Doyle R. Brown, J. M. Brown, Will Brown, W. H. Burks,

J. E. Cahoan, John Loid Callis, Hester A. Callis, Scott Carey, J. W. Casaday, Mary E. Chamblee, Herman Chandler & wife, Robert C. Channell, W. P. Chappell, T. M. Cildwell, J. C. Cobb, L. J. Coble & wife, R. H. Collier & wife, Jonah Cones, E. A. Conklin, J. T. & M. E. Crecelius, E. A. & L. M. Crecelius, F. C. Crow, G. A. Culp, John Culp, Annie Culp, D. D. Culp, Marshall & Sadie Currin, Marshall & Montgomery Currin, V. V. Curtis, Milburn Curtis,

Victor Dauinroy, J. Q. Davis, H. DePriest, L. C. Dodson, L. C. Dodson, Henry C. Dorman, C. Dozier, E. L. Drake, Gordon O. Drewry & wife, East Arkansas Lumber Co., Vicie I. Epperson, J. D. Epperson,

S. M. Fife, J. T. Fitzgerald, Earuth A. Frazer, O. E. Frazier, Hubert Freshour, E. M. Freshour, Everett Freshour, Rube Gatewood, V. E. George, P. E. Gilbert & wife, Roy E. Glover, Lin Goode, George E. Goodrum, I. M. Goodrum, O. R. Graham, James R. Green, Lennie Grubbs, L. N. Grubbs

Winslow A. Hagard, William F. Hall, Fred Hall, Dan Hall, Mack Halsey & wife, E. H. Hancock, E. G. & R. E. Hankins, R. B. Hart, Birt Hatley, Edmon Hatton, Tommie Hatton, T. H. Haynes, John Henneke, Simon Herren & wife, Ruby Holman, W. F. Hornback, C. L. & J. W. Hoskins, Jake & Alvin Huffman, E. S. Huffman, Phepps Huntley, R. C. Hurley

G. W. Jackson, A. T. James, Russell James, Jesse Johnson,

Charles A. Jolliff, J. E. Jones, F. M. Jordan, R. D. Keirsey, H. B. Kelley, Henry R. Kight & wife, Robert F. Lackey, Lee Realty Co., W. H. Lemmel, J. L. Lewis, Guy T. Linsman, Kas Little, Mary Jones Little, E. Long, H. D. Long, J. C. Lucius,

E. J. Marshall, R. H. McIntire & wife, B. C. McKnight, Martin Menz, Glynn B. Middleton, Raymond B. Milligan & wife, J. G. Mills, S. R. Mitchem, Wesley Moore, V. J. Morehand, Paul Mulcahy & wife

National Refining Co., A. L. Neal, Jr., Virgie Neal, A. L. Neal, Harry Neal, Lula Neal, Ausburn L. Neel, Napoleon Norman & wife, D. L. Nunnery & wife, John Oliver & wife, T. E. Olree,

W. R. Parter, Mary A. Patterson, Mary A. & C. L. Patterson, L. D. Pelts, J. M. Petty, D. M. Piercey, M. L. Pike & wife, T. G. Poe, W. R. Porter, Jones Porter, Ed Porter, Vernon M. Porter, W. I. Power, W. O. Powers, John W. Price,

M. L. Rainbolt, Cloride Reed & wife, James M. Reeves, J. M. Reeves, M. F. Richardson, C. H. Robins, Shirley A. Rodermund, Linus Edwin Ross, F. M. Ross, D. C. & Josie Rutherford.

J. N. C. Salmon, R. L. Scott, A. A. Sexton, E. N. Shade, E. W. Shade & wife, Guy Shelton, Erline Shelton, J. A. Skinner, Bert Skinner, Carl E. Smith, T. B. Smith, N. N. Speakes, Lynn Speer, Asier J. Speer, C. I. Stallings, J. C. Stewart, Della Stout, Frank Stover, Mose Stover & wife, Mose Strong, Sail Stubbs, Charley Sullivan,

Robert & Rose Tabor, C. F. And Ida Tabor, W. O. Talley & wife, Ed Tarleton, The Colored Ed Res Ass'n, J. V. Tittle, V. K. Tittle, G. W. Toon, Ray M. Trexler, O. C. Tucker, C. E. Tucker, T. T. & Marie Turner, James Allen Vaughn, Jim Mat Vaughn, Matthew Vaughn, M. H. Vernon, J. P. & R. W. Vickrey,

W. N. Waldrop, S. W. Watson, Herschell Watson, L. L. Weaver, W. E. Webb, Hunter Wells, G. M. Whistte, W. A. White & wife, W. A. White, T. W. Whittle, W. G. & Birdie L. Wicker, I. G. Wilkinson, James F. & Lula M. Williams, Sam H. Williams, and I. R. Wright & wife.

CHAPTER FOUR

The History of Deering, Missouri

By the Sixth Grade History Class of 1934-35, R. R. Eddleman, Instructor;

OUR SOILS AND MIXED RESOURCES

It is not known when the soils of this community were first formed, but since the vicinity lies in the Southeast Missouri Lowlands and is a part of the Mississippi River Lowlands, we know that it was once a part of the Gulf of Mexico. For thousands of years this Delta country has been built up by the river until it is now over 250 feet above the Gulf. To the west lies Crowley's Ridge. The soil is all transported. After the great ice sheet which covered most of the northern part of our continents was over, the Mississippi River carried millions and millions of tons of this glacial soil into the Mississippi River bottoms and deposited it there. The soils of this community had become cultivatable, when in 1811 and 1812 the New Madrid earthquake once more lowered the surface of this region. Many quakes and nearly every person in the southeast Missouri Lowlands Deering was so changed that they helped to make this community very swampy.

Pemiscot county takes its name from the Indian language. The word Pemiscot means "Liquid Mud" and is taken from Pemiscot Bayou south of Deering where the Indians used to canoe, to catch fur animals for the French fur trading fort at La Petite Prairie (north of the present site of Caruthersville.) When ditches came, much of their work was again undone, and today except during floods on the St. Francis River only dry beds remain. These ditches were begun after the 1913 high water.

The soils are very fertile and adaptable to most temperate crops. Cotton is the chief crop at the present, but mixed farming will likely be done in a few years.

This region contains both soft and hard timber. As late as 1900 this entire community was covered with a dense growth of fine timber. Many of the trees found here are natives to the Rocky Mountains, Appalachian Mountains, and even Canada. They were brought here by the Mississippi River. In fact little or no native timber is found as they have been covered up in the process of farming our soils!

The native game includes deer, bear, bobcat, panthers, wolves, and other common fur bearers. Today only a few deer, wolves, and some other small animals are found here in what was once a hunter's heaven.

The climate is seldom very cold, while the summer temperature rarely reaches 100 degrees. The rainfall is sufficient for almost any crop. (1)

OUR COMMUNITY'S SETTLEMENT AND GROWTH OF INDUSTRIES

About 1903 the first railroad came to Deering. The train was old "Three Spot" which collected logs from the bottoms. This railroad was our only railroad until 1912. The Wisconsin Lumber Company used it with tram cars often pulled by animal power. This railroad was known as the Deering and Southwestern (D. S. W.). The "Old Timers" called it the "Dern Slow Wiggling Railroad Company." Between 1901 and 1902 the Frisco Railroad was built. It was from Pascola to the curve north east of town. It ran upon rails which were laid on large logs with sand packed between them.

The first mill was a circle sawmill which might have been called a ground-hog mill. It was replaced with a modern band mill in 1906 that burned in 1913. A new mill was built and it operated until 1928 at which time it was closed.

For a year the freight had to be hauled from the curve into Deering. A connection was then built by the Wisconsin Lumber company. The railroad from Deering to Rives, Missouri was built in 1903. The D. & S. W. was extended to Caruthersville in 1913. In 1919 the Frisco sold to the Cotton Belt which controls this line today.

At that time railroads were almost the only means of transportation as only by following the ridges or high spots in dry weather was it possible to travel by land. Roads were almost unknown except for log drives. Dense forest at first, covered the entire community.

The early mail was carried from Pascola to Deering, on horse back, down the railroad track. When a train or section gang was in sight the mail carrier, on his pony, had to take to and hide in the woods. One of the first mail carriers was Mr. Miles Miller who still lives northeast of town.

There were enormous tracts of good timber here when Deering was first settled by W. M. Deering. It was first settled as a sawmill center when in 1899-1900 the Wisconsin Lumber Company began work here. It is said that six yokes of oxen were mud-boating the boiler from Hickory Landing (2) for the big mill here when they bogged down in the mud. Upon investigation it was found that the boiler was barely on Wisconsin Lumber Company land. Since it was impossible to move the boiler farther, it was decided to build the mill and town at this place.

The first settlement was located east of the present town and about where the present Pondertown is. The Wisconsin Lumber Company soon built the D. & S. W. R. R. And began operations. This "R. R." or "tram" went back into the swamps and hauled out the logs which were sawed into lumber at the big mill. The first mill was a circle sawmill. In fact it might have been called a ground-hog mill. It was replaced with a modern band mill in 1906. (3) In 1913 the first band mill burned one day while the mill hands were at dinner. A new mill was built. It was operated until 1928 at which time it was closed down because timber was scarce. The special lumber for the second mill was bought in Louisiana by Mr. Pingle who was then superintendent. Mr. Tom Turner built the mill. The following superintendents have been in charge of the Company's affairs at this place. The Wisconsin Lumber Company superintendent succeeded one another as follows: Mr. Medca, Mr. Shew, Mr. Pingle, Mr. Moore, who was the superintendent from 1917-1923, and Mr. R. M. Collier from that time up to the present time.

When the timber failed the Wisconsin Lumber Company became interested in agriculture. Their experiments with cotton farming proved profitable, and in 1929 a large modern cotton gin was built. The company has been active in fostering better schools, churches, roads, and other public welfare activities. (4)

OUR PEOPLE

Deering was settled by white people and they still form by far the largest part of the people in this community. The present settlers have come from various nearby southern states for the most part. The population remained almost all "white" until most of the timber was cleared out.

Directly after the Wisconsin Lumber Company began farming the lands, they brought in Mexicans to clear the lands and Negroes came to help grow the cotton. Today the Mexicans are gone and the Negro population has never been large.

Our populations have been mixed, but the Kinsall murder and a few minor troubles, have been the only race problems which have been bothersome.

OUR COMMUNITY CHURCHES

The Methodist Episcopal Church, South, was organized at Deering in April 1909 by Rev. T. F. Fallin. Other ministers who followed were: S. L. Young, S. A. Bennett, A. Ellis Barrett, J. W. Williams, J. L. Wolverton, J. A. Scamahorn, W. A. Edmundson, Charles T. Young, E. M. Cook, Harvey E. Stone, C. M. Swape, and P. L. Pritchard. In the boom days of the "Big Mill" Deering was a station, (5) but since then has been on a circuit. (6) The church died down after the mill left. Until finally, in 1932-33 no minister was sent here. In November 1933, the church was reorganized by the present pastor Rev. Fred Woods.

The present total membership is 47.

The church school has an enrollment of 118, with an average attendance in February 1935 of 111.

The women's missionary society has 17 members, and the young peoples league has 30 members. W. A. Hudson became Church School Superintendent, January 1935.

There are preaching services every second and fourth Sundays, the church being on a circuit with Braggadocio and Bragg City.

In a Sunday School census, taken in March 1935, it was found that there were 180 white people in Deering—55 of them attended Sunday School, 125 did not, 61 were members of churches, 36 were not old enough to be church members, and the remaining 83 were members of no church. There are also churches at Bakerville, Vicksburg and Mid-City to serve this vicinity.

The Beulah Grove Colored Missionary Baptist Church was organized May 4, 1902. At one time there were 210 members of the church. The present membership is 94. The average Sunday School attendance is 30. They have a woman's Missionary Society and B.Y.F.U. They have preaching services on second and fourth Sundays. Rev. E. T. Hull is the present pastor.

The African Methodist Episcopal Church was organized in 1923. The membership has never been very large, with a total at present of 14. They have about 15 at Sunday School. There are a Woman's Missionary Society and an Allen League for young people. They have preaching services on first and third Sundays. Rev. R. D. Carter is the present pastor.

The two colored churches use the same building which is a gift of the Wisconsin Lumber Company. It is located in the Negro section of Deering which is South of the Cottonbelt Railroad. This section contains about 42 colored people. (7)

THE GROWTH OF DEERING SCHOOLS

The first school at Deering was held in what is now the church. School began at Deering about 1904. Miss Aunie Adams was the first teacher. She is now connected with the Hornersville, Missouri post office.

The school was located on the extreme east side of Deering. Under a big oak (8) in what is now Pondertown.

The first school building was a small frame building which was remodeled from time to time and used for many years. It has been remodeled and made into a very pretty church building. The Methodist Church uses it today. (9) The next school was remodeled from a boarding house of the mill days and called the Big School. Today is a three-room primary school in the Northeast part of the town.

The earlier teachers up until 1911 were: Miss Adams, Miss

Bell, Mr. and Mrs. Bess, Mr. George Klinkhardt who is now at Hayti and Miss Powell who taught here in 1911. Mrs. R. H. Collier was also a teacher at this place.

Mr. M. E. Brashler was principal of the first high school (1922). The school consisted of three teachers.

In 1925 Vicksburg, Deering, Seldom Seen, Little River, and Maple View School districts consolidated with 14 sections of Dunklin County land to become Consolidated District No. 6 of Pemiscot County. This made a district worth $1,250,000 and containing 57 square miles of land. Two buses were purchased and transportation was begun in 1927 and today there are six buses in use and all of these over crowded. Since 1928 the enrollment has more than doubled itself as there are now 1,028 school children in the district. The school grew from three teachers in 1926 to twelve teachers in 1927 and today there are eighteen. New teachers are being added each year to keep up with the enrollments. The Central School today consists of the three room Primary School, and the Central School building which contains an auditorium and gymnasium, a large study hall, offices, shower rooms and a supply room besides eight classrooms. It is a beautiful structure built at the cost of $68,000 in 1927. Louis Ittnor of St. Louis was the architect.

There are three ward schools: Little River (built in 1934), Vicksburg Ward, and Maple View Ward. Only the work of the first grades is done in these ward schools.

Several years ago the district opened a school for Mexicans on the upper plantation. (10) Rev. E. M. Cook taught the school. It was discontinued when all the Mexicans had left the community.

A colored school is operated in Deering. It has been in operation for several years and is well equipped.

The schools of this community sponsor Troop 95 Boy Scouts of America, Troop 1 Girls Scouts of America and are doing a nice piece of work for both troops.

Sound motion picture equipment is owned by the school and used to furnish recreation for the community.

THE TOWN AND ITS GROWTH

The buildings in our town which are important in local history include the oldest dwelling (Mrs. Dunn's home), the old mill, the Teacherage, the Doctor's Office, Wisconsin Lumber Company Office, the Cotton Gin, the Railroad Station, the beautiful Central School, Little School (primary school) and the Old Amusement Hall (now a ware house).

The big store began in 1904 when a Mr. Zallsman, became the town's first merchant. The commissary of the Wisconsin Lumber Company was at the time located just north of the railroad tracks near the new depot (built in 1925). For several years the streets ran cat-a-cornered to their north-south and east-west direction at the present. The big store has always been on Main Street. The street today is called "Front Street."

Mr. Zallsman was followed by a number of head merchants and today Mr. J. M. Bowen is the store manager for the "Company."

The present office of Dr. A. J. Speer was formerly located near the old mill and served as a butcher shop and hall as well as a lodging place for office men here. Today it is on "Back Street" and the upstairs serves as a dwelling. It is lovingly called "Dog House" as a reminder of butcher shop days.

The first post office was established in 1904 but the new building has been used since 1925. The real name of this place is registered with Wisconsin Lumber Company and International Harvester Company as "Deering Sawmill," but the U. S. Post Office Department name is "Deering." Miss Bensinger is now the Postmistress of Deering.

The Hotel building which was torn down during the summer of 1934, was an old community land mark. The Wisconsin Lumber Company Office (sometimes called Pay Office) and the large water tank are also land marks of our town.

Among the things which the Wisconsin Lumber company sought to do was to furnish recreation for its workers. So about

1911 or 1912 the "Amusement Hall" was built. It was a large structure. It contained a bowling alley; pool hall, dance floor, and confectionary as well as a barber shop. Later a motion picture show was held regularly in this building. At one time the high school here was held regularly in this building. During the mill days it was the scene of much gaiety. The building was partly destroyed by fire in the fall of 1926. It has been repaired and made smaller. Today it is used as a food and train warehouse by the Wisconsin Lumber company. It is located back of the Wisconsin Lumber company store, on the side street.

In 1918 in an effort to furnish more recreation for the local people, the Wisconsin Lumber Company built a base ball park and playground. It was surrounded by a high broad fence and contained swings, seesaws and other play equipment for children. A large grandstand was built and a base ball diamond laid off. Then better roads came and people could find other recreations, interest became less. The playground was finally abandoned after several years of worthwhile service.

The town has a running water supply approved by state authorities. Electric power in homes is to be found here. A recent census shows 225 people, 61 homes and 28 autos. Deering is located 4 miles south of Highway of 84 about midway between Hayti, Mo. and Kennett, Mo. It is 15 miles west of Caruthersville, Missouri and the Mississippi River and is 6 miles east of the 90th meridian. It can be reached by good roads from all points.

Footnotes:

1 Taken from facts in a letter by Mr. A. S. Duckworth, State Teachers College, Cape Girardeau, Mo.

2 A fairly high solid portion of ground and settlement west of Deering.

3 This mill was at one time the second largest mill south of the Mason-Dixon line according to most sources.

4 This chapter is in part quoted from material written by G. G. Goodman, who is connected with the Wisconsin Lumber Company at Deering.
5 A church with a minister who serves only that church.
6 A number of churches having one minister.
7 This chapter is largely written from the findings of Rev. Fred Woods.
8 This great oak has been pointed out by many as a vicinity landmark. It was cut about 1917.
9 Moved and remodeled for a church in 1915.
10 There are two plantations belonging to the Wisconsin Lumber Company (the upper and lower plantations)

CHAPTER FIVE

Dogskin and Vicksburg

As early as 1891, this little settlement was referred to as Dogskin and two of the pioneer settlers were J. W. Cawthon and J. M. Faris. No one really knows how it got its name, but there is a fable that in the early days it was a hunting camp, and that one of the hunters had a reputation of not caring for his dogs. They were poor and underfed, and the other hunters joshed with him that his dogs were just skin and bones, thus the name Dogskin was derived from that.

When the early citizens applied for a post office, the postal department refused to let them officially name it Dogskin. J. P. Vickrey was the school teacher in the little one-room school house, so they decided to name it for him, thus calling it Vicksburg. A little after this time, Mr. Vickrey left the area and went to medical school, only to return in a few years as their country doctor. Vicksburg had a post office from 1913 through 1916 and the postmasters were John A. Vaughn, Jessie L. Potts and Milburn M. Masters.

The Vaughn, Callis and Bullock family were kinfolks, arriving at the turn of the century. In 1901, Will Gibbs and his wife Rebecca (Acord) Gibbs moved here from Vanduser, Mo., with their daughter Lela. Tom Callis and Wade Callis came with them. Lela says that farm houses were scattered throughout the woods, and that there was a school house that was used as a Church of God on Sunday. The old cemetery was on the Garrett farm, originally the John Wright farm, and that her mother is buried there. She states that some of the early teachers were Grace Allen, Montie Juden, and Nettie Gather, along with Mr. Vickrey.

The courthouse records, in deed book 23, page 455, show that on January 17, 1902, E. L. Davis and his wife, L. B., deeded one-half acre of land described as: "Beginning in the SW 1/4 of NW 1/4, Section 28, Township 18, Range 11 to be used for a school."

J. B. McDonald and Jim Vaughn both told me eventually that school house was abandoned and one was built a little south and east of it. There was a fence all around it to keep the animals out, and the fence had steps going over it on the southwest and northeast corners. Teachers in the school after that were Mr. Bingenheimer, Ruby Williams, Nell Lemons of Braggadocio (later Nell Long), Mr. and Mrs. J. J. Johnson, Claude Day, Mamie Ledbetter, and Mr. and Mrs. Earlie Carter.

The first store building was built by Uncle Billy Bonds, father of Otto Bonds, and was occupied by Jack Hughcock from Denton. John Allen Vaughn and Matthew Scott later owned it, but they sold it to Frank Stover. Another store later had Bill Hall as the owner. This first store building was on Grandma Bullocks farm, which was later the scene of the killing of John Naile, father of Jadie Nail. He was killed by Cap Neal.

Ruby Sudduth Turner taught in the school 1938-1941 with grades one through four, and she had an enrollment of sixty students, with an average daily attendance of fifty-one. The school closed down in 1942 and she began teaching at Deering C-6.

CHAPTER SIX

My Life in Deering and Pondertown

By Mrs. Isom (Willie Garrett) Baxter, 28 October 1970

Fifty-four years ago, the 28th day of October 1916, Deering was all fenced in because there were no stock laws. They had cattle guards so the cattle could not go across the railroad and into town. They had a little house up here by the old church building, and a Mr. Price, a crippled man on crutches, opened the gate at 6:00 a.m. and every afternoon at 6:00, he closed the gate. It was fenced with wire and they had two large wooden gates that would swing open and they were locked with a padlock. If you wanted to go to town after 6:00 p.m., you would have to climb the gates, get what you wanted, and then climb back across to go home.

Deering was opened into from the east; there was no road leading to it from the west at all. When my aunt passed away, they took her out on a flatcar pulled by a motor car to take her to the cemetery at Kennett. This is the type of car the section foremen used. Most of the people that died here were buried in the old Hazel cemetery, or else in Braggadocio or Caruthersville, being taken out in wagons.

Pete Robinson owned the first car that was ever owned in Deering and Isom owned the second. Isom's was a little one-seated Sikeston Roadster. Pete's was a Hudson.

We had a pole road that ran from Deering to Dogskin to Braggadocio. This road was made by laying poles side by side and that is what the wagons would travel over. Part of this road can still be seen. Go down to the old Clarence Lipsey place, and it is the first road to the left that takes you to Braggadocio. The poles are still there, but there is dirt in on them now. The length of the pole was the width of the road.

Well, Pete would put his car on the flatcar at Deering and then at Braggadocio he would unload it and drive it to Caruthersville or wherever he wanted to go; then drive back to Braggadocio, load it up again and bring it home to Deering on the train.

The train ran twice a day, once in the morning and then back in the afternoon. If you wanted to go to Caruthersville shopping, you would catch it of the morning, shop all day, and come back home in the afternoon.

The Wisconsin Lumber Company had the big sawmill here in town. They had a big company store and the post office was in the store. This was the big two-story building which burned a few years ago. This was the only store that was here. Mr. Clark was the manager of the store and Mrs. Acuff was the postmaster. They sold everything in the store that a person needed.

Then they had a barbershop. Originally it sat behind the big company store and Roy Day was the barber. Later on, when the barber shop ceased to function, they pulled that little building up near the big store building and moved the post office from the store over to the little building.

The building that is now behind the store was the old recreation building. In the back was the dry-cleaning shop. In the front they had a self-playing piano, pool tables, bowling alley and served ice cream. This was where everyone went for relaxation, etc.

There has only been one church in Deering, and that is the same Methodist church building that is still standing in its original place.

There was a little two-room schoolhouse. It sat on the north side of Deering and I went to school there. Later, they built another room on it and made it a three-room school. It taught all grades and you went to school until you felt like you knew all they could teach you, and then you quit. Mr. and Mrs. Bess were our teachers. He was black-eyed and black-headed and his wife was blue-eyed and redheaded.

Then they built the big two-story building which still stands. You would go to the small building for the first few years, then start in the big building in the third grade.

The only way you could get out of Deering was by the railroad that ran from Caruthersville to Hornersville; the people here mainly going to Caruthersville.

Everything around Deering was in woods and timber and old wild cane. Every morning the mill whistle blew at 4:00, then 5:00, then 5:45, and then at 6:00 and everybody was to be at work at 6:00 when it blew. The 4:00 whistle was to get everybody up. The 5:45 whistle was a short blast as a warning that it was fifteen minutes until work.

My daddy worked for Wisconsin Lumber Co. and then when he quit working for them he started farming and we moved about one and one-half miles east of Deering at that time. This is where we were living when I got married.

My uncle was a grader for the Wisconsin Lumber Co. Uncle Jonah Garrett had been here for years, coming when he was seventeen years old. He is the one that urged us to move here.

The depot was here when we moved here. They had large plank floorings out in front of the depot and the small cars would travel along the floor, picking up the produce the train brought in, then hauling it over to the company store, returning back and forth with the merchandise until it was all delivered. The railroad station was a busy place and everyone coming or going passed through it.

All the farmhouses that are scattered on the farms nearly used to sit in Deering. They moved them from town out onto the farms as the lumber was cut and the land cleared.

There was a big two-story hotel that sat on the east side of the company office. The Jackson family ran it first, then Daisy Blue took it over. Her husband was Johnny Blue and he worked on the train. Bob Hargrove was the conductor on the train. Dink Johnson was the engineer on the train.

Wisconsin Lumber Co. owned the whole town and you rented your house from them. If you needed a loan of money, you could go sign for a doodlum book and then go to the company store and spend the paper money inside the covers of the book. Then, when payday came, they would deduct the amount of your doodlum book from your pay.

We had a company doctor. His name was Dr. Wells. If you were a single man, they took $1.00 per month out of your pay; if you were a married man, they took $1.50 out of your pay each month. This is all the doctor would cost you unless he delivered a baby to your household. Then you paid him $10.00 for that extra service. You never paid him another thing.

The doctor's office was a two-story building behind the old barber shop. Negro Alice was the one who kept the building clean for him. She lived in Deering for years and years, and later worked for some of the white women in town.

After Dr. Wells was Dr. Speer, then Dr. Kelly, then Dr. Farnsworth. After that we never had a doctor reside in Deering. Dr. Vickrey lived in Braggadocio. All the Deering doctors lived in the town of Deering.

We had electricity in Deering and had electric lights, even though the people out in the farm areas did not. The Wisconsin Lumber Company generated this electricity for us.

The houses along the front part of town were painted. The other houses were not painted. Lots of the houses were four-room houses with really high ceilings. They would be double planked on the inside to cover the cracks on the outside, then papered over that.

Each house had a fence around it and a gate leading out to the plank sidewalks that ran along every street in Deering. These were made of wide planks cut about four inches wide. Then, there was a plank sidewalk running up to each front door.

Most of the houses that set on the back streets were three-room shotgun houses. These were not painted either, but were still serviced with sidewalks.

The town was blocked off into squares, and I can't guess how many houses were in town, but there was a lot. It was heavily populated.

You could have chickens, cows or horses or anything you wished right in your yard. Your yard was fenced and your animals would all stay in your yard. Nobody in Deering that I can remember had buggies or surreys.

Pondertown was in existence when Wisconsin Lumber Company had Deering. Isom stayed with Mr. Williams who lived in Pondertown and ran a small store. Isom had a buggy with rubber tires, which was something long time ago.

Isom's mother and daddy did not come here. He lived with Mr. and Mrs. Williams until he went to World War I. When he got back from the war, we got married.

When we got married, we invited all the people in Deering to the wedding. We lived one and one-half miles east of Deering, on the farm. Everyone came for supper and stayed for the wedding. The house was full and people were on the outside. Mother cooked hams and killed chickens and made cakes, etc., and we really had a feast.

They kidded me later for how nervous I was. I stood there before the justice of peace with my hand alongside my dress. Gradually my fingers started gathering up my dress and by the time the wedding ceremony was over my dress was clear up to my knees. Mrs. Williams and Claiborn Canard's mother helped my mother do this cooking for the wedding.

Out in Pondertown there was also an old hotel. Mrs. W. M. Williams's mother and father kept borders there.

The church is an old landmark and also the office building and the old barbershop. The church had good attendance then, as people had no other place to go. They had choir practice on Wednesday night and church on Sunday morning and Sunday night.

We used the recreation hall to dance and visit. They charged a nickel to bowl a game and a nickel for the piano. Everyone danced and had a good time.

The big office is just like it was when I came here. It is just like it was then. The old blacksmith shop set on the south side of the lumber shop. Charley Book was the blacksmith. The old brick building on the south side of the tracks was part of the old sawmill. It was a brick building then, and part of this building is still there. The big white doors still are there on the north side of the building.

They used two-wheel carts with a mule from the mill to the yard. These carts would go from the mill to the yard and be graded, then stacked on the railroad cars for shipment.

In the wartime they were so short of men that women worked in the yard. They wore their overalls and would stack the planks after they were graded and do the work of the man. Mary Williams worked on the lumber yard. She drove a mule. Also, Willie Blue worked there.

You could buy a poor grade of lumber really cheap.

Colored town had a school, a church, a hotel, and a recreation center. They had a piano and an ice cream parlor just like we did. They did their shopping at the big general store, but otherwise stayed on the south side of the tracks. They buried their dead in Deering, having a cemetery out in their area. Some tombstones still stand there. After dark, you never would see a Negro in the white part of town. Colored town was large in size, almost as large as the white part.

The white women did their own work, not even hiring the colored women for several years. Gradually, they did develop into this, Negro Alice being their favorite.

Dr. Wells was also a justice of the peace. He married Isom and me. Dr. Wells told us, "I married you. I delivered your first baby to you, and I'm not going to divorce you."

Mr. Pingle was the boss of the Wisconsin Lumber Co. He lived in the big two-story house just west of the general store. This later was turned into a teacherage. It was torn down in the 1950's. After Pingle left, R. H. Collier took his place and lived in the same house.

When the hotel was torn down, the lumber from it was used to build the Tinkerville school house, four miles west of Deering. This school was named Little River. Then a new boss's house was built on that site.

Earlier I said that the Pingle and Collier house eventually became a teacherage. But before this, there was a teacherage located on the north side of town, a big two-story house.

The hotel was a big two-story building and I can't remember how many rooms it had. The big dining room was larger than this four-room house and they put big tables and chairs in it and put the food on the table family style, and everybody sat down like a great big family

Mary Putman Williams worked there once, and there was a Negro woman named Ethel who helped there. Mrs. Baxter's mother furnished milk and butter for the hotel.

The company store was petitioned off back at the meat market. The white people were waited on from one side of the iron barred area, and the colored people from the other side. Butcher Dykus served all of them from the same meat box. Large hunks of ice kept the meat fresh.

They had an ice house that sat back behind the company store. It wasn't very large and they brought in ice daily on the train. I don't remember how much it cost, but you could buy a dime worth and have enough for a long, long time;—that is, if you had a dime.

The wages then are about $3.00 a day

They had a ball diamond which was on the east side of town. Every Sunday afternoon they had ball games, and had the teams in Deering playing each other. They had swings there for the children to swing in.

You could go to the big ditch south of town to fish. The fishing was good and you could plan on having fish for dinner anytime you went. The banks were always covered up with colored women fishing.

There was one old colored woman, who lived here, called Aunt Paul, who lived during slave times. She would relate the story of how her husband was sold away from her and her two sons and that she never saw him again. She lived to be really old. Aunt Paul used to go to the schoolhouse and talk to the children at school. She was a really large woman.

The mill also employed the colored people and the mill paid them the same as for the white people. Although they came to the general store to trade, they were back in Negro Town before sundown.

The roads were so bad in the old days that it took us two hours once from our house about two miles away. The wheels on the wagon would gum up with gumbo and we would have to stop and punch the gumbo from the wheels. The roads were just trails and there were no road ditches to drain off the water. The roads were terrible until the sun came out and baked the dirt again. With all the large trees, this was a slow process.

There were wild animals around. Of the morning when the 4:00 whistle blew, the wolves would start howling just across the field. People had to keep sows and pigs and cows and calves put up to keep the wolves from them.

There were bobcats in the area. Mr. Baxter would walk his children to school to keep a panther that was in the area away from his children. I never saw any bears.

There were plenty of wild turkeys and wild hogs. People killed these for meat in the wintertime. The wild hog meat wasn't as good as the fattened hogs, but it surely beat nothing.

The women didn't play pool, but they did bowl. Marie Umphrey who married Charles Jackson really like to bowl.

Mrs. Acuff was the postmaster that I first remember, then Miss Jenny Bensinger, then Mrs. Ann Brown and now Miss Mildred Brown. Mrs. Acuff's husband was dead and she married a widower by the name of Arnold and they moved from here.

Christmas was a big Christmas tree at the church building. Everyone attended the program, as all the children were participants and the parents came to see them. Lela Gibbs played Santa Claus one time, dressed up in the red suit, and the young boys threw firecrackers at her.

On the Fourth of July we all had a picnic basket lunch on the ball diamond. They had flags up around there, and the children were all given red-white-blue caps that they wore. Then they had a ball game following the celebration.

When a person traveled or lived at Deering, they were there and the only way to leave was the same way they came. They felt like they were penned up at the last outpost.

Sewing machines were in all the homes. The mother made the family's clothes. Lots of the material was from the cloth feed sacks that was washed, starched and ironed, and made into cute little dresses for the girls. A mother's talent at the sewing machine was more the display long ago, than the expensive purchase at the city's department store.'

The first school bus they had was owned by Joe Curry. It was like an old hack. It was black and had three seats. My brother, Barney Garrett, drove one of them.

Mr. Norvell Stover had an old truck which had seats in the back with canvas curtains which would pull down when it was raining. The next year, then, Mr. Curry bought the two school buses which would seat about twelve each. These made the run from Dogskin to Deering.

Mrs. Curry's husband was a janitor at the school. She, after Mr. Curry died, married Dan Potts and they now live at Hayti. This is Mildred Farr's mother.

There was an old cemetery down close to Clarence Lipsey's house just south of the old Pole Road. Go on south from the Lipsey house, cross the ditch, then it is on the left side of the road (the east side). This was the Pete Robinson farm, and Pete is buried there. A baby named White was buried there. Monroe Farris is also buried there.

The colicus epidemic hit Deering and the whole Jarrett family died except for one child. They buried them at Braggadocio. Her husband was in the penitentiary, they sent for him, he was released and came home. As far as I know, he never had to return to the pen.

This area out east of Deering was named Pondertown for a man named Ponder who owned lots of it. He had a partner named Harrell. There was a little store in Pondertown at that time. Mr. Drake also had a store in Pondertown

CHAPTER SEVEN

Deering: My Hometown

By Mrs. Burl (Mary Putman) Williams, April 1970

My family came here in 1907 from DuQuoin, Illinois. We crossed the river at Cape Girardeau. We came in a wagon up to Nigger Woods Swamps where Papa's sister, my Aunt Mat, was living. This was up near Anniston. My Papa was a timber man and he came on down here, and that first winter, my older brother Charlie and I stayed with Aunt Mat at Anniston. My mother was deceased, and we were the only two children.

Then when Uncle Walter came back up from Deering to Anniston to get us, we all went to Deering on the Frisco Railroad to Pascola. It was night time as we were getting into Deering, and the town was all lit up with its electric lights. The hotel was really ablaze. Where we came from up near the Ohio River, we had seen these showboats that ran on the river all lit up, and I thought that was what Deering was like. I even asked Aunt Mat if I could go to the showboat!

Well, we stayed at the hotel. That first night Fred, Claud and Charlie had a room. Carrie and I stayed in the room with Uncle Walter and Aunt Mat. Charlie never did use good language, and after a while (we were already settled down) he shouted into our room, "Uncle Walter, come in here and blow this damn thing out." He had been trying to blow the electric light out.

I don't remember how long we stayed there with Aunt Mat,

but Papa had a tent, and he had it set up about where the high school building is now, out by that big oak tree.

There was a little slat-topped building that was a store and it sat about halfway between where the store is now and where the depot used to be. And of course, those big wide walks went all over town. When I came here there were this store building and a hotel. I'm not sure that the depot was here when I came.

The old brick building that is still standing of the old Wisconsin Lumber Company is what they called the fuel room. You know they always cut a slice off of a log. They ground this up and it went to the fuel house, and that is what they used to make the electricity. The engine room was also brick, but the mill itself was a wood building.

I don't know who the first blacksmith was, but later on it was Charley Book. Perhaps a Mr. Moore was there first. Mrs. Book ran a little cafe in one of the old Wisconsin Lumber Company cars. She only did this for a few years.

They had these cars for the log camps and they had a hook in each end of them. The machines that laid the logs onto the dollies could pick them up and put them on one of those cars and move them to a new camp. They were called camp cars. They had a whole lot of different log camps.

As the land was cleared, they moved lots of the houses in town out to the farm. The long row of houses out west of town was called Upper Smokey Row. The houses that they moved out to the lower plantation were called Lower Smokey. This was out southwest of Deering about three miles.

We moved away from here in 1927, and went to Morehouse for four years, then moved back and have been here ever since.

The streets in town never were named. The house I am living in was built in February 1920, and I don't guess there were any more new houses built until they erected what they called the superintendents and principals house. They are the ones that the Crows and Browns live in today. This house was built for Charlie

Enman who was one of the inspectors and shipping clerks for Wisconsin Lumber Company.

During the war I worked in the lumber yard. I loaded buggies with dry lumber. When the lumber first came from the mill, it was called green lumber. This was stacked to dry out. There were big wide lanes between these stacks. They used mules to pull the carts inside these lanes. There was a mule barn just west of the mill, and beyond that was three houses which are still standing today. Elrod, a colored man, took care of the mules. He lived in one of the three houses.

There was a little cart and the mules were hitched to it. They backed it up and laid this other cart of lumber onto it, and those carts had to be balanced because they were two-wheeled. I believe we put something under it until it was loaded. This little cart then carried the lumber to the loading dock to be shipped out.

One day Willie Nixon and I wrote our name and address on one of the boards of one of the biggest loads that was shipped out of here. I got a letter from a boy in Canada, and he said that load of lumber was being used to make boxes to ship food to Europe for the boys in service.

Not very many women worked at the mill. There were two crews doing the same things. Our crew had Willie Nixon, her mother who worked part-time, Eva King, Floyd Davenport and Frances Drury. I loaded the buggy, Eva walked stack and Willie broke off. The inspector would measure the boards and tell how many feet were in it. These boards were from twelve to sixteen feet long. She picked it up and took it to the end, she would let that down, and one on the breaking off would catch it on the wheel and bring it around, and I would place it on the buggy.

The mill worked one shift a day from seven in the morning to six in the evening. The work we women were doing wasn't too hard.

The first school building in Deering was the building that is now the Methodist Church building. It sat on the west side of what we now call the Neel Road.

The first church services were held in the home, until we had a meeting place, which was the school house. After the store was built, I believe that was 1910 or 1911, I'm not sure, we had church services in the big room above the store. Then when the two-room schoolhouse was built, they moved the abandoned school building up to its present location.

This new school building was a two-room building, later having another room added. They had all grades up through the eighth there. If you wanted to go to high school, you had to ride the train to Caruthersville, attend classes, and then ride the train back out in the afternoon. Very few did this.

In 1913, Walter E. Bess and his wife Effie Odell Bess was the first teachers in this little school. She taught the first, second and third; he taught the other grades. He was originally from West Plains and she from Willow Springs. I am referring to the very first school building, the one that later became the church building.

Deering had a killing one day. A colored man, Andrew Simmons, was the meat cutter in the general store. I guess he had been cheating, I really don't know. There were three people in the store that day and he watched them until he got them all on the same side, or he thought they were. Mr. J. C. Clark was the manager of the store, and he didn't see Mr. Clark when he picked up some papers and went to the office. Mr. Si Clough came into the store to get some groceries and a little girl, Mary Sands had come in.

Andrew came out from behind the meat market, and Dow Edgington was opening the safe. Mr. Clough was waiting for Claude Kendall to get some change from Dow. Well, Andrew came up to them and said, "You know, I thought you'd get me today, so I'm getting you first." So he shot Dow first, then he shot Claude and stomped him. Sachel "W. L." Enchlin yelled, "What's happening," and began to run, but Andrew shot him too, in the leg, but he did get away.

About that time, Mr. Brashler, who was the school superintendent (this was after they got the high school here), shot at the

Negro from the office window and killed him out under one of those cottonwood trees. That is where he fell. He was trying to make it back home. He and his wife had the colored hotel over in Negro Town. They got her out of town, and also got his body out of town. He is not buried at Sandy Ford. This was in 1916, I believe. If I remember correctly, there was no trial for this. I think Mr. Brashler was a deputy sheriff, but am not positive. This took place while the post office was still in the general store building.

Juanita Ransom was an only child. Her daddy was the agent over the depot. Mrs. Ransom went to see Mrs. Bess one day, and told her that if Juanita needed a spanking for Mrs. Bess not to give it to her because Mrs. Ransom would do it herself. Mrs. Bess was redheaded anyhow and she said, "Mrs. Ransom, I'll tell you, Juanita has never given me a bit of trouble, but if she ever needs a spanking, I'm capable and I will do it."

There was an old bell on the top of the school building, and I think this is the bell that is in front of the high school today.

This two-room school building, later a three-room, had an extremely wide sidewalk extending outward from the south door, which was the main door. Then there was a board walk the whole length alongside the south side of the building. When this building burned, Mr. Earlie Carter, who was a teacher in the brick building, grabbed his camera and took pictures of it as it burned. The children inside the building had just gone through a fire drill, and everything went orderly without any injuries whatsoever. The building burned very quickly. This was in the spring of 1940.

The houses and buildings from west to east, along Main Street, were (1) Dr. Speers house (2) Miss Byrds house (3) Superintendent of the Lumber Company house (4) Amusement Hall and this building really sat northwest of the store building (5) General store (6) Wisconsin Lumber Company Office (7) Deering Hotel (8) Methodist church building.

The building commonly referred to as the doctors office first sat on Main Street between the store and the office. It was a meat market then, and had the doctor's office upstairs. Lots of the Chicago men would stay there. Then they moved it back behind the store building over close to where Ruby Speer lives today. The doctor moved his office downstairs and there was an apartment upstairs. Mib and Pauline (Condit) Masters lived upstairs at one time. Then after the school building burned, they had school classes up there. The other classes were in the fire station and up over the store building.

Out by the church building was a little house called a "Hose House." They had a house like this on different corners of town in case of fire, and the hydrants were all around. The water tank at the mill provided the water. Very few houses had running water piped inside.

All along this Main Street was a big board walk. Then when you got to the corner where the church building is, there was a boardwalk that went directly north up to the school house.

When they put in the lunchroom on the brick building campus, the children from the little school had to march from their building to the lunchroom. And during all those years, in rain, sleet or snow, the school bus always dropped the children at the campus of the brick building. The little folks had to walk to their building. On a few occasions it might have carried them, but not very many.

In the school picture that is in the Wisconsin Lumber Company book are two teachers. The one on the far right is Miss Alley or else Miss Green and the one next to her is Miss Stout.

The picture of the hotel in this book looks just like the hotel looked. The front door ran into the lobby, with the living quarters of the ones running the hotel downstairs and off to the side. They had three bedrooms and no bathroom. There was a big washroom with big roller towels. The dining room was behind this, then there was a long porch, a pantry and a kitchen. This was all downstairs. While the mill was running, the mill hands filled the hotel. After it closed down, the unmarried school teachers lived there for a while. When the hotel was torn down, the lumber from it was used to build the Little River school house.

Mr. and Mrs. Bess were the first man and wife teachers here. Then Mr. M. E. Brashler came and he was here when the brick building was being built.

Our Methodist minister, Everett Cook, also taught the Mexicans. You know they brought Mexicans in to clear the land. Mr. Cook spoke Spanish. The Mexicans had a camcar out on the railroad. The ones that did not live in it, lived in shacks down close to the lower plantation.

They had a hotel, a school, and a church over in Negro Town. Their old church building is the recreation room attached to our Methodist church today. Their church building sat closer to the railroad tracks and the school building sat further back. The old school and hotel buildings were torn down.

Sandy Ford is the Negro cemetery. Aunt Paul is buried there. She was an old, old slave. She didn't die until the 1930's. One summer when the watermelons were in, somebody told her that if she would carry a watermelon home on her head, she could have it. So she picked it up and put it on her head, and here she went, no hands, and she carried it home. She and her son Joe lived together. Joe is buried at Sandy Ford, too. Aunt Paul was a fat woman, but she was also a very huge woman. A typical Negro Mammy.

Alice is not buried out there. She is buried in Kennett. Alice was here when I was a little girl and she stayed for years and years. She did housework for everybody. She was Alice Walker, then Alice Reid, then Alice Skinner. She really was good help.

James worked at the lumber shed. His wife was Lizzie and she is still living. The Negro school teacher was Lillian and I can't remember her last name. She was the only teacher they had at the school and she taught all grades.

When the Negro school disbanded, they all went to Gobler and Jackson Conley taught down there. When Conley went to school at Caruthersville, he rode with Lynn Speer and Willie Brown. I think the Conley family moved in when the land started selling.

Dogskin, Cowskin and Pull Tight were all settlements between Deering and Steele. I think they called Little River from the Little

River slough. Deering was named for William Deering who owned part of the Deering-McCormick equipment. This company was affiliated some way with International Harvester. And they were somehow connected to Wisconsin Lumber Company. I know when the mill pulled out, they transferred a friend of ours to International Harvester up there.

>(James Charles Putman was born 24 October 1893 and he added a few details to his younger sister's story. He states that his father drove oxen to clear some of the wooded land in Deering. There were two reasons for that. One was that their yokes didn't hang up on the brush like a mule's harness would. The other reason was that a mule's hooves are solid and work like a suction cup when he steps in deep mud. He finds it hard to lift his legs out of the mud. An ox doesn't have such trouble with his split hooves. Charlie himself laid the ties from Deering to Caruthersville with one horse so that the railroad could be extended. He states the railroad that went five miles west of Deering when he came here in 1908 was called the "Railroad Dummy Line." Then when the Deering South Western Railroad was built they nicknamed it "Damn Sorry Wages." He says the freight station was in operation until 1958. Charlie said there were swams of mosquitoes with blue-steel bills. They lit on you a-bitin'. He states that they ate quinine the year 'round to prevent malaria.")

CHAPTER EIGHT

Draining the Swamps

Five Floodway Ditches from North to South

"Swamp Angel" has been defined as a man or woman with web feet, whose diet is quinine and whose only mission in life is to dodge malaria and trap muskrats. This region, known as the "Bootheel of Missouri," or some refer to it as the "Heel of the Boot in Missouri," reflects life in this regard. Optimistic timber men and farmers moved in, cut their trees and planted their crops on the high knolls that could be found, and tried to inhabit this swampland. A small village would be established when four or five families settled in, and thus began the establishment of civilization in the swamps of Southeast Missouri.

Those were the days when the cavaliers went courting in a rowboat; or when the papa lazily rolled over and caught a bass for breakfast from the cabin window. These morass dwellers were perfect amphibians, and as much at home in the water as on land. No wonder they were called "Swamp East Missourians."

In Southeast Missouri, where the Ozark foothills give way to vast flat lands that stretch more than 100 miles into Arkansas, two great Rivers, the Mississippi and the Ohio converge. Also, several Ozark streams, most notable the Castor and St. Francis rivers, flows into this region, known as the Bootheel of Missouri.

Soon after the beginning of the twentieth century a group of visionaries realized the potential benefits of converting the swamps into habitable land. They knew that if the swamps could be drained, the soil beneath the water, some of the richest in the nation, would become available for farming. This undertaking would become the world's largest drainage project.

The Little River Drainage District began in 1905, and is the largest drainage district in the United States. It serves an area some ninety miles in length and varying in width from ten to twenty miles. Otto Kochtitsky was hired by the board as the first chief engineer and the law firm of Oliver and Oliver as legal counsel. On November 15, 1909, the Board of Supervisors adopted the "Plan for Drainage." The board was J. H. Himmelberger (president), C. W. Henderson, Alfred L. Harty, S. P. Reynolds and A. J. Matthews. George S. Hansford served as secretary-treasurer.

The drainage work was long and tedious and required the expertise of some of the best engineering minds in the nation. The drainage was accomplished from 1914 to 1928 through construction of 957.8 miles of ditches and 304.43 miles of levees. When it was finished, more than one million cubic yards of earth had been displaced, a greater amount than was moved during construction of the Panama Canal. Some people have described it as the eighth wonder of the modern world. The district comprises some 540,000 acres, although, through its facilities, more than 1.2 million acres of land are drained.

The swamp's dense forests contained millions of feet of marketable timber. Some oaks reached circumferences of twenty-seven feet and some cypress of ten to twelve feet. In the late 1800's, lumbermen recognized the value of the abundant timber and bought up most of the land. But after the land was cleared of its oak, hickory, gum, ash, elm, cottonwood, hackberry, maple, and cypress, the lumbermen found themselves having to pay taxes on land that was no longer productive to them. The farmer came in, produced abundant crops and the land became known as "The Garden Spot of the Mississippi Valley."

Drainage of Pemiscot County - St. Francis Levee District

October 1918 to December 1922

This resume' was prepared by Howard L. "Cy" Clough of Caruthersville, Missouri, Construction Engineer for Elliott and Harmon Engineering Company of Peoria, Illinois, the contracting firm for this assignment. Details were retained or recalled by Mr. Clough, though he substantiated some facts by renewing acquaintanceship with Mrs. L. E. Thrupp and Mr. Harry Farrar of Caruthersville, Mrs. Tom Hemingway of Caruth and Mrs. Kenneth Deweese of Hayti. By purchasing maps and copies of records of that era, from the Office of Recorder of Deeds of Pemiscot County, the legal aspects and descriptions were substantiated.

As this article was prepared for the Missouri Historical Society of Pemiscot County, Mr. Clough injected information regarding conditions existing in Caruthersville and the county in 1919 in a comparative manner to May 1971. He set forth his personal thoughts, living and working conditions and other activities while on this job. He hoped to enhance the interest in the history of this project by the use of names, firms local and otherwise, of those who contributed to this great undertaking of draining Pemiscot County.

This was a County Court set up. The following County Court Judges were active during the time of construction, Mr. S. E. Juden, Presiding Judge, Mr. T. R. Cole, Associate Judge District #one, and Mr. E. W. Shade, Associate Judge District #two.

Upon my return from World War I, on June 20, 1919, I checked into the main office of Elliott & Harmon Engineering Company on Fredonia Avenue, Peoria, Illinois and found that Walter A. Birkett, for whom I had worked prior to my going into the United States military service, was on a project in Southeast Missouri near Caruthersville.

In a few days I caught the train—about the only means of

transportation—to Caruthersville by way of St. Louis and Hayti, Missouri down near the Arkansas line. The trains were quite lacking in the luxuries of modern trains. There were a few oil lamps, no air-conditioning, the seats were uncomfortable, and odors from food in sack lunches and what could be purchased from the "butch" were at times most annoying. The roadbed was all that was necessary to keep the equipment on the track at slow speeds. This train that I rode was the "main line" between St. Louis and New Orleans via Memphis. The train did not come to Caruthersville. The passengers got off at Hayti which was about five miles west.

I was met by Walter A. Birkett, the Chief Engineer, and W. C. Owens; the latter I had never met before. On our drive over to Caruthersville, in a Model T Ford, we passed a tower machine just north of town that belonged to the Corps of Engineers. This machine was probably putting out 20,000 yards per month using cord wood for fuel. I had never seen one of these before which provoked Owens to "good time" me. He proceeded to make me the brunt of several jokes regarding equipment and processes used in this area.

While walking down the main street, I ran across Claude Nelson, a real estate representative here. I had known him in the army at Camp Dodge, Iowa. He had been transferred to the depot brigade and I was sent overseas. It was good to renew acquaintance with him in this territory that was new to me.

The community was a rather rough place. The country had just been voted dry. Bootlegging was a thriving business. Prices were reasonable, along with the demand. Whiskey was being hauled to Memphis by car and boat. There were numerous boarding houses, several restaurants, livery stables, Sawyer's Drug Store, Gill Drug Store, Citizens Trust bank, Bridgewood Corner Saloon at Third & Ward, Globe Clothing Store and Musgrave & Mason in the 300 block of Ward Avenue.

We stopped by the Elliott & Harmon Engineering office which was over the Post Office. There was the equivalent of three rooms across the front of the building which was facing West Third Street.

We then checked into a rooming house, located behind the office building, which was known as the Jumper Rooming House. This was a stately three-story house of clapboard with a watchtower atop giving view of the Mississippi River. I remained there about two years. The house still stands and is still occupied.

About six o'clock the next morning we all gathered at a restaurant across the street from the Post Office, then to the office. Other contractors there were Willis, representing A. V. Wills & Sons of St. Louis; Frank Kinzel, representing McWilliams Southern Dredging Company of Chicago; Tom Hemingway, owner and operator of a dredge; R. B. Hart, a friend of Mr. Birkett's from Chicago who was dealing in real estate in Pemiscot County. We thought of Mr. Hart as a "character". He lived with a family by the name of Mr. Paul Bester at the south end of town. This location was near the present Fifteenth Street. Mr. Hart had a very strong pipe and a pocket full of matches. Now the matches served a double purpose—lighting the pipe and something to whittle on during his idle moments.

Mr. L. E. Thrupp, District Engineer, was in charge of everything and everybody. As he was doing all the computing, he was somewhat behind in his work. I took over the job of computing for him and we got caught up in about three months.

At this time all the work of this nature was the result of a group of landowners organizing a district under jurisdiction of the County Court. They in turn hired an engineering firm to make the necessary surveys, estimates of costs, etc. The Court taxed the property for the improvement and collected the taxes. This is quite different from the way it is handled today. The Corps of Engineers now handles all the work of this nature. They are furnished money each year via appropriations. It is very evident that our forefathers had a tax burden TOO, along with an occasional depression that forced a turnover in farm lands.

At the end of three months, Mr. Birkett gave me one man and put me out to running levels. My first job was on Drainage Ditch #eight, Lateral 27 which was already staked out but needed levels run over the center line from ditch #30 for one and one-half miles east through Cooper Lake. This location is near the Sample farm in Butler Township. After completion of this, other jobs of similar nature were designated for my attention. I had completed the Cooper Lake assignment in one day. Tom and Ed Jennings left us in the fall of 1919 and went to Memphis. Bob Blair was assigned to lay out work and I was put on the job of take-up at estimate time, once a month. This, with probably seven machines operating, gave me considerable work at estimate time. Mr. Thrupp and Mr. Birkett stayed very busy with other details.

Bob Blair did not stay with us very long and I took over the lay out as well as the take-up for the entire job.

We had two Model T Ford touring cars with one crew to each car—that is, when we could keep them running.

Most all the land was heavily timbered. Land not timbered was cleared but full of stumps. There were no paved roads in Pemiscot County. In the summertime, we usually traveled the roads every day, including Saturday. However, in wintertime, train travel being cheap, we would catch a train at 5:30 in the morning and ride north or south. We would get off at Steele or Holland, or some other station; wait at the restaurant for daylight; then we would walk to our work. The bad part of this was the coming back at 9:00 in the evening which was after dark. That made for a long day! It was necessary that we carry transits, levels and level rods, axes and tapes for the day.

Wages were low. I paid my helpers $2.25 per day for six days a week. This scale prevailed for the entire six years that I worked in this vicinity. At various times I worked the following local men: Carmen VanCleve, R. C. Powell, Winfield Webb, Dell Reno, Olin Tilman,

Melvin Ashley, Herman Medlin, Dee Morgan and Arthur Williams. From Braggadocio I worked Carter Bray, and from Pascola I worked Ben Adams.

The system or plan we used on taking cross-sections was simple and fast. We could run from twenty to forty sections a day using three rod-men and me as instrument man. Usually I would send the boys out to stake out the lines; then I would go out and run the sections. We would wade the ditches where possible; where impossible, we used a small "john" boat. A shot was taken on the water surface quite frequently. All measurements were taken below the water surface with a sounding rod. Areas above the water were shot direct with the instrument. Ten by ten cross-section papers was used. We did not use any duplication but just plotted field section direct to the cross-section as we took it. I believe this idea came from Walter Birkett. When we ended up we had a completed section with bottom and side slopes established and ready to run the planimeter over. No field book was needed except for line work.

In taking up the sections for estimates, we picked up at the station of the last estimate; we took cross-sections; plotted same every 100 feet. In addition we took soundings in between. All sections were plotted as taken. Any high sections were thus determined as they were taken and the dredge operator could thus be made aware of high places in the ditch.

All of the machines used hand-placed dams to hole up the water in the ditches so they could float and dig. They each had side and rear spuds to assist them in digging and keeping the machine lined up. As I remember, they were all old but in fair condition. The dredges were all built of timbers, old and new. They were all steam operated burning coal for fuel. They started work early in 1919. The McWilliams dredges evidently commenced first at the north end of the county and worked to the southwest ending up in the vicinity of Deering.

As we proceeded with the work, a schedule was kept. This progress schedule was kept on the wall at the office. One could see that all work was on schedule and kept up with once each month.

Commencing in the vicinity of Highway 84, West of Hayti, they changed the style of dredging the main channel at this point. Previous to the arrival of the dredge, it was agreed that some changes were necessary from this point to the end of the dredging. It was going to be necessary to dig a flatter slop, which the dredges could not execute. Therefore, from here on down, floatation was necessary but no attempt was made to execute the three-to-one side slopes. The bottom grade and floatation were all that was done. A deal was executed for a dragline belonging to W. E. Callahan Construction Company, at Deering, to execute a flat slops to the end of the project.

The Deweese Machine was built during the spring of 1919 near Hayti; it was put to work digging south of Main Ditch No. 6.

The Blazier Machine was built about the same time and put to work on Lateral No. 2, near Braggadocio, and continued digging south.

The Straddle Machine belonged to Foote Brothers. It commenced digging on the upper one mile of Main Ditch No 6, then moved south to Lateral No. 3, Drainage District No. 3, and dug south 2 miles from Route U.

The A. V. Wills Dredge was built at Steele and dug southwest from the upper end of Steele, and picked up on laterals as proceeding southwest. They later took this machine on the Elk Chute Drainage District job to work in that district on what was known as Belle Fountain Ditch.

The Tom Hemingway Machine was built on Half Moon Lake, Drainage Ditch No.1 of District No. 3. They proceeded south and southwest digging out laterals on Drainage District No.3.

Frank Stanley, Superintendent for W. E. Callahan Construction Company, moved in a skid and roller machine in the vicinity of Cooter. This was a dragline that traveled on wooden skids and rollers. I have seen only one other machine like this; it was used to strip gravel near Springfield, Missouri. During their stay at Cooter and vicinity, they replaced the engines from a steam rig to Fairbanks-Morse Diesels; this machine had quite a long boom; was very efficient when operating in dry weather.

The ditch dump road, adjacent to Ditch No. 30 and No. 6 of Drainage District No. 8 was built with the material from these excavations. In my opinion, this piece of road was the worst in the whole of Pemiscot County. On one trip with two Model T Fords, we had to detour west about three miles when we came to this stretch of road, and then through a bad slough to get back to the main road. This terrible road condition existed for about three years.

The road from Caruthersville to Hayti was always in very fair shape. Also, the road from Caruthersville to Braggadocio was usually in very good condition in the winter months. Other roads throughout the county were, at times, practically impassable in the winter months. The maintaining of the roads was up to the farmer who owned the adjacent property. However, if he did not live on the property, the road was usually not maintained.

All of the dredges had floating rigs for feeding and housing the crew. These were generally in the form of a quarter boat floating behind the dredge at various distances. I am not able to recall the names of the different cooks except the one for the A. V. Wills & Sons Dredge at Steele, Mo. This was Mr. and Mrs. Brown. They were parked at the highway south of Holland for quite a long time. On numerous occasions I stayed all night at this machine.

The work hours on all dredges were on a twelve-hour basis. That schedule applied to the runner, crane man, deck hand, and fireman and occasionally an extra hand. I believe they changed shifts at 6:00 a.m. and 6:00 p.m. and attempted to run continuously on all shifts, 24 hours a day and seven days per week. I believe the meals were sent out to the machine from the quarter boat, except for the meals at shift-changing time. The Engineers were always furnished meals when it was made known that they were on the job.

Frank Kinzel, Superintendent for McWilliams Dredging Company of Chicago, left in 1920. I later met him in Tampa, Florida where he had charge of operations on a large suction dredge at St. Petersburg and a machine or two on the east coast. Harry Farrar, who was local Assistant Superintendent for McWilliams, finished operations on this project in 1922. He now resides in Caruthersville.

Drainage of the area covered by these ditches had been under contemplation since about 1905. The work that we had been sent in here to do was contemplated to begin about 1918. It was completed about 1923. Much work has been done since that time; the number of districts has been increased; drainage being an ever-present problem, thereby requiring perpetual maintenance.

Elk Chute Drainage District

By Howard Clough, October 1971

The Elliott & Harmon Engineering Company of Peoria, Illinois, after completing the Pemiscot County project, moved their offices to Deering, Missouri for purposes of draining Dunklin County. When A. V. Wills & Sons completed their portion of the Pemiscot County work, they proceeded into the Elk Chute Drainage District portion of the project and completed that portion of the Elk Chute project known as the Belle Fountain Ditch which went across the drainage district from East to West, just north of the South boundary. We also had some of District No. 9 ditches to complete with other equipment.

This Elk Chute project had about 50,000 acres in the area, bounded on the south by the Arkansas State Line; on the east by Pemiscot County; on the north by Little River Drainage District; and on the west by the "double ditches," now totaling five ditches to the Arkansas lines.

In the late fall of 1922, I, Howard L. (Cy) Clough, with my wife, Antoinette Aquino Clough, moved to the community of Deering, about twenty miles due west of Caruthersville, Missouri. We secured a square frame house, on the "back street of houses." It might have had a double wall but I am not sure. I know that we had to have plenty of blankets in the wintertime. This house had four rooms with no bath. It faced north toward a row of similar houses. It had rough floors and no conveniences whatsoever. We furnished it with new furniture from Blytheville, Arkansas. We had a coal shed about fifty feet from the house with elevated board walks leading to same. There were elevated plank walkways all over town, a necessity on account of high water each year. Each house had a front porch and a back porch. We got our water supply from a driven well in the yard. We used a King heater for heat and a coal-oil stove for cooking purposes.

After about one and some half years here, we moved up on a street next door to Mr. Manton who was office manager for the railroad. It was a different type of house and had three bedrooms. Electricity was furnished by the Wisconsin Lumber Company; there were no phones except at the Company store; the Company furnished a doctor. An entrance gate on the East Side of town was locked every night at ten. The village had a hotel, a barber shop, a saw mill and the Wisconsin Lumber Company had a local office. The Wisconsin Lumber Company had a small railroad for logging purposes; there was also the Deering Southwestern Railroad that ran between Caruthersville and Hornersville. The Company facilities were all operated by the Company forces. I think the mill probably got out timber for five or more years.

The W. E. Callahan Construction Company, of St. Louis, Mo., was the contracting company on the drainage project. Their plant was a three-room office building; a large shop, and a commissary building. I headed up the Engineers on the project and had the room on the north of the office; the District office was in the center; the Contractor had the room on the south end.

When possible, I repaired all my instruments that I used. They consisted of two transits, two levels, four axes, six machetes and ditch blades. We also had a blue print machine, from the Caruthersville job, that was operated by the sun. The Contractor had about four Fairbanks Morse #41 speeders; the Engineers had only one, but it was ample.

We worked six days per week and the Contractor worked seven days per week. We left every day about six a.m. in order to get ahead of the log-loading crews on the main line of the railroad. The job was about twenty miles north and south and could be covered each day.

The timber has been cut and only the stumpies remain before clearing the land. Almost all of them are six feet tall, as that is how deep the water was when the men stood in boats to cut the timber.

The Contractor had Wes Gierth at the shop; C. F. Waites was a master mechanic; Gabe Smith was in charge of clearing and grubbing at the north end of the project; Art Gierth was in charge of the clearing and grubbing the south and west portion; Tom Downs was in charge of all blasting of stumps; Harry Comer had charge of the pulling of stumps with a team of horses. John W. Radford was Superintendent of the project; Tom Rivers came in from the job at Elaine, Arkansas to assist. The District offices always had two people working. I had three to four on the Engineer party. One of the owners, W. E. Callihan, visited the job frequently, usually sleeping at the office.

Deering was just a small town, probably less than 1,000 people. The Negro labor, which they used to operate the mill, lived on the south side of the tracks. Mr. Collier, a Wisconsin Lumber Company official, lived along the "front line of houses," more pretentious structures. Mr. Clark, operator of the commissary also lived in a house on the "front line."

The various camps on the job consisted of a cook shack and a bunk house. These were all built on wagons and moved from one place to another, as required. Each camp had a teamster with a good team. His wife would do the cooking. Once each week, the commissary car would be taken out loaded with food and repair parts. The wagon would meet the car at the appointed time on the railroad. For water supply, a new well would be put down each time the camp moved.

The machine ran continually except when down for repairs. There were two men to each shift, and the foreman. The man coming off shift Saturday morning usually went to his family that lived in an adjacent town. He would be off for twenty-four hours. The operator coming on a shift was on for twenty-four hours. There were no overtime and no time-and-a-half.

The machines were all 3-yard-Monighan Walkers, old style walking gear, single cylinders, with a Charter gasoline engine. Before the job was finished, all engines were replaced with Fairbanks-Morse two cylinder engines.

I believe we had only one serious accident on this job. A Mr. Beck suffered the loss of a foot while walking over the swinging gear. The company later gave him a job as foreman on the All American Canal west of Yuma, Arizona.

We started off with number 48 machine on the upper end of the job digging downstream. The work was all the same—building a levee and digging a borrow pit. Number 49 started out from a point northwest from Gobler, digging south. Number 45 machine started out near Rives and dug south toward Hornersville. Number 50 dug south from Rives to the State Line. My job was to see that all machines had the right-of-way stakes, and after being cleared, then restaked.

The engineering on this project was not too difficult. The traveling was the most difficult since great distances had to be walked after getting off the speeder. We had to carry all of our equipment to and from the job site. This of course included the transit and level. The crew I used was as follows: Ben Adams - Pascola; Carter Bray - Braggadocio; Dan Clough - Peoria, Ill;

Winfield Webb - Caruthersville; Roy Medlin - Caruthersville.

Labor was cheap as scales go. I paid my men $2.50 per day for a twelve-hour day.

I want to tell you about the oxen that were used on this job. It was the first and only oxen I had ever seen used on any project. They were first used right below Deering across Main Ditch No. 8. Of course they were only good in wet country and this particular job was a REALLY wet job, especially in the winter months. Mud was "knee deep to a tall Indian." The drivers would jump from log to log, cracking the whip and yelling at the animals. At night they were sort of bedded-down and fed. They moved very slowly, but compensated for it in working in areas where other animals could not travel. These animals were worked in the Deering area for about two years. I do not recall the owner.

I had the first radio in this town. I purchased it in 1924. I got it in St. Louis, wholesale for $25.00. It was a Crosley with two sets of head phones. We could get stations all over the United States. It took me one day to install the antennae on the house and coal shed. I built a cabinet for it. The first station I got was Havana, Cuba.

Others I can recall and their place in the set up at this time: Oscar Leathers from Rives—operator of a loader; Jim Ward—Wisconsin railroad engineer from Rector, Arkansas; Bob Hargrove—Conductor on the Deering & Southwestern railroad; Jim Hargrove—Switchman on the Deering & Southwestern railroad; Dawson—Superintendent of railroad; Manton—Officeman for railroad; R. H. Collier—Supt. for Wisconsin Lumber Company Mill; Clark—Supt. of Company store; "Bud" Minton in charge of logging for Lumber Company

It was my understanding that all of the construction equipment on the job came from Poplar Bluff, Missouri—also most of the men. I also understand that when they shipped out from Deering they went to Bragg City, just north of Deering. I understand they built, and walked out from the derrick, thirteen machines, on the job at Bragg City, Mo.

Numerous clearing camps were established over the entire project by the Wisconsin Lumber Company forces. They built railroad spurs and established a camp at the end of each spur. All spurs were left in until the drainage project was complete.

I need to tell you about the shooting we had one morning. 'Twas over at the "Big Store," which was also known as the company store. A Negro by the name of Andrew Simmons, who was the company butcher, had apparently been engaged in stealing from the company. On this fateful morning he walked past me, with his butcher's apron on, saying "good morning" as usual, to the east side of the store. I had given a check to be cashed to Dow Edgerton, a white clerk in the store. He went to the safe with Andrew almost behind him as Dow opened the safe door. Andrew shot him twice in the head and continued shooting. There were two clerks, a little girl and myself ducking and running. He stalked one of the clerks and killed him. I made the door, jumped out and off the porch while Andrew shot out the windows on the right hand door. I ran home for my pistol and when I got back the Negro was lying dead on the walk in front of the store. Andrew had run out of bullets outside the store and a law-officer, who was also the principal of the school, shot him down five times, four times of which he got up.

All of this work took place in 1923, 1924 and the first six months of 1925. The country abounded in wild game. During a deer season probably five deer camps would be located throughout the area. Game to be had for the hunting consisted of deer, 'possum, racoon, rabbit, wild ducks, geese, turkey and squirrel. At this time the limits were fairly high.

After complete take up in the spring of 1925, high and low spots in the levee and ditches were corrected by the contractor. I had 100 foot lengths of levees and ditches taken up and plotted for inspection. Mr. Walter Birket from the Caruthersville office, and Mr. John W. Radford inspected work and made final approval.

I then went to Memphis to discuss with Mr. Oakey, of Elliot & Harmon Eng. Co., the job at Clewiston, Florida. We could not agree so I went by train to Tampa. "Skeet" sold out our household goods and joined me in about a month. At this time I was thirty-one years of age. I had been with Elliott & Harmon Engineering Company for six years.

CHAPTER NINE

COME TO "THE HEEL OF MISSOURI"

Where Diversified Farming Pays Big

by Wisconsin Lumber Company, 1925

Low-Priced Land for Live-Stock and Poultry Raising, Dairying, Corn, Cotton, Alfalfa, Clover, Small Grain. Mild Winters, Healthful Climate. Near-by Markets, Good Schools, 17 Years to Pay
Fertile Farms at Reasonable Prices, Well Located for Stock-Raising and Dairying. Soil Adapted to Corn, Cotton, Small Grain, Fruit and Garden Products.

The Wisconsin Lumber Company tract includes about 60,000 acres of unusually fertile land in the heel of Missouri, which comprises Pemiscot and Dunklin Counties. This land has many distinct advantages in the way of soil, climate, location, and a liberal and unusual purchase plans that make it possible to own a productive farm and home at a reasonable price.

This soil is adapted to a large variety of crops and will produce excellent yields of red clover, sweet clover, timothy, millet, and an abundance of pasture. Annual alfalfa yields of four to five tons an acre is common in this section. The fertility of the soil, combined with a long growing season and a mild winter makes this section of Missouri a practical and highly desirable dairy country. It is equally attractive for hog and poultry raising, general diversified farming, or the cultivation of corn and cotton.

The photographs reproduced on pages 12, 13, and 14 of this book are on our land. The remaining illustrations are not on our land, but were taken in the neighborhood. These attractive homes and productive farms were a wilderness of hardwood timber a few years ago and are now worth from $125 to $200 an acre. It is only a matter of a few years until our 60,000 acres of land will be covered with homes like the one shown in the illustrations, because our land is of the same quality and well drained.

This land is not placed on the market to be sold to speculators who would expect to profit by an advance in price without developing the land. It is offered only to practical farmers who are desirous of securing a farm of their own and on a basis that will permit them to pay for it on longtime payments. A man who knows how to farm and shows his good intentions by moving onto his land will be given every opportunity to succeed.

The Wisconsin Lumber Company purchase plan is original and unique. It is designed to permit the new settler to make good before he is called upon to make any substantial payments. He is given contract for deed and guarantee of satisfactory title upon completion of his payments by the Wisconsin Lumber Company, a subsidiary of the International Harvester Company. A purchaser, therefore, could not buy from anyone who had the interests of the farmer more at heart than this company. Please read the following pages of this booklet and if there are any questions that arise in your mind, which are not fully answered to your satisfaction, do not hesitate to write us. Requests for information are cheerfully answered and do not obligate you in any way.

17 Years to Pay—A Selling Plan That Permits a Man to Pay for a Farm and Make a Comfortable Living While Paying.

Our plan and terms are entirely different from any other land plan. The prices are reasonable and payments and interest has been worked out in a practical way so that the settler can improve his land and place it upon a paying basis before he is obliged to make substantial payments on his contract. In other words, he is given sufficient time to develop the land so that he can make it pay for itself. You will observe that there are no payments due on the contract the first two years and the third year the payment is only $1.00 an acre on $60-an-acre land. The remaining payments are spread over a period of fourteen years in easy installments. You know just where you stand all the time and your land should increase in value each year. Why work hard on rented land when you can get a place of your own in one of the most fertile sections of the Mississippi Valley on practically a rental basis?

While our lands are in a new and undeveloped country, it is not necessary for a settler to go through the hardships that are usually encountered by pioneers in a new country. You can have a telephone if you want one. We have good schools, churches, nearby towns to trade in, picture shows: in fact, everything any reasonable person could ask for or expect in a country just being developed.

Good roads, both hard-surfaced and graveled, are being rapidly developed. It will be only a few years until you can use your car all winter. In fact in many parts of South-East Missouri automobiles are now used 365 days in the year.

Location of Our Land

Our lands are located in the heel of Missouri, as you will see by referring to the map on page 15. They are on the Deering Southwestern Railway, St. Louis-San Francisco (Frisco) Line and the St. Louis Southwestern (Cotton Belt Route), 234 miles south of St. Louis and 85 miles north of Memphis, Tenn. There is the very best of passenger and freight service, north, east, south and west.

St. Louis has a population of 812,000, with an additional 70,000 in East St. Louis just across the river. Memphis has a population of 172,000. These centers, together with many others in the surrounding territory, provide excellent markets for dairy products, livestock, poultry and eggs, fruits, and other farm products.

You can ship milk and cream, poultry and eggs to St. Louis or Memphis and they are delivered within a few hours after they are placed on the shipping platform. We also have Chicago, the northwest, and the cities of the south and east as a market. Livestock leaving here at night are in the St. Louis market early the next morning and in Chicago the second morning long before the market opens.

General Description

The timber either has been cut or is now being cut from the lands we are offering for sale. After all the timber has been removed, there still remain many standing trees. As a result practically every piece of land has some timber standing. In most cases it is sufficient for rough lumber for outbuildings and to provide a wood lot for some years to come. Small mills are available for sawing rough lumber at reasonable prices.

The timber growth consists largely of gum, cottonwood, soft maple, elm, sycamore, ash of several varieties, hackberry, oak, and cypress. This is a very good indication of the quality of the soil. As a general rule the stumps will rot out in about four years, with the exception of the cypress, which takes a year or two longer.

The usual plan is to clear the ground of underbrush and plant corn among the stumps. Corn or cotton planted under these conditions, and cultivated only twice, has resulted in some very good yields—50 to 65 bushels of corn per acre are common.

Climate

The climate is an important factor to the farmer. The heel of Missouri has as good or a better climate than many other parts of the United States. Although Dunklin and Pemiscot Counties have no marked peculiarities of the climate as compared with other sections of the state, there are differences in the amount and distribution of rainfall and in temperature which are of considerable importance to the farmer. In this respect, the above named counties have an advantage even over the counties a short distance farther north. These differences permit the growing of certain crops which cannot be grown farther north, the growing of two crops in rotation in the same season, the cutting of four and sometimes five crops of alfalfa, and the placing of some crops on the market earlier than is possible from other sections of the corn belt.

The long growing season also prolongs the use of pasturage, which eliminates the necessity of storage of large quantities of hay, ensilage, and roughage for stock. The winters are mild. It seldom goes below zero; in fact, our temperature in winter usually ranges from 10 to 60 above. There is just enough snow and cold weather to make it a good country to live in.

Our average growing season between the late frost in the spring and the first frost in the fall is more than 200 days. This permits the cultivation of cotton and other crops that do not thrive in the north. The long growing season also permits a greater diversification of crops than is possible where the season is shorter. The farmer can, therefore, take every advantage of the unusual fertility of our soil. The average annual rainfall is from 40 to 45 inches.

Maps by the U. S. Department of Agriculture, department circular 183 (Pages 11 and 12) indicate the spring and fall killing frosts in all sections of the United States. The April 1 line of the last spring killing frost passes to the west, north and east of Pemiscot and Dunklin counties. The October 21 line of the first killing frost of fall passes to the west, north and east of these counties. According to these maps, therefore, the average period between frosts is 204 days which substantiates our statement of approximately 200 growing days in a year.

Good Water

Good water is essential on every farm and it can be obtained in the heel of Missouri without great expense. You can drive a well and get an abundance of good water at from 15 to 25 feet. On account of the low cost of providing wells, a farmer can have wells at convenient points about the farm. This is a feature that is readily appreciated by the farmer who raises considerable livestock.

Soil

What the farmer wants now-a-days is rich soil rather than large acreage. Since the beginning of time, the Mississippi River and its tributaries have placed an annual deposit of silt in Pemiscot and Dunklin counties. This silt deposit was the cream of the soil from the northern states and as a result we have a fertile, black, sandy loam that is many feet deep and will produce all kinds of crops in abundance.

We no longer have the annual deposit of silt because the river no longer gets out of its bank and levee. Our lands are now well drained and the soil is capable of producing as many different crops and of as high a quality as any general farming section in the United States.

Drainage

Drainage is important and in that respect our lands in Pemiscot and Dunklin Counties will pass the most rigid inspection. The Mississippi River, which is located to the eastward of these lands, is diked or provided with a levee to prevent overflowing. The drainage, by a system of ditches, is in a southwesterly direction to the Little River. It is impossible in this description to give the readers even a remote idea as to how thoroughly this drainage system has been planned. It has been pronounced by experts to be one of the best drainage systems in this country. In respect to soil and drainage these lands are far more desirable than undeveloped lands in other sections selling at the same figure.

Practical Demonstration Farm

Maintained by International Harvester Company

The Agricultural Extension Department of the International Harvester Company has established a demonstration farm at Deering, Missouri. This farm is operated along practical lines to show what can be done on soil in this vicinity. A diversified plan of farming will be followed, equipment and machinery used, and crops grown on the same basis as if the farm were operated by an individual.

The Company has a farm manager, but he must handle the farm in such a way that it will pay and show a profit. The equipment is the same as that which should be used on any farm of its size.

The Harvester Company Demonstration Farm is maintained for the benefit of the farmers in Pemiscot and Dunklin Counties. The manager has instructions to give all possible assistance to settlers, for which there will be no charge. You are invited to avail yourselves of this opportunity to become fully posted on up-to-date method of farming and take every advantage of the experience gained on this farm.

The Company will cooperate in every way with the settler. We want you to come to us with your problems. Your success means our success; so do not hesitate to call on us for any assistance we can give you.

The Company is making plans to have on its Demonstration Farm, to be sold to our settlers who will provide pasture, proper feed, and shelter for the winter, good grade dairy cows, and pure bred sires. They will be sold to settlers on terms so that returns from the cows will pay for them and leave a profit. The Company will also arrange to sell to the settlers good brood sows and pure bred boars at reasonable prices, provided the purchasers will first assure the Company that they have a proper place to keep this stock and have sufficient pasture and feed for the winter.

In addition to the Harvester Company's Demonstration Farm

there is also a county extension agent who is ready to cooperate in every way to get best results. The county extension agent has the cooperation and aid of the United States Department of Agriculture and the Missouri College of Agriculture. He is, therefore, equipped to give valuable assistance and is well posted on the most up-to-date methods of farming in this section.

Wisconsin Lumber Company Time-Payment Plan

A Payment Plan That Assures Success

A great deal of time, effort, and scientific study have been expended in order to perfect a time-payment plan that would assure success to purchasers with a reasonable degree of certainty. Many different plans were carefully analyzed and discarded. Some were too cumbersome and involved. Other did not arrange the payments to equalize the possibilities of the land to the best advantage. The plan finally decided upon is as simple as A B C. Every purchaser knows exactly what he is under obligations to pay and the payments are not a burden in any single year. The first two years when the land is new and the settler is getting a start, there are no payments aside from taxes. The third year there is a small payment and from then on the payments increase as the earning capacity of the land increases and the purchaser has been able to build up a reserve in the way of livestock, equipment, etc.

The payments on $60-an-acre land are shown at the bottom of this article. On land purchased at a lower price, the payments should be proportionately smaller and at a higher price proportionately greater. Even during the last ten years the purchase is paying no more, on an average, than the rental on equally productive land in the corn belt—and in the end he owns a farm clear of debt.

The payments include interest at the rate of six per cent, and we allow six per cent on cash payments, and six per cent on all additional payments in excess of the regular annual payments as shown. A purchaser can pay any amount from $50 up at any time and he will be credited with six per cent interest from date it is paid. This is better than a savings account because it pays two to three per cent greater interest and is being invested in his own land.

A practical farmer should be able to make a good living and pay out before the seventeen years are up and he will then own a farm clear that should be worth from $125 to $200 an acre. No man who does not own a farm of his own can afford to overlook this opportunity. In many instances it will pay men who now own high-priced land to sell out and come to the Heel of Missouri and grow up with the country and prosper. It is an unusual opportunity for the man with a large family of boys who are all ambitious to have a farm of their own. If land is too high in the locality where you live to realize this ambition, come to the Heel of Missouri—where prices are reasonable—where you can really live and prosper.

Cash Payment

In working out our plan we made no definite rules with reference to a cash-down payment. We want a purchaser to pay as much down as he conveniently can. He should, however, have sufficient money in reserve to run him for at least a year. The cash-down payment can be arranged satisfactorily. A man's qualifications as a practical farmer are of greater importance to us than the sum he can pay down, because we want the settler on our land to make good and prosper. We will sell some of our land without a cash payment down provided the purchaser has sufficient money to carry him through the first year and to make the necessary improvements so that he can live on the land.

Free Railroad Fare

To the purchaser of eighty acres or more, we will refund his railroad and sleeping car fare by applying the amount on his first year's taxes, provided he makes a cash-down payment of $500 or more. Payments are due December first of each year, in the following amounts per acre:

First year, none; Second year, none; Third year, $1.00; Fourth year, $2.00; Fifth year, $3.00; Sixth year, $4.00; Seventh year, $5.00; Eighth year, $6.00; Ninth year, $7.00; Tenth year, $8.00; Eleventh year, $9.00; Twelveth year, $10.00; Thirteenth year, $11.00; Fourteenth year, $12.00; Fifteenth year, $13.00; Sixteenth year, $14.00; Seventeenth year, $15.37 and the Seventeenth year is the FINAL year. Taxes are in addition to above payments.

CHAPTER TEN

Doctor Asier Jacob Speer

By Jack Lewis

From the very beginning, Deering had capable doctors who worked for the Wisconsin Lumber Company. A fee taken from the worker's pay check paid for this service. Dr. Charles A. Wells, a native Missourian, held that position for more than ten years. Dr. Alphus B. Allatun also practiced medicine in the village, and George W. Moore was the druggist. When the town was no longer a company town, then there was not a company doctor. Dr. Asier J. Speer heard about the little town down in swamp east Missouri who needed his services. He gave up his robust practice in Bollinger County and moved to the little village of Deering.

 Dr. Speer was born in Martin county, Indiana, December 10, 1874, the first child of four to William R. and Arinda Speer. While a small boy he moved with his family in 1885 to Zalma, Missouri. Dr. Speer was reared to adult age on the old homestead farm and he continued to attend school until he had reached his sixteenth year. Then, in 1890, he began to teach school, his first position as a teacher being at Revelle, near Lutesville, Missouri. In 1891, he entered the Southeastern Normal School, at Cape Girardeau, completing the prescribed course in one year and heading his class in all written examinations. He graduated April 8, 1903 from St. Louis College of Physicians and Surgeons. Immediately after graduation Dr. Speer located at Zalma, where he initiated the active practice of his profession. He controlled a large and lucrative

Doctor Asier Jacob Speer
10 Dec 1874 - 21 Nov 1940
He faithfully served the citizens of this area for fifteen years, leaving a lucrative practice in Bollinger County, Missouri for this job.

patronage at that place and in the surrounding country. He was widely renowned as a highly skilled physician and surgeon in Bollinger County.

Dr. Speer kept an alligator as a pet, placed the reptile out on the front porch one fine morning to soak up some sunshine. Somehow he managed to escape confinement and made his way to the nearby Castor River. He was never recaptured, however, and needless to say, would-be swimmers in the river were few and far between for some time afterward.

Asier was a direct descendant of Richard Speer who was born in England, January 28, 1762. Richard came to America while a single man, and fought with the American Army in the Revolutionary War. He was a farmer by vocation, and married Delpha Bivins, a native of N. C. Richard Speer died in 1846. To him and his wife were born nine children, of whom Jacob is the seventh and is the direct ancestor of Asier Speer.

Jacob Speer, a substantial farmer of Bollinger County, Mo. was born in Lawrence County, Indiana, January 1, 1824. When he was 35 years of age, he learned the stonemason trade, which he pursued, at intervals, for several years. On February 13, 1849, he was united in marriage with Miss Jane Fields, a native of Indiana, born in 1836. They had nine children: William R., Sarah D., Mahala, Louisa, John, George W., Alonzo, Ollie and Henry. In 1879, Jacob Speer and family immigrated to Missouri and located in Bollinger County where he purchased 200 acres of land.

William R. Speer, was born December 12, 1850 in Indiana, died December 12, 1932 at Greenbrier, Missouri. He and his wife had four children, Asier Jacob, Daggy, Lemuel and Gertrude. This completes the lineage of Asier Jacob Speer back to the emigrant ancestor.

In 1917, Asier was elected to the House of Representatives from Bollinger country, Missouri and served as a member of the 49th and 50th General Assemblies. He was chairperson of the committee of Education and Public Schools and a member of the following committees: ways and means, swamp lands, drainage and levees, public health, scientific institutions and rules. It was probably due to his work on these committees where he heard of Deering and decided to move to this area around 1925-26.

On August 10, 1899, Asier was married to Bertha M. Black at Greenbrier, Missouri. She was the daughter of John and Eliza (Reed) Black and she was reared and educated in Missouri.

Asier and his wife were blessed with fifteen children:

1. Charles Vernon born Nov. 20, 1900, died Sept. 13, 1901
2. Ruth Arinda born Apr. 22, 1902, died 1987, md. William Henry Frazelle.
3. Ida Grace, born March 10, 1904, died January 14, 1964, md. Marion Denfip
4. Waldo French, born Oct. 13, 1905, died July 31, 1988, md. Lena C. Frazelle who was born February 12, 1907 and died 1993
5. Hester Eliza, born August 29, 1907, died Nov. 22, 1981, md/1 Charles Lewis, md/2 Waco Wright.
6. Manford Jacob, born August 8, 1909, died December 24, 1966, md. Opel Welsh
7. Justin Linn, born August 25, 1911, at Zalma, Mo. died Feb. 13, 1993, md. Clora Cox born October 24, 1901, died July 27, 1983
8. Lemuel Howard born March 31, 1913 died in April 1931.
9. William Park "Bill" born November 12, 1914, died August 13, 1976 at Detroit, Michigan, married Rosemary Thomas
10. Asier Otto born January 22, 1917, died young
11. Asier Ale born Feb. 8, 1918, died 1998 (age 80 years old) Lacrosse, Wisconsin, md/1, Irene Kennedy, md/2 Helen Petracha Aug. 25, 1956.
12. Clement Daggy, born May 4, 1920, died young
13. Georgia Imogene, born March 16, 1922, died Oct. 17,

> 1981, md. Harold Oakley
14. Eugene Fenton , "Peanut," b May 29, 1924 at Painton, Mo., md. Virginia Edwards, born June 29, 1925 died July 1997.
15. Phillip, "Kayo," born January 31, 1927 at Deering, Mo., md. Sylvia Petersen, born July 31, 1929.

Dr. Speer joined the Methodist Church in 1900 and was an active member while living in Deering. He was a member of the Odd Fellows and Modern Woodmen Lodges, and was president of the Southeast Missouri district of Odd Fellows in 1939 and 1940. He was a Republican.

Doctor Speer died in a hospital, November 21, 1940, in Texarkana, Texas where he had ridden the train to seek treatments, at the age of 65 years, 11 months, and 11 days. The wake was held at the family home in Deering and his funeral was held in the Eastwood Methodist Church on Ward Avenue in Caruthersville. An overflow crowd attended his funeral and lined the steps to the street. His burial was in Little Prairie cemetery in Caruthersville, Mo. His wife, Bertha then married as the second wife to Rev. S. E. Walker. She was born 20 June 1882 and died 8 November 1949 and is buried in Walker Cemetery at Bloomfield, Mo.

This poem was written in memory of him by a neighbor, Mrs. G. C. Hipp.

> *God took from our garden a full bloom rose,*
> *And left our hearts heavy with grief.*
> *He knew that the toils of this life was too much,*
> *And he bid him come, where there is rest and relief.*
>
> *A friend to mankind this one that we lost,*
> *No other can take his place.*
> *He went to his patients no matter the cost,*
> *And there was always a smile on his face.*

To some he was "Doc," to me he was "Dad,"
For he knew just what to do.
For I went to him with my troubles and cares,
When worried, downhearted or blue.

He is done with the sorrows and worries of this world,
And he has come to a better place.
I hope that I too, can make heaven my home,
And again behold his face.

Dr. Asier Jacob Speer was my Grandad. He maintained an office in Deering which was directly north of the big general store, but he did most of his work as a doctor making house calls, as he was the old-fashioned General Practitioner that flourished during his lifetime.

During the depression of the 1930's, he went about the countryside doctoring the sick in his usual manner. He was unable to collect the money owed to him. He would take pay for his services in a hog's ham, a stand of lard, chickens, lumber or any asset his family could use. He also let men do labor for him such a cutting trees and building log cabins.

The only curse word I ever heard grandad say, about noon one day, when he came home from delivering a baby, we had all set down for dinner and granddad was filling our plates. Boyd Wright burst in the house yelling, "Doc, come with me quick. The Graham boy has cut his throat and is going to die." Grandad didn't reply to Boyd's summons and he yelled again to Grandad to come on. Grandad's reply was"No." Boyd said "Why are you not going to help him?" Grandad looked up at Boyd and calmly said, "If the dam fool had no better sense than to cut his throat, he ought to die." Boyd left and Grandad kept filling our plates with food. The Graham boy lived. He had only cut the skin enough to bleed and scare his parents.

I remember the night our great-grandmother died. We were upstairs in our bedroom playing, jumping on the bed and having pillow fights. Grandad climbed the stairs up to the room and with calm voice asked us to stop and sit on the bed with him. He explained to us that his mother, Arinda who was very old and badly sick was dying. He asked us to come down with him to her room so we could say goodby to her. Later that night she died. As long as I knew her, she never spoke, she would just sit in the living room and smoke her pipe. We were all afraid of her. Kayo and I did not go to the funeral. Instead we went to visit my Aunt Ruth Frazzell, southwest of Deering on a farm back in the woods and played with her children. It was the only time I ever ate popcorn covered with buttermilk and the first time I slept in a barn loft. They were poor but happy. Arinda was born in 1850 and died in 1936.

Grandad's office was on what I always called back street or second street. It was a two-story building with a stairway on the outside of the building. On the top floor he kept the coffins that were made at the blacksmith shop and the local women covered the insides with cloth to make them better looking. My grandmother would tell us it would be more comfortable for them on their way to heaven.

In 1937, Mib and Polly Masters needed a place to live and it was the only place available, so Doc had the coffins moved downstairs to a back room. They moved in, but vacated as soon as a house became available.

Irene Burns, who lived at Gobler, told us about how Grandad saved her life. She was having her first child. She was a very small woman and was having trouble having the baby. Grandad was gone three days for this delivery and Mrs. Burns said he never left her side. When he saw she was in critical trouble, he put all the china plates in the house in the oven of the wood cook stove, got them really hot, and put them all around her body to keep her warm. The baby girl, Paula, was finally born.

I remember my first day going to school. It was to the school house in a field northeast of back street and it was in the woods. It seemed like a mile out of town, but it wasn't. Kayo and I left out this day walking on the wooden side walk. We walked by the big store building, turned north and walked by the barber shop and bath house and toward grandad's office. When we were about half way between the barber shop and his office, the bell rang for school to start. Kayo (Phillip) told me we would get a whipping as we were going to be late. Of course, I started to cry and he told me to shut my mouth. I asked what we should do and he said, "Let's put our tablets and pencil under this loose board and go to the north woods and play hookey. I was all for it. When they rang the bell for dinner we went back to grandmothers' to eat dinner and she asked us how we got so dirty at school, and we said playing with the boys and girls. We told her they were bad and she believed us. After dinner we left to go back to school and back to the north wood to play. No one ever caught on about what we did and on several occasions we would use this trick.

Grandad was a very large robust man with long arms, bald head with a little hair on the sides. Almost everyone I have ever known liked him very much except for a few of the families whose members he did not know how to help. He always was ready to go, day or night, in a car, or horseback, or in a wagon. At this time, the doctor had to go to his patients. He had an office, but as I remember he didn't get to use it very much because they wanted him to come to them. He had a milk cow and it was Bill and Ale's place to take care of and milk her. He had chickens and always two or three hogs for meat. They were killed in late fall when it was getting cold. Nearly every house in Deering had the same kind of animal.

His house was the first in town to have self-powered electricity. He bought a dynamo that had a generator and lots of batteries for storage of the power. Everything in the house worked off of this. It was direct current. He had a telephone, the old crank type.

I remember one time I was going through the house and my Uncle Bill stopped me and asked me to hold the two wires hanging down while he checked the telephone out to see why it wasn't working. I did and he reached up and took the crank and started to turn. I started screaming, for electricity was going through me and it shook me all over. Grandmother came yelling for him to stop, he was going to kill me. Bill was laughing and just having fun and wasn't going to go that far.

Mrs. G. C. Hipp and Grandmother Speer liked to be clowns. They would dress in their costumes, paint up their faces, and go to any event where they could entertain. They were asked to entertain quite frequently and were loved by the community.

For Christmas one year I got a new red wagon. I was at the high school building on the sidewalk, the only walks in Deering that were made of concrete, and Gene Book was with me. He was older, as I was only six years old, and was pushing me in it and I was steering it going around the south end of the building. I didn't make the turn and rolled over on the walk. I tried to get up and I didn't know what was wrong with my arm but it was hurting. Gene put me back in the wagon and pulled me to Grandad's house and he was home. He told my mother (Hester) that my arm was broken and he would have to set it. In those days they used splints of wood and bandage. It wasn't so bad as my mother and grandmother let me have everything I wanted.

It had not healed when I went up to the Zack Hasting house, the big house on the corner, and was playing on the swings at their house. I just couldn't hold on very well, and sure enough, I fell out of the swing, hit the ground hard and broke the other arm. This time they had to take me to the Ross house on 84 Highway, for Grandad was there delivering a baby girl. He set my arm there and sent me back home. I had both arms broken now. My mother and grandmother had to feed me every bit that I ate for a while.

Several years later, a lady came to where I was employed at Wal-Mart, and she asked me if I remembered when she was born. I said, "Yes." She said she didn't have a birth certificate and was having trouble getting her social security started. She asked me to write down the events as best I could and tell them I was present when she was born and Doctor Speer was the doctor. I did as she asked and gave it to her to mail in. Some time later, she came to me and said everything worked. She was getting her check as they had accepted what I wrote.

Eugene Book was killed in service during World War II, either on Normandy or in the African campaign. I believe he was the second person from Deering who was killed in World War II. The first was Doyne Huie. He had graduated from Deering High School and two or three of the seniors joined up, my Uncle Ale being one of them. This was before the war started. Ale was sent to Pharmacy School. Ale served twenty years in the Navy, and married a woman from Lacrosse, Wisconsin and he died there in 1998. Doyne Huie was on the battleship Arizona in Hawaii. He is still there entombed with others, killed in action.

I can remember Mr. Collier, the supervisor, who rode a big red horse around Deering. We children made sure we stayed out of his way.

I can't remember my teachers in grade school very much, but Kayo told if I was going to get a whipping from a certain one, that when she whipped she couldn't hit very hard because she had to hold up her drawers with one hand while she spanked you.

The McCarns and Shortmacks were boss of the railroad work crews. The McCarns had several children my age, like Warren, Glenn Wayne and J. R. We played together a lot. The Shortmack children were older, more the age of my Uncle Peanut and Uncle Ale.

All the boys I know, had at one time or another, tried to climb the water tank in town. It was about 150 feet up to the top and on top of the tank was a ball with a direction finder for which way the wind was blowing. I remember climbing to the walkway around the tank but my Uncle Peanut climbed to the top and sat with his legs around the ball. Everyone in town would know you did it, and when you got home you could expect a spanking from Grandmother. I can never remember my Grandad ever laying hand on any of us.

Every Sunday when Grandad was home he would have us children to the living room and sit on the floor around him and he would read the Sunday comics to us. If one of us was sick that one would get to sit on his lap. So it was always a fight to see who would get to sit on his lap.

Some of the colored people in Deering that I knew in my early age were Aunt Rosie who did most of the cooking for Grandmother and the rest of us. Aunt Paul had helped some, but what I remember of her was one day, she was the Deering store and this salesman was kidding her. She was about one hundred years old at this time. He kept talking about her to the store manager. She could hear every word he said. He looked at her and said, "If you can carry that one hundred-pound sack of flour home without putting it down until you get home, I will pay for it." She lived about a quarter mile away across the railroad tracks then in the colored town. She said to this salesman, "Yas, Sir." She reached down, picked it up, flipped it on her shoulder and went walking home. The salesman tried to tell the manager he was joking, but wound up having to pay for the flour.

Jeff Freeman worked at the big store and he always wore a white shirt and a necktie. He worked there for many years, and lived in colored town across the railroad tracks. He moved to Catron, Missouri when Earl Byassee went there to manage a company store.

James Caldwell worked at the lumber shed for years. He lived in colored town. I really liked them all. There was a colored church there. Two or three times a year, Grandad would take us there for service.

I remember playing tricks on Mack McMahon when he was over the mule barn. Telephones, the kind you dial, had just come in, so everyone could dial and no one would know where it came from. Mack would always run to answer the telephone when it rang. So to trick him, we four or five boys together, would make white flags out of handkerchiefs and put them on a stick. This was how we would signal one another. One of us would be at our phone, and when Mack was seen at the back of the barn, that one would lower his flag. The next would do the same, till the one at the phone saw it lowered, then he would then dial the mule barn number. When Mack heard, he would go running to answer it. As soon as this happened the first flag would rise up, the next, the next, till our phone man saw the one next to him, rise up and he would put the phone down. Some days all Mack ever got to do was try to answer the phone, till he found out what we were doing to him. We didn't get a whipping for this, but we got a good talking to, and were forbidden to touch the phone again.

Granddad was the Doctor for the section men on the railroad stationed at Deering. For his services as their doctor, he was given a free pass to travel on the railroad anywhere it traveled. He would ride the train to go to doctor people and also use the train to go for treatment for himself, after he got in bad health with heart trouble and high blood pressure.

CHAPTER ELEVEN

My Recollections of Deering

By Mary (McIntosh) Stillman-Wright

My Dad got to Vicksburg, because Frank and Mose Stover had built a nice home out there. They had this cut over land and they hired Dad to put them in a sawmill so they could cut the good timber that the big mill left. I was five months old when we left Braggadocio and moved to Vicksburg.

There was no school and my brother was going to be eligible to start to school in July. Mr. Charles G. Ross was the county superintendent of schools, and he got this little school started and J. P. Vickrey came to teach school. Edgar started to the little school and so did Mamie Stover and the Ledbetters and some Brewers.

Braggadocio put in a bid to be the county seat as they were the most centrally located place in Pemiscot County. In order to do that, they had to have a doctor and Grandpa Kersey was in medical school and he passed the state board in Missouri. He was given the certificate title of a doctor, and he came here in order to be the doctor so they could have the county seat. That's how grandpa Kersey got to Braggy, and he had served 12 or 14 years, his kids were all married and he wanted to retire. So he got Mr. Vickrey to become a doctor. So Mr. Vickrey went back to St. Louis University and got his degree. He wasn't married when he came here, but he married Delia Meeks over in east Tennessee where they came from. Their daughter is Helen who married Bailey Rutledge. Helen took care of Grandma Meeks.

When I started to school at Deering I went to that old frame school building way down on the north corner. Mr. Brasher was the superintendent and he had to crowd us in there and worked all the time to get this brick building. Mr. Brasher was an officer and veteran of World War I. He was a very staunch man with the military training and very patriotic and devoted to the country. He was a strict disciplinarian

I started to Deering in the fall of 1925 and I was in the ninth grade. I had graduated from Braggy that spring, and they only went to the eighth grade, then they transferred the students to Hayti. My mother got the chance to buy the big hotel at Rives and we moved down there that summer and Edgar worked in the store and office and then he went of to Chillecateaux Business School.

We were able to move in a wagon, as there was a wagon trail from Deering out to number five, which was the sawmill furthest south, and we had a nice box house. It was built for the boss man, and I went to school out there two years. We had church on Sunday in the school building. Number two was A.B. Smith's sawmill with a school and big commissary. William Forest shop is painted red, and it was the old store building at Bakerville, which originally had been the old school house at number two sawmill.

Deering had no connection with A. B. Smith, but my dad, Dunk John McIntosh, and Smith were business pals. Smith would get the timber rights to the stumpies and that is what he dealt with at his many sawmills. Dad was a sawmill man, and he built and operated sawmills all over this area. He traveled around from Smith's sawmills and checked on their operation. Smith never named his sawmills, but called them by number. T. R. Cole had a sawmill at Pascola, and my Dad would check on it ever so often.

At Deering they brought in everything new from the north. It was strictly a lumber town and they had a big band saw. They had the finest of equipment in Deering. What they had at Deering did not compare with the little sawmills scattered around the country. It was run by electricity and they used wood chips to generate the electricity, which went off at 11:00 at night and turned back on at 6:00 the next morning.

Mother, who was Nettie Kersey McIntosh, was able to buy the hotel at Rives where they had a stave mill. She had 100 men to feed and she slept about 40 of them in the hotel which had 26 rooms upstairs. You could put two and three men in a room, then they had sleep jackets and they all ate there in the big dining room. She had two black women there in the kitchen. She did the managing. She had two girls that were maids that cleaned the rooms, then they came down and helped serve the noon meals. Now for the men that were in the logging woods, they would pack their food and send to them.

My uncle owned the farm east of Deering that everybody refers to as the place where a Civil War battle took place. Edgar, Leonard and I would take our jelly buckets and go down there and pick up buttons and shells, and items like that which had been left behind. We never did find any arrowheads on this farm, but we found them in Braggy. We would take those things to grandpas at Braggy and he put them in the drugstore, and they gradually disappeared.

Deering was already flourishing and I am sure that all that big band saw was shipped in there from somewhere else. The DSW railroad was built early during its operation. The company got black help and they had the colored town over there. After the Kinsall murder, the colored people from Deering went to Gobler. Dr. Vickrey was taking up land around Gobler of the cut over land and dad ran the sawmill. He constructed two sawmills for Doc Vickrey.

William A. Cannady was an old bachelor and he had a store at Cannady Switch. He also had a store on Highway 84, just north of the A.B. Smith sawmill at Mid City. It was a long slender store building and he stocked it full of all the necessary items. I worked for him at one time.

I was born at 7:00 on a Sunday morning, in 1912, in a log

house about a mile and half from the Gill place, east of Braggy on a farm owned by Farris.

It was about 1925 before I went to Deering, but Grandpa would have patients from Deering. I remember a Morgan family from Deering that came over here for Grandpa to doctor. He would ride the moose. Dad rode the moose, too, during the two years we lived at sawmill number five.

Northwest of Deering there was a log trail set in there through the woods and it was panther woods, and it was dangerous, and we would talk to try to scare off any animal. It was always safe to carry some kind of a gun. When my grandma died in 1922 or 1923, they sent a wagon for mother. It was sleeting and Uncle Luther and Dad couldn't run the sawmill. They heated up bricks and irons to keep mothers' feet warm while the wagon took her back into Braggy.

We could catch the moose and ride from Deering to Braggy. There was also a good pole road that ran between the two towns. Dr. Vickrey and Dad supervised getting that pole road laid. They were just wagon trails. That road then was just an old dirt road and in the winter you couldn't get a car over it, but with a good team of mules you could get over it.

Deering had just one big mill, it was a big mill, and it was a band mill. They cut over all of that land down by Gobler. They left stumpies and little sapling trees. The big trees were 300 or 400 years old and they were b-I-g. The cypress was the main tree.

The old folks would sit up and play cards at night and then go to church on Sunday. This was the only pastime they knew. The rest of the time it was work.

You know how Deering is built in a square block. Mr. Stout's daughter and I got in his car one day, and she got it started, but she did not know how to stop it. We went around and around the square, and every time she passed him, she would yell, "How do you stop it, pop?" Finally she understood him when he said to turn the key off. That was about 1927.

Front Street at Deering was nicknamed "Silk Stocking Row."

When I was there in 1925, Mr. R. H. Collier was chief honcho of the whole operation. He lived in a beautiful two-story house with a double car garage and two big cars in it. Frank Manton lived next to him and he was the head cashier for the railroad. He had others under him who sold tickets. Mr. Dawson was head of bookkeeping and Mr. Meyers was head of the lumber measuring and stacking. Mr. Clark was the manager of the store. Mr. Gwin, of the Gwin family of Hayti, kept books. Mr. Bennett, who was club-footed was also from Hayti, as was the Pophams. After Mr. Collier's house burned, they built a house for W. A. Hudson.

They built the two-story white house out west of the school complex for Grover Wicker who was the farm manager. His daughter Polly, and my sister Joy, were the best of friends. This house had a big shed at the back and a barn that later burned from spontaneous combustion.

They had a lot of houses in Deering that they picked up and moved out to the farms. Most of these were the three-room shotgun houses.

Reuben Dunn's father was the section crew manager, and they lived across the street right behind the hotel. Mr. Copple managed the big machinery in the field, after he had been the big mill manager.

My parents started me to high school in Braggy, staying with Uncle Robbie and Aunt Bertha. She was a lovely woman, but her kids were all there was in the world. And I was having to stay with her, and I didn't like it at all. W. A. Hudson was the superintendent at Braggy, and he moved to Deering to assume the position over there. He persuaded my parents to let me go to school in Deering. Mrs. Norton was running the teacherage, and my mother fixed it up with her that I would stay there and take care of her three children for my room and board. And so this is when I became associated with Deering. I would dress the three children before I went to school, come home at noon and feed them, and take care of them after school. Then Mrs. Norton sent my mother a bill for two months rent, which my mother paid. It made three of the teachers mad, and they moved out of the teacherage, rented a four-room house and let me move in with them. They said I could pay them the $25 per month rent and have to do nothing but study my lessons.

There was four in my freshman class and nine in my graduating class. Jadie Naile and I were the cutups at any and all parties. They even let us get up at school and entertain the students. They all liked him, especially the teachers.

Let me back up and tell you one more story about the lumber mill at Deering. Before the entire operation started, the big men in Chicago at Wisconsin Lumber Company, tried to buy some land around Braggadocio to put the mill. No one over there would sell them any land, as they did not want the mill at Braggy, because they were going to move in their labor from that northern city, and they didn't want them.

McCormick-Deering made a complete town of Deering. They had a lodge hall for the masons, a recreation building, a bowling alley, and every comfort anyone could want. I guess they thought that made up for the fact that the town was isolated from the rest of the world and the only way to get in and out was on the old railroad.

I understand there was a Mr. Ponder who had a store at Pondertown, and that was how it got its name. One of the most prominent families of Pondertown was the Charles Alva Jolliff family, who moved there in 1927 from Lepanto, Arkansas. They bought the grocery store from Mr. I. R. Wright, father of Waco and Boyd Wright who later had a grocery store at Oakville, and of Myrtice Russ who also lives in this area. The Jolliffs were hardworking people and staunch members of the community. He served on the school board for approximately twelve years. Their children were Claiborne, J. C. and Scottie. Boyd Wright also had a grocery store on the road connecting Deering with Tinkerville.

SECTION TWO

DEERING—
AN AGRICULTURAL
METROPOLIS

Mr. Charles B. Baker was a man of great foresight and he had plans for the future of agriculture in this area. It was with true grit and determination that drove him into his ownership and involvement with Deering. He ran the farming on the plantation system, calling it the upper plantation and the lower plantation, and some land he rented to individual farmers. This enterprise was named Deering Farms, Inc.

His association with International Harvester led him into a small dealership with them. The first red equipment he stocked was kept in this town in the 1930's, and had the "McCormick-Deering" name on it. Later he moved it to Kennett, Missouri and named it Baker Implement Company.

Tractors replaced mules in farming and Mr. Baker filled the country with his mechanized farming equipment. When timber was cleared and tree roots dynamited, Mr. Baker made a sale. His business expanded and he established stores in Southeast Missouri and Northeast Arkansas.

In Deering, he purchased a fire truck and constructed a building for it. A large lumber shed was added, along with a beauty shop, and a small restaurant. In 1941, W.P.A. labor built a new high school building. The service station and bulk oil plant also went into business

In 1996, Baker Implement became the seller of the largest volume of International Harvester agricultural equipment in the United States. It all started right here in Deering.

Charles B. and Hattie Baker had two daughters. JoNelle married T. A. Brown and Charolyn "Bid" married Taylor Miles. Both sons-in-law were involved in the business.

CHAPTER TWELVE

Charles B. Baker

May 2, 1894 - March 29, 1993

In a lifetime that spanned nearly a century, Mr. Baker wrote a remarkable history of achievement in a wide area of fields, from agriculture to business, from religion to scouting, from civic improvement to statewide service. He served as the first president of the Kennett Chamber of Commerce, was an organizer and first president of the Missouri Cotton Producers Association, was chosen an organizing director of the National Cotton Council, served as president of the Missouri State Chamber of Commerce and was a longstanding worker in developing and improving Boy Scout and Girl Scout projects on the Southeast Missouri Council levels.

He was born in his family's two-room log cabin on a farm near Senath, son of Elijah and Francis Almeta (Romines) Baker. After growing up on this farm in the Nesbit neighborhood that had been in his family for a century, Mr. Baker, at the age of 20, became a teaching principal in the Senath Public Schools after attending the old Normal College at Cape Girardeau, which later became Southeast Missouri State University.

On Christmas Day, 1915, in Cardwell, he married Hattie Dial. They were the parents of two daughters, JoNelle Brown and Charolyn Miles, and had five grandchildren, fourteen great-grandchildren, and four great-great grandchildren. His daughters, sons-in-law and grandsons have been active participants in his businesses and activities.

While engaged in teaching, he managed a farm, which soon led him to a position with General American Life Insurance Company as regional agricultural supervisor for some 250,000 acres in a four-state area. In 1938, he launched his own businesses, which over a span of fifty years would include farming, ginning, farm implement sales, insurance and propane gas distribution.

Commercial enterprises were not the only activity to engage this Bootheel pioneer, and he measured his success by the activities that were civic, charitable and religious in scope. An active member of the First United Methodist Church in Kennett, he was a Sunday School teacher for many years and served on and headed church boards over a long period. Recognized for his contributions to the church and its institutions, he received an Award of Merit from Central Methodist College.

Mr. Baker's special interest was Scouting, and he was engaged for many years in developing this activity in Southeast Missouri. Serving as both chairman and member of numerous executive committees, he received every award given by the Boy Scouts of America on the local, regional and national level. He spearheaded the development of summer camps for both Boy Scouts and Girl Scouts, heading development groups that led to their establishment and improvement.

A 32nd Degree Mason, he was a member of the Scottish Rite and the Moolah Shrine as well as the Southeast Missouri Shrine Club.

One of the pioneers of cotton farming in the Bootheel, he helped organize both the regional and national development groups for this crop, receiving both state and U. S. Recognition for his long service to agriculture.

Whether it was the Dunklin County Red Cross, the county's Civil Defense Council, the U. S. O., 4-H clubs, Future Farmers of America or the Kennett Board of Education, Mr. Baker volunteered his time and talents to a wide range of civic and service groups and organizations, serving as the first president of the Senath Lions Club and later in the same office in the Kennett Lions Club.

Charles B. Baker, 1894-1993

Mr. Baker was a man of foresight. After going to college, then teaching school, he went into the business world and made a big success of it. His first and biggest adventure was Deering Farms, which he created from the old Wisconsin Lumber Company. He purchased the town of Deering and 2500 acres of land in 1935 and made it a thriving agricultural town, and sold it in 1956.

He was an organizer and director of Kennett Development Corporation at the time of his death.

Several years ago Mr. Baker founded the Charles and Hattie Baker Foundation, which annually has assisted students in securing college educations.

(Taken from an article in "The Daily Dunklin Democrat" March 31, 1993)

CHAPTER THIRTEEN

The Plantation of Deering

By Charles B. Baker, 24 April 1976

The first time I was ever at Deering was about 1907 or 1908 to play in a baseball game. I was on the Senath Independent ball team and we had to go in a wagon to Hornersville, then catch a train to go to Deering to play the game.

The second time I saw Deering was in 1928 after I had begun to work for the Missouri State Life Insurance Company. They had lands surrounding the town and so occasionally I would go into the town. Some of the men who worked for Wisconsin Lumber Company that I saw were the manager, R. H Collier; the farm manager, Grover Wicker; the manager of the store, Earl Byassee and others.

When I first started working for Missouri State in September 1928, I lived at Senath and I had Dunklin County as my territory. In December of that year, they moved me to Malden and I had all of southeast Missouri—117,000 acres. I worked for them until around 1938. My family moved to Kennett in 1930 and have resided here since then.

They began to try to sell me Deering in the summer of 1935, and at that time they wanted $240,000 for everything they had down there and I wouldn't pay it, but I kept talking to them from time to time. Then on the 13th of December 1935, I bought it all, including the inventory and everything they had for $110,000.

Deering was not intended to be built where it was. When

they were moving the equipment in, they finally got as far as they could, and they decided to build the town at that spot. The president of Wisconsin Lumber Company told me they were traveling with the equipment, traveling west from Caruthersville, and originally intended to go another two miles on southwest, which would be about a mile or so northeast of the little town of Gobler. The mud was so bad and the animals worn out. They just stopped where they were.

Wisconsin Lumber Company was a subsidiary of International Harvester Company. It was started down here about 1904 with a big sawmill. They were cutting timber primarily to make the spokes for their carriages and wagons. They also needed wood for their reapers and other equipment. So the first thing they did was build a big sawmill, the biggest one in this part of the country. They would load the logs on the railroad cars and pull them right up into the second floor of this sawmill and unload them. It was a big operation.

The hotel here in Deering was called just that by the folks up in Chicago. They had to have some place for the officials to stay when they came down. People around here called it a rooming house. The ballfield where I played baseball that day was located on the other side of the Methodist church. The preacher of the church did not behold to Sunday ball games. So that particular afternoon he did not join the rest of the people of Deering in watching the ball game. He sat on the balcony of the hotel, in plain sight of the ball field. I feel sure he looked toward the ball field quite often. Incidentally, that same preacher, a few years later, married my wife and me. The hotel was torn down before I bought Deering. My firm used the lumber from the hotel and built the Little River School.

The big office in Deering was in existence when I first came to the town. I remember it quite vividly.

From the time the mill went idle in 1928 until I bought Deering in 1935, they tried to farm the land. They didn't know anything about farming, and they tried to run it with the same personnel they had used in the mill.

They tried to sell the land, requiring the buyer to pay only the taxes the first year. A lot of folks bought that land but had no finances to go with it, and they lost it. Only a few of the fellas who bought that land for taxes have it today.

Another thing that hindered the sale of it was that we had a big early frost in 1935 that killed a lot of the cotton. People would come in from the south to look at the land, and they would say it was too far north to grow cotton. The land just wouldn't sell.

The officials in Chicago told me they were losing from $70,000 to $140,000 a year and were getting tired of it. That's the reason they sold it so cheap. I made two trips to Chicago and I met several of the officials of the company. The president of the Wisconsin Deering Company was down here continuously with me and we finally made the deal.

The lawyer in Chicago was having a hard time trying to write up a contract because they didn't exactly know what the company had down here. So I told the vice president I was dealing with if he would send the lawyers out of the room, and send in a secretary, I would dictate a contract. This he did, and in a few minutes we had a contract that covered everything. In essence the agreement was that they would sell me everything they owned in Pemiscot County, both real and personal, for $110,000. The lawyers said if I was willing to accept it that way, it would be all right with them, but that it was the most peculiar contract they had ever heard of.

Sidney Souers, executive vice-president of Missouri State Life Insurance Company, his father and mother, my wife and I were partners in the company and we named it Deering Farms, Inc. You see, I had no money and I had to get somebody that did to go into partners with me.

I bought only the cleared land, and of the 2600 acres, only about thirty acres was not cleared. They had used sharecroppers in their farming operation, and I didn't like sharecroppers, so I made them all tenants and rented the land to the same people they had used.

I sold them their mules and equipment, helped them get their seed, and financed them in their farming operation. We raised cotton, soybeans and alfalfa. We didn't raise much corn as this land was not adapted for corn.

When I bought Deering, I got what was left of the sawmill, including two railroad engines. When we started the crop in 1936, money was scarce, so I put two fellas to hauling the scrap metal to Memphis. From the sale of this scrap metal, I raised most of the money that was required to make the crop of 1936. Then I sold the engines.

We had to finance all of our tenants, and to save making a charge ticket every time they bought something, we issued them brozine [sic] and they paid their bills with this. Wisconsin Lumber company had used coupon books, but I knew of other companies that had used these coins, so we had them made up. They were in five dollars, one dollar, fifty cents, twenty-five cents, ten cents, five cents and one cent denominations. If a man needed money for his weeks supply, he would go to the office and sign for it, and he would be given the coins. Then he could go in town and spend it at each place as he needed to. When he got his pay, which came through the office, he would then repay his debt.

I became the International Harvester dealer in 1938 or 1939 and I had some tractors and equipment at Deering. The parts store was in a little projection that we built on the west side of the store and the equipment sat in the empty lot on the west side of the store. Then I expanded the implement business and moved it into Kennett.

In those days it was necessary to establish different kinds of businesses in Deering. The farmers could not travel by wagon or train to Caruthersville or Kennett for everything they needed. So it was for convenience sake, rather than a financial reason, that the Deering operation became a plantation.

The cotton gin had already been built before I bought the

farms. We enlarged it, and then in 1936 we built a gin at Tinkerville which we called the County Line Gin. Paul Hutchins developed a very good cottonseed which he named Paula Cottonseed, so we built a delinting plant next to the cotton gin so we could process the Paula cottonseed. We shipped this seed to New Mexico, Arizona, Texas and even sent ten sacks to Afghanistan.

The lumber shed began operation in 1937 with Kimble Swindle in charge of it. I can't remember who else was connected with it, but I later sold it to E. P. Crow and he operated it for several years, until he dissolved the business around 1970.

Zack Hastings, who lives here in Kennett, was the store manager for a while, then Hezzie Highfill, who now lives in Senath, was there. Bill Lester was a meat cutter. L. B. Lincoln and Bennie Williams were both store managers, as was Jack Clayton.

The school was paying its teachers about $60 a month, and I could pay $75, so I hired lots of them. Jack Clayton left school teaching and became the store manager, and later became farm manager. Bill Richardson, who originally was from Blytheville but had moved to Pine Bluff, Arkansas, moved to Deering and became farm manager for me for many years. W. A. Hudson, who was the superintendent of Deering Schools, left the school and became general manager. Later he bought a business at Malden and moved there.

We put in an oil business and a service station. Floyd Farr, who now lives in Kennett, ran the service station, and later Gene Willis managed it and later bought it. Mib Masters worked in the office and at the cotton gin. Other office help was Langdon Clark, a young man from Kennett, and T. A. Brown started in 1937 after he graduated from business school in Memphis. Clarence Carnell and Nathan Wood both worked in the Deering office.

It was around 1943 or 1944, and two men went to James Rounsaville who was our bookkeeper, and they knocked on his door one night. He opened the door and when he did they stuck their foot in and both of them had pistols drawn. They made James and his wife go down to the office and open up the safe and get the money. We actually did a banking business at Deering, being so far from town, we cashed checks for all the community, and at times had a considerable amount of money. That night they got $18,400.00 in cash and checks. About five weeks later, the law officials caught the people who did the robbery and they were sent to the penitentiary. Two of them were sentenced for fifteen years, one for five years and the other one, I think, was paroled. He didn't actually take any part in the robbery, but they divided the money in his store which as over on Highway 61 and they gave him some money for the hideaway.

East of town, where the blacktop road makes a curve and goes south for about a mile, and then curves back again east, on the east side of the road we have found lots of shrapnel and balls out there. Tradition has it that it was a Civil War battlefield, but I don't know any details about it.

I sold the Deering Gin and Mercantile Company, which was a different company from Deering Farms, to Bert Richardson and Taylor Miles and they operated it in 1948 and 1949, then I bought it back. Then in 1956 I sold the entire operation to A. T. Earls for one million dollars, sold the oil business to Standard Oil, sold the lumber shed to E. P. Crow and I think Mr. French who bought the store.

During the time that I had the Deering plantation, I also had a plantation at Catron and a farm of five hundred acres at Bragg City. This was called Delta Realty Company.

CHAPTER FOURTEEN

The Farm Managers

Number One—Grover Wicker

by Mrs. Russell (Pauline Wicker) Burns

My daddy, Grover Wicker, went to work as plantation foreman the first day of January in 1930, and it was the end of a semester in school. They didn't have a place fixed for us to live, and he drove from Hornersville to Deering and Bud and I rode with him to school every day and started to school over here. He would take us to the restaurant in the hotel to eat our lunch. Lela Gibbs worked there and they run out of meat one day. When we got there, they served lunch meat, and daddy told Bud not to make a hog out of himself. Lela came around and said, "You let him eat all he wants." She was just going to charge daddy half price for Bud, but she changed her mind, as he ate as much as daddy and I put together. They got our house ready and we moved. The weather was so bad that spring month, that my sister, who is eleven years younger than I, only got out of the house one time. The ground stayed rotten and marshy all winter.

Robert H. Collier, Superintendent for Wisconsin Lumber Company, lived in that two-story house on Main Street. He was married to Ruby Hargrove whose daddy was a conductor on the railroad, and she was a school teacher. They had three children—a girl and two boys, and one of them was named Robert.

Daddy got rid of those Mexicans that lived on the lower plantation, and moved in several white families from Hackleburg, Alabama. They had moved the Mexicans in to help clear the stumpies off the land and to get the land ready for farming. Daddy said he wasn't going to work anybody that he couldn't understand what they were saying. Most of them were migrant workers and lived basically in the railroad boxcars.

Joy McIntosh and I was very good friends in school. When she was a junior and senior, she stayed at my house more than she stayed at home. My mother never knew until she got up the next morning how many lunches she had to fix. I have seen her fix as high as nine lunches in the morning, because lots of our friends spent the night with Bud and me after our basketball games. My mother was Bertie Rauls before she married and she was from down around Hornersville. The Wickers came over from Tennessee and South Carolina.

After daddy got to Deering he was the plantation manager. He didn't take anyones place as they had just started clearing up this land and this was a new position. They had closed down the lumber mill and were getting the stumpies off the land and was ready to start farming. I have chopped many a row of cotton going around those stumpies. When we moved to Deering there was a colored man that used some kind of gig lever running those logs through, and his cap as still hanging there just as he had left it, and the mill had been closed since 1928.

Three people on the plantation died the first year my Daddy was here. At that time, it was depression and nobody had insurance. They had to build boxes and Daddy had to see they were buried. Lots of them they took down around Hornersville and buried and a lot they took to Caruthersville or even to Braggadocio to the Culp cemetery. Ola Howard, a lady that taught me when I was in high school, would prepare the bodies for burial.

Aunt Paul, the ex-slave who lived at Deering, came to our house, and, oh she just, worshiped my mother. And she would come to the house and we had a little dog, a little terrier, that was the hairiest little dog you ever saw, and she was so afraid of that dog. She would yell, "Miss Bertie come and get this dog." She taught me how to iron a long sleeve shirt. She ironed the yoke first, the collar, then the side of the sleeve that had buttonhole, then the back next, up the fronts, and the sleeves last. I still iron shirts that way.

Aunt Paul is the one that carried a watermelon on her head out to her house one day. Another time, she carried a barrel of flour on her back. When she got to the railroad, she turned around and waved to that salesman. And they made him pay for it, too, as he had bet she could not do it. She showed him!

For recreation, I played on the basketball team, and I played tennis. And we had what was called a University of Missouri agriculture club and I belonged to the pig club. They would give us one gilt and we had to give the university back two gilts. And the girls were in the agriculture club also.

The teachers had a good time at the school teacherage. Now see, the first year Mrs. Jonakin was here she came to Deering without Mr. Jonakin. He still lacked a little being out of college. The company built them a new house. I liked her, but I surely did like him. He surely was a fine man. The woman who ran the teacherage was named Mullins and she had a daughter that went to school with us, in fact, she was on the basketball team.

R. M. Stokes was a good teacher. Every day you went into his class he had a test with two questions and you had to have studied your lesson to know the answers. All the students liked him.

My daddy was an amateur veterinarian and that was what he was going to do and he was at the Hornersville depot and my mother came down to the depot and cried, "What is your daddy going to do with the business without you." So Daddy didn't catch the train, but went back home, and worked with his Dad until he came to Deering.

Charley Book had a blacksmith shop and he had this sick cow and she quit giving milk. He had a son, Arthur, a great big husky boy, so dad told him he was going to have to hold that cow so he could split her tail and put some stuff in it and fix it up. Well, that cow pulled Arthur all over that lot. I was sitting on the fence watching them, and finally daddy said, "Pauline get down here and get a hold of that cow." All I did was put my fingers in her nostrils and she stood still. Charlie furiously said, "And you let that cow pull my son all over this pasture."

They had two mule barns—one on the upper plantation and one on the lower plantation. Arnold Mason was one of the hostlers and Burl Williams was the other until he left that and went to be a janitor of the school. They had many, many mules and in the flood they had to bring them all to Kennett. Six young boys rode the horses and they drove them all the way to town.

Did we ever have mosquitoes at Deering? We took typhoid shots all the time. And there were a lot of big snakes. The Hudson's came to our house one night, and their son Howard proceeded to take care of my little sister Carrie by putting cold cloths on her forehead. Finally someone asked him if he had the measles, as that was what was wrong with her.

Mr. Collier was so precise. He would come out and ride on the farm. One day he came out and daddy told him, "I'm going to tell you something. You just sit up there like a wart on a log. At least you could ask the man how his family is, or how he is. The next time we ride up to somebody, you ask him about his family."

I tell you whom daddy liked and his name was Andy. He came from Wisconsin Lumber Company main office in Chicago every fall when they went to gather the crops. Oh, he was small but he was smart. The company issued coupon books to the people and all this credit had to be accounted for so the debts could be paid. He was really good.

I went to school at Deering and Mr. Brashler had already left and Mr. W. A. Hudson was the superintendent. He held that job at Braggadocio and then they hired him at Deering. Where he came from originally, I don't know. I graduated in 1934 and there was thirteen in my class. I walked to school, as I lived within a mile of it.

My husband was Russell Burns and he went to school and

graduated in 1934 with me. We had two children, Jack and Sonny. Sonny teaches history and Jack teaches science. He loves his history and has books all over the house. He especially loves the Civil War history.

One Mexican family had lived in the house where we moved into when we got married. On my front porch was a flower box and I planted flowers in it. Daddy came by one day and asked, "Do you know what you have got those flowers planted in?"

I answered, "Well no, it was here and I just thought flowers would look pretty in it."

He replied, "The Mexicans, when their children got really sick, would build the casket. This family had two little children that got really sick. One died and the other didn't. Your flower box was the casket they had built for it."

We had the flood in 1937, and when Russell and I got up that morning we had 400 acres of cotton, somebody cut the levee on #eight ditches, and by 11:00 all the land was covered like a swamp. Lot of people that farmed that land walked off and left, but we didn't, we paid back every penny. It took us a while, and we had to skimp, but we did it.

Another ex-slave lived at Deering. She was Rose Stockton and her husband was Mose Stockton. She worked for me when Sonny was born, then she left and moved somewhere, but when Jack was born she came back to me. Now Rose was from Marked Tree, Arkansas, and worked for the people in Marked Tree that practically owned the town. Rose was also a midwife, and Russell has taken her many a night, when it was raining, and she had to go. Now when they lived on the farm where we lived, Russell furnished Mose seed, a mule and a little shovel and he made the gardens. They were quite old. She wasn't in slavery as long as Aunt Paul. Rose moved to Kennett with my mother. Daddy went to work for the Cotton Exchange Bank as farm representative when he moved from Deering in 1935. They wanted him to stay, but he left.

Number Two—William "Bill" Richardson

By Pat Richardson

My father, Bill Richardson, had left this area in 1930 and moved to Sherrill, Arkansas (out from Pine Bluff) and worked for Emory Matthews of the General American Life Insurance Company. Originally, he was from Blytheville, Arkansas, but had moved to Missouri, following his twin brother, Bert, into this area. Two of his other brothers, Bart and Russell, lived in the Bakerville area, and were also farmers. His brother, Oliver, was manager of the Missouri Mercantile Store in Bragg City. The other brother, Ted, lived in Chicago and had a photography business there. Dad's sister, Pauline McLeod, lived in the Bragg City-Bakerville-Deering area. She was a widow for more than forty years. The other sister Beulah, married to Ben Hawkins, resided in West Helena, Arkansas where he was connected with the Chicago Mill and Lumber Company.

At this same time, in 1935, Mr. Baker hired Mr. P. A. Hornbeck as construction engineer. It was his job to finish removing the stumps from the land that was not completely cleared. Dad, Mother and I moved just west of the school complex in the two-story white house. We lived there from 1935 to 1942, and my daddy was the farm manager for Deering Farms, Incorporated during those years. He oversaw the farming on the upper and the lower plantations.

When he began, there were 105 teams of mules. One of the mule barns for housing them was behind our house. It caught fire and was completely destroyed. The tragic thing about the accident is that Mr. Baker had two riding horses stabled in the barn, and they did not survive.

This was in the time period when tractors were replacing mules on the farm, and it wasn't long until bright red International Harvester equipment was delivered to the farm. Dad, and all his workers had to adjust themselves to this new way of farming.

The workers on the farm needed supplies during the week. They would go to the business places and sign a ticket for what they got. This ticket would be taken to the main office and run through the bookkeeping machine. This got to be a very tireless job, as some days there would be up to five tickets for each family. So to avert the work load, Mr. Baker had some bronzine coins minted. They were redeemable at any of his business locations. The head of the household could go to the office, sign a ticket for the coins, then spend them in town. This constituted only one bookkeeping entry. We called the coins "bronzine," as they were made of bronze.

Dad's job as farm manager kept him busy, as the land was great in the production of cotton and soybeans. There was no slack period in the planting or harvesting of these two crops. He usually was involved with both crops at the same time. The only good thing is that the soybean crop harvesting was a once-over job.

The cotton was picked initially about the first week in September when the first bolls opened. The women and children were eager to earn some money, so they withstood the heat for this reason. Then it was picked again, this time in a field of white cotton. I often heard my daddy say, that by picking it that first time, it helped it to open faster. Finally they "pulled bolls" in the wintertime, because the freezing weather would help the last green bolls open and yield some cotton. This would help the farm hands have money for groceries during the winter, and also kept the cotton gin busy.

I attended the Deering school. I loved all the music classes, and was in the first band that we had at school. We had classes in July and August and were dismissed in September and October for "cotton picking vacation." Now, how they put 'vacation' on that phrase, I'll never know, because picking cotton was no vacation to me.

In 1942, my dad resigned as farm manager, and purchased 160 acres on the Rice Road and we moved there and I was still in the Deering School District and finished school in 1948. He was farming for himself, and renting about 600 acres of land to go with his 160.

I went to college at Ole Miss at Oxford, Mississippi where I graduated with a double degree in music and band director. In their later years, mother and daddy moved to Kennett. Dad died with a heart attack March 9, 1961, and my mother moved to Jonesboro, Arkansas to be near me. They were married November 11, 1920 at Blytheville, Arkansas.

Number Three—Jack Clayton

By Zoetta (Clayton) Whitener

An exciting time for the Jack Clayton family, at least for me, was moving from Clarkton, Missouri to Deering, Missouri in 1937. We moved from a sandy area to a "sea of water." The only road was water with stakes on both sides of the road to mark your spot. Our vehicle was a big truck and water lapped up almost to the bed and also lapped up almost to the floor of our house. While waiting for the unloading, I kept hearing a strange sound, and finally across the road at the top of the ditch bank I saw a snake eating a frog for lunch. Remember, I was only seven and these were things I had never seen nor heard, so it was exciting.

My mother had just moved from a new house with solid hardwood floors, so suffice it to say, she was not happy. But it was the depression and they both had gotten jobs at the Little River school. Dad was to teach the fourth and be principal. My Mother was to teach the first. Mildred Farr taught second grade and I was in her room. Gutherie Skaggs taught third. They all had thirty to fifty kids in their rooms.

After the flood water went down, every kid in school had itch, lice, boils or whatever a flood brings. We had to burn smudge pots around and under the houses for mosquitoes. The house floors were not all that closely built.

We then moved to a house across the road from the school house. While living there we had a tornado. We were in school and my Dad had all of us to go under the ditch bridge and lay flat. We could raise our heads a little and see the monster coming at us, but right behind our house it did an abrupt jump up over our house, over the road and over the school house, then touched back down and created havoc for quite a few miles.

Let me give a word of advice to kids of school administrators. My Dad didn't want anyone saying he was not doing his duty so whatever mischief happened at school, I was one or the only culprit. One day after being innocent but being accused, I went to Tinker's Store and bought everyone at school a piece of penny candy and charged it to my Dad. Every one of the clerks got a kick out of this, and my Dad had to pay up. Maybe that's the reason my Dad became Deering Farms store manager and never did get back into the educational field again. My Mother stayed for thirty-eight years in the teaching profession.

My Uncle Dwight Whitaker, his wife, Chub and son Darrell moved to Little River. He had been teaching third grade. When my Dad left he became principal until they moved to Pontiac, Michigan. Loren Lincoln then took my Dad's place.

After a few years as store manager my Dad became farm manager and we moved again. This time it was to the two-story house just west of the school campus, and we lived there during the World War II years. There were machine storage sheds and a big barn behind our house. One day after a big load of fresh hay was stored in the barn, it caused spontaneous combustion and caught the barn on fire. They would drive the horses out, but the horses ran back in. Finally, they put something over their heads and saved most of them. My two pet horses, "Pal and Pat" were killed, also, my mother cat and her new babies.

Later, my Dad decided to do his own farming and we moved to the Rice Road next to Bill, Bertha and Pat Richardson on the opposite side of the road. My grandpa and grandma, Arthur and Lou Clayton, lived in the next house on the same side of the road. My Grandpa grew watermelons and they were good. He grew a patch for me. I believe this was my pay for helping him chop and pick his acre of cotton. We took grab rows. He couldn't see too well and goose locked his row. I picked mine and the grab row, then turned around and started back on his goose locked row. Every now and then he would want to stop and get the tractor so we could go to the store for a Nehi soda. Now, Grandpa couldn't drive, so I was the driver. I didn't even know reverse, but my grandpa would have a long bilious black stogie in one hand and holding on to the tractor seat with the other one. Not knowing reverse, we just kept turning until we headed back the way we came. He surely was a brave soul to ride with me. Of course, we waited until everybody else was gone before we did this. None of this was bad for Grandpa as he lived to be ninety-five and died in his sleep.

After I went to college, at SEMO, Mother and Dad moved to Cape. A few years after that Dad died, my mother moved to Desloge where we live. I married Don Whitener and we have two children. My mother is 93 years old and is living in a retirement home and is very active.

I always felt that our school system was a good one with good educators and also was a hub of the community. I remember the suppers at the school cafeteria where the men cooked and cleaned up. So many, young and old, went and just enjoyed being together. My memories of all facets of Deering, especially the people, and events are still fresh in my mind. I enjoyed it all.

After Mr. Clayton was farm manager, the plantation system changed and Mr. Baker rented all the farm land to individual farmers. Mr. J. T. Lindsey, with his wife Loy and daughters, Mary and Betty, moved into the farm manager's house. Mr. Lindsey continued farming his land near Bragg City, but also farmed several acres of the Deering Farms land.

CHAPTER FIFTEEN

Mildred Callis Farr—School Teacher

by Eugene Farr

Mildred Callis was born June 10, 1913, the daughter of Wade S. Callis and Anna Elizabeth Knapp, who were married June 5th, 1912. The Callis's had migrated to Southeast Missouri from Kentucky while the Knapps came from the Sardis, Ohio area. Both the Callis and Knapp families, along with others from Ohio and Kentucky, including the Bullocks, moved down the Mississippi River to Pemiscot County. Their home furnishings were unloaded from the river boats at Caruthersville and then transported by the Deering-Southwestern Railway to Braggadocio, where it was loaded on wagons and taken to the community in which they settled - now known as Vicksburg. Mildred's grandmother, Mary Josephine "Josie" Callis married William "Bill" Bullock, grandfather of our cousin, Porter Bullock, of Wardell, Missouri, and his brother, the late Lester Bullock (husband of our Illinois cousin, Ollie Lipsey Bullock). Josie's marriage to "Bill" Bullock followed the death of her first husband.

In the first decades of the present century, the land in the bootheel area of Missouri was covered by either large swamps or dense forests. The community of Vicksburg was surrounded by wooded land owned by the Wisconsin Lumber Company of Deering. Many of the local folks found employment with that company. Once the land was cleared and the swamps drained some of the most fertile farm land in America was ready for the plow.

The story of the wedding of Mildred's parents is an adventure in itself. Because of Anna Knapp's age (14), Wade Callis (18) took his soon-to-be bride by horseback to Blytheville, Arkansas, for the ceremony. They both rode the same horse, a trip of some distance in those days, and to another state. The wedded life of Wade and Anna (Knapp) Callis was tragically short. On October 12, 1913, some four months following Mildred's birth, Wade Callis was killed in a hunting accident.

Eventually, a young man by the name of James Joseph Kerry began showing an interest in the young widow. James and Anna's courtship consisted of three dates: Date number one was a horse and buggy ride. Anna was accompanied by her young daughter, Mildred. Date number two was the setting of James Kerry's proposal of marriage to Anna. Mildred was again present. Their third date was the marriage day. Mildred stood by her mother during the ceremony. Following James Kerry's early death, Anna married for a third time. This time she married Thomas Daniel Potts, formerly of Houston, Texas.

Mildred's grandparents were large landowners in the community. Mildred recalls fond memories of the dairy, orchards, and peanut farms on her grandparents' place. She says in those days, most of the farms were separated by heavily wooded sections of land. There was free range for livestock. Farms were fenced to keep out the animals rather than keep them in.

As a respected member of the community, "Josie" Callis Bullock, was primarily responsible for the naming of Vicksburg. In 1913 she was asked to write to the Post Office Department requesting a Post Office be established for the community - heretofore known as Dogskin. The Post Office promised the facility provided the name was changed to something more dignified. The name Vicksburg was chosen to honor J. P. Vickrey, a local school teacher of the times. Mr. Vickrey later became a doctor and practiced medicine in Braggadocio for many years. The post office operated from 1913 until 1916 when it was disestablished.

When she reached school age, Mildred began her education in

a small one-room country school. The school was taught by one teacher and included grades first through the eighth. After finishing the eighth grade, Mildred transferred to Deering to attend High School.

She was a student of Deering High School when she met her future husband, Floyd Farr, son of William Emory Farr. The Farr family had recently moved into the area from Hackleburg, Alabama. The year was 1930. The event, a pie supper sponsored by the church to help raise money for the school. A pie supper (or box supper) was an excellent means for young folks to meet. The young ladies would bake the pie or prepare a boxed supper and the young men would bid on the box brought by the girl of his choice. The highest bidder won the pie and the privilege of sharing it with the young lady. Floyd's first attempt to meet Mildred in this fashion failed. He was outbid by his cousin, Clarence Lipsey, who later married Lula Mae Stover, another local girl.

Floyd continued his pursuit of Mildred. His next ploy was to use his sister, who was a classmate of Mildred's, to inform Mildred of his desire to date her. Once they began dating, Floyd pressed for an early marriage; however, Mildred had long ago made up her mind to become a teacher and convinced Floyd she would not marry anyone until she had earned her teaching degree. True to her word, she entered Arkansas State College, at Jonesboro, Arkansas shortly after graduation. Floyd made frequent trips to Jonesboro to visit Mildred while she was in college.

Finally, at age eighteen, Mildred Callis married her twenty-one-year old beau, Floyd Farr. At the time of their marriage, Floyd worked on the railroad and was away from home except on weekends. With the help of her mentor, Mr. Hudson, the Deering School Superintendent, Mildred secured a teaching position at a small country school outside Deering. In this small one-room school house, Mildred began a career that would span forty-four years.

Mildred's memories of those early teaching days are many. Thrilled at having a school of her own, she could hardly wait until its opening. One summer day, near the beginning of the school year, she was cleaning the school house in preparation of its opening. While engaged in this task she received a visitor, a local farmer. This was during the great depression of the '30's. The government was trying to reduce the amount of cultivated acreage. To reach its goal the government offered incentives for farmland left fallow, the amount of money depending on the number of acres left unplanted.

The farmer had a hand drawn map of his farm with lines and squiggles dividing sections that would and would not be put in cultivation. Some sections were very odd shaped. His question was how many acres of his land should be left fallow. Mildred promised him an answer the next morning, but try as she did, she could not figure the measurements using the homemade map. She then decided to redraw the map on her blackboard. It was not long before she realized she was hopelessly lost in the morass of figures. Quite dejectedly, Mildred, in a ladylike manner, sat at her teaching desk and began to cry. Fortunately, Mr. Hudson, accompanied by his math teacher came by and rescued her from her dilemma.

Word of Mildred's mathematical skills quickly spread and soon there were farmers seeking Mildred's advise on how many bushels of corn would be realized from a wagon full of the recently harvested produce. Another time, a local farmer appeared with a load of newly cut timber wanting to know how many ranks of wood were contained in his load of logs.

Life for the young couple improved. Floyd left the railroad to begin his business career as manager of a service station then owned by Deering Farms, Inc. Mildred recalls it was about this time, Floyd came home one evening leading a milk cow followed by a young calf. Although she had lived on a farm her entire life, she had never milked a cow. Neither had Floyd. They decided to learn together. So with buckets in hand they journeyed to the barn. Mildred sat at one side of the cow with Floyd on the other. And, with the calf trying to get his share by nosing from the rear through his mother's legs, I am certain the poor cow was quite puzzled with all the attention being directed her way.

Floyd next purchased an all-night Cafe and Service Station in the town of Hayti. They lived in Hayti some ten years with Floyd managing the station while Mildred taught in the local schools. It was in the late 1940's. They finally settled in Kennett, the largest town in the bootheel where Floyd entered the automotive sales business, later acquiring a franchise of his own.

In 1945 Mildred gave birth to their first child a daughter who was named Barbara. In 1947, their second child, also a daughter was born. The second daughter was named Patricia. In December 1971, twenty-four year old Patricia died of cancer. Her death deeply affected Mildred. On June 14, 1984, Floyd died. Shortly thereafter, Mildred moved to St. Louis County to be close to her daughter, Barbara and her family.

Barbara, who had married David Fulton in 1966, was following in her mother's footsteps by becoming a well-respected teacher in her own right. Barbara held a teaching position at the University of Missouri, St. Louis Campus, when she was asked to head the Montesson Private School located in Chesterfield, Missouri. Montesson is not only one of the most respected school districts in the State of Missouri, but its reputation for excellence has gained national attention. The district has now expanded into St. Albans and is known as the Montessori-St. Albana School System.

Barbara is a unique lady in her own right. A few years ago she was chosen as one of the top fifty outstanding young business women of the St. Louis Metropolitan area (an area encompassing some 2,000,000 people). Then in 1988, the year Chesterfield received its city charter, Barbara was chosen as Chesterfield's Business Woman of the Year.

Despite hr own recent battle with cancer, Barbara has continued to devote many, many hours to the management of her school. She is devoted to her husband and children and looks forward to becoming a grandmother for the first time in March when her son, Kyle, and his wife, Ginger, is due to become parents. Both Kyle and Ginger are teachers.

Kyle is not the only third generation family member to choose teaching as a career. Barbara's daughter, Kara, a recent graduate of

Rice University, is in her year long internship at Chesterfield Day School-St. Albana School System. This is strong testimony to Mildred's influence. Over her forty-four-year teaching career, she has had tremendous influence on many of her students, many who still keep in contact. But no greater homage could be rendered to Mildred than having her daughter and grandchildren following her footsteps.

Our family's heritage is enriched by Mildred's contributions, and her family has become a strong link in our family circle. We are delighted she joined us some sixty-five years ago! Mildred presently lives in a Chesterfield area retirement community near the home of her daughter.

CHAPTER SIXTEEN

Sentimental Journey

(This story was written and presented by Ophelia Wade to the Fiftieth Anniversary celebration at the reunion of the graduating classes of Deering High School of 1947 and of 1948. It is typical of all the classes of Deering and that is why it is being included in this book).

In July 1935, the front schoolyard of the three-room schoolhouse is full of very small youngsters. Some are playing childhood games and others are just standing there watching. The three adult women teachers are trying to get everything straightened out, and they have sheets of papers in their hands. The school bell rings, and the wide-eyed youngsters are told to line up in a single file. Those to go into the primer in a line extending back eastward from the school, those in the first grade in a line westward from the front door, the second graders toward the south. So many do not realize what grade they are in. And, too, several of the smallest will not let go of their older brother or sister. There is mayhem. The bell rings again. The teachers go down the line, checking off names. Children are moved from one line to the other. The hot sun beats down upon all of them, and the teachers decide to take them into the school rooms and straighten out the "mess" in there.

All of the new students, those who have just reached the age of six, are led into Miss Byrd's room. She was a gray-headed woman, rather short in stature, wearing glasses and very authoritative. She was my teacher. She gave all of us a black box of crayons and a picture to color. She did this to keep us quite while she enrolled us, one by one. Several times she had to go into another room and consult with older brothers and sisters for data on each of us.

The Carter sisters were there that day, with pastel organdy dresses and black patent leather slippers. I was in my homemade dress with my brown scuffed shoes And Betty Mangold with her sweet smile was there. It was depression days and everyone was scrubbed clean, in clean clothes, although some of them were somewhat worn. It was reminiscent of the days and times we were encountering.

Jumping rope was one of the favorite games and Nina Barksdale could jump the rope the best of anyone. She was small and they just could not throw "red pepper" fast enough for her. Louis Hillhouse came into class one day, a new student, from Arkansas. We kept having a little girl from the area wander into our playground and she was Ruth Sudduth who was only five, but was eager to start to school. Her mother had to come to school and take her home quite often. Virginia Bounds lived just across the field from the school and she walked back and forth. We also had an older girl come to kindergarten, and I never could understand why a woman so large would be our little kindergarten. I kept wandering that when you finished school, did you have to start all over again. Such youthful meandering of the mind!

My first grade teacher was Miss Smith. The thing I remember about her most was she taught us Tap Dancing. I think Jean Carter still knows some of the steps. I was clumsy and gawky then, just like I am today, so I was not a good pupil. She put me on the back row when we had our dance recital. She had more girls than boys, and she wanted me to dress in overalls and be a boy, but I refused. So I got to wear a red-and-white pinafore type dress, with underpants to match. Lurlyne played the boy. She wasn't much better at tap dancing than I was. We only took lessons one year.

I only stayed in the first grade for two days, and they promoted me to the second grade. No, I wasn't that smart. They lacked three desks and chairs having enough room, so two others and I were promoted to the second grade. Our teacher at the beginning of the year was Miss Pauline Condit, but at the end of the year it was Mrs. Mib Masters, and it was the same person. It seems that she married while teaching us in the second grade.

At this little isolated white three-room school building, we had lots of playtime. We had an egg hunt every Spring. The boys also flew kites during the warm weather. We had lots of fun singing and putting on operettas. Inside of the building it was the first grade to the left, primer to the right and second grade at the north end. There was a wide hallway that had pegs for hanging coats. The building was originally a combination hotel and restaurant and was only two rooms. The third room was built onto it when they converted it into a school house.

The schoolhouse was white clapboard. It had a big coal bin on the east side of it. Out back were two large outdoor privies labeled "boys" and "girls." The cleaning compounds they used to sweep the floor at that school gave it an unfamiliar smell of cleanliness. The school bell that was used at this school house is in front of the high school building today. During the bicentennial they painted it red-white-blue.

The school buses would unload all the students under the giant oak tree of the two-story brick building. The students in the primer, first and second would then walk the wide plank walks to the little three-room building. One day after walking from the school to the bus in drizzling rain, Mr. Hudson, the superintendent got on our bus and noticed our wet shoes. From then on, the bus would come down and pick us up during bad weather. After Mr. Hudson was not the superintendent, Mr. J. F. Taylor took his place and served during the remainder of our school years.

Then I was promoted to the third grade and left the little white schoolhouse in the northeast corner of Deering. Now I was ready to enter into the big massive two-story school house on the main campus where the buses parked every afternoon. Miss Camilla Day was my teacher and I liked her a lot. But all of a sudden, our enrollment in our class became very small. So they sent Miss

Hotel Deering, Deering, Mo.

Hotel Deering was built primarily so the officials of Wisconsin Lumber Company would have a place to stay when in Deering. It was a thriving business until the lumber mill closed in 1928. It was torn down in 1934.

Cervenka, the new music teacher, over to the three-room school and she brought back about eight second graders. Pat Richardson, Ruth Sudduth, Maudene Carter, Zoetta Clayton, Agnes Alexander, and Pauline McCarn was in that group. So Miss Day taught them their second grade while she taught us our third grade. They sat in one row on the south side of the room. It was probably the comradely we had with them then that bound these two classes together.

One day we decided to give Miss Day a pounding of sweets. I think Herman Jennings was the mastermind of this. He told all of us throw our cookies, candy, fruit, etc. to her. We did, and Miss Day's eyes got big, and I think she was about to discipline us when it probably dawned on her that we meant well by it. So she picked up all the goodies and stored them in her desk.

In the third grade, we made some clay pueblos like the Indians lived in out west. We also made some clay flower pots and painted them with bright colors. It was in this grade, while standing next to a girl at the blackboard, I saw my first lice crawling down some persons dress. I can't remember her name, but she lived in a tent in Mangold's grove. Later one of her little sisters named Violet died. They said she died with her eyes open and someone put a coin in each of them. Just before she was buried, they said, her father reached in and took out the coins. Gee, that I should remember that. The community asked the family to move, and the father said he did not have the money to buy tires for his truck. Several people went together and pooled their money and got the tires for the truck and the family was sent on its way. This was at the height of the depression.

Miss Day moved from Deering and the next third grade teacher was Miss Christine Myers. She was a very short woman and wore spike heels. She was slightly taller than her pupils, had black hair and very pleasant mannerisms. Miss Myers was the girl's grade school basketball coach. She let all who desired to dress out and we had quite a large team. There was Maxine Ayers in the sixth grade, large for her size, who usually was our top scorer. The team wore the castoff uniforms of the junior high school. We were a sight to behold in our baggy one-piece, sleeveless blue breeches.

Unmarried teachers stayed at the teacherage which was just a little west of the big store. Miss Grinstead had a permanent single-occupancy room there. Roy Ashabranner roomed there, along with several more of our teachers, including Miss Geraldine McCormick and Miss Aline Johnson.

The little town of Deering was a plantation town. It had been created by Wisconsin Lumber Company who had a lumber mill there. It had electricity in the very early 1900's, had big plank walks on which to walk, as the ground was muddy and soggy most of the year. It had its own town physician, a recreation room, post office, general store, office building and Dr. Speer lived there. There was a big bus barn just north of the school which housed ten buses for transporting the children to and from school. Some of the bus drivers were Reuben Dunn, Mr. Hankins, Red Corbin, and yes, even G. C. Grimes. Oak and cottonwood trees were all over town and cotton fuzz blew all over town, especially on windy days.

The houses in which the railroad men lived were just south of the railroad tracks which ran from east to west on the south side of town. For years, the only way to leave or enter Deering was by rail. We lived at Bakerville, and my older brother and sister had to walk the railroad tracks southward to catch the bus about three miles south. But the road was finished when I started to school, so I started to school riding the black "Crackerbox."

The winters always seemed to be cold, and the girls wore long brown stockings for warmth. Almost all the children enrolled in school were from agricultural families. It was the depression years and all of us wore home made dresses. Practically every student wore slippers or shoes with holes in the soles, and we stuffed cardboard inside.

We had our fun, though There was a valentine box every February, and we had a Christmas pageant each December. Mr. McMahon would bring his trained horses to perform for us. His daughter, Shirley, tap danced on a table over them.

This experience of having some of the second graders with us when we were in the third grade might be what started the bond between our two classes. Who knows? But anyhow, we passed to the fourth grade and this is when James McDonald became a member of our class, as he had been retained because he was so short. There were lots of boys in the fourth grade—James and Herman whom I have mentioned before, and Richard Barksdale, John W. Huie, Alvie Williams, Jack Lewis, William Edwards, A. J. Townley, Doug Bivens and others. I ought to know as they all gave me their prize marbles and I had quite a collection of them. While the boys played marbles, we girls played jacks.

When I was in the fourth grade, my Mother started me taking piano lessons from Mrs. Masters. Very soon, I realized this wasn't for me, so as soon as piano recital was over, I was allowed to stop taking them. But first, I had to memorize and play "Long, Long Ago," a song I can still play.

Miss Cervenka was a tall, straight-back, strict woman. She would tolerate no nonsense and if you misbehaved in her class you were instructed to hold your hand, palms up, and she would fold your fingers back as far as she could and pop each hand with a ruler. This calmed down lots of the youngsters, but for some of the older, tougher boys, it just made them meaner than ever, as they would do that just to enjoy seeing her administer her punishment.

She had come to Deering from Chicago. The school had a baby grand piano and she played "Narcissus" on it and she introduced us to Tchaikovsky. She had black hair that glistened with hues of green, purple, red and green. She was a wonderful teacher, and her career of teaching ended when she fell down the steps and broke her hip. I understand she returned to Chicago and started writing music.

I have told you before I was not good at tap dancing, nor at the piano. Well, Miss Cervenka made me aware that I could not sing either. She tapped me on the shoulder one day and asked if I would mind not singing with the group as I could not carry a tune. Very early in life I learned that I would not pursue any degree in the musical field.

Our home room fourth grade teacher was Miss Pauline Myers, and she really had a room full of students and several of them were big, husky boys. And the loudest and most unruly was named Jesse James. We could get out of a lot of class work because of the taunting he did to the teacher. I don't remember his being in school after the fifth grade.

No story about our early school years would be complete without mentioning the tornado of 1938. Several of the buses were loaded and leaving school when they noticed it, and they turned around and went back to school. Our little bus just kept going, driving right into the path of the tornado. Guy B. Tucker, a high school student was the driver, and just as he let us off at the Bakerville store, the tornado struck the Sanderson house and killed their son. It also destroyed my cousin, Melba Jean Richardson's house, and did destruction to several houses.

Bobbie Sue Lawson says the students at Little River school were instructed to all join hands and lie flat on the ground. She said the tornado mysteriously lifted up just before it got to the school and nobody was injured. It was a devastating tornado, as many houses were damaged or destroyed.

I had played around in the lower grades of school. My older sister Lurlyne had played school with me at home and I didn't have to study in those beginning years, so the fourth grade was especially hard for me when I had to learn how to study. I almost failed that grade.

"The Lion's Den" was our school paper and it was distributed to grades 3-12, to the oldest child of each family. I loved to submit articles for it, and finally once, my poem was published. I think this is when I decided I wanted to be a writer.

Mr. Joe Redwine was our fifth grade teacher. He was shorter than most men and was a sissy from day one. But he was a good teacher because he made me realize I had to stop flirting with the boys and begin studying. He was really a good math teacher and that is when I realized I was very good with numbers. Lots of the math he taught us then was later called "modern math." Then we had J. R. Corbin as our math teacher in high school. That's probably why our classes did so well with the subject of bookkeeping.

We always had a school picnic at the end of school and most times went to Walker Park in Blytheville. The students would play all day. At noon, the teacher spread the food the students had brought and we had lunch. And then the buses would bring the tired dirty children back to school for all of us to be transported back to our homes. My mother was always assigned to make chicken salad sandwiches, but I never was able to find one of them when we ate.

The lunchroom was built and we started having hot lunches November through May. Since there was no air conditioning it was too hot for them to cook during the summer months, so we still took our sack lunch to school during the hot weather. I still hate peanut butter to this day, as that was the one thing we could take that would not ruin. And if anybody remembers how to make those fried chocolate pies, would you please write down the recipe for me. Mrs. Huie was the first manager of the lunchroom, then Mrs. Williams took her place when they moved to Gideon. As Bill Watson described it, "For the cost of 25 cents a week, we marched through the serving line, sat at bench tables, and ate the most delicious lunch imaginable. A typical meal consisted of mashed potatoes and gravy, meat, another vegetable, bread and a large cookie."

The building was also where the art classes met. Alvera Tollison and Inez Bentley were our art teachers. Mrs. Enoch Tollison's father worked on the train, and many times she would send a bundle of clean clothes out to him by two of the boys in the class.

The little white schoolhouse burned one cold snowy December day, I believe in 1939, and all the students were led outside and nobody was hurt. It did destroy all the contents of the building. My younger brother Bob, and two sisters, Val and Eula, were students in that building when it burned. These classes later met in the big room above the store building and above the doctor's office. They shared the same playground behind the store building.

Our class in the fifth grade became larger, as some students from Vicksburg school, which only went to the fourth grade, joined us. Mary Lois Brewer and the next year her sister Mattie Sue Brewer and Bobbie Robbins joined the group. The Vicksburg school had four grades in one room with only one teacher. Some of the Vicksburg teachers included Mamie Ledbetter, Flo Brewer and Ruby Sudduth Turner. It was the teachers' job not only to teach the three R's, but keep a fire in the big wood burning stove. The drinking water came from an outside pump, and the privies were also outside. "Sand burrs were so thick on the playground that recess was not much fun," says Sue Brewer Jordan.

The sixth grade was finally the melting pot of these two classes. Several from Little River school, such as Lydia Branch, Charline Tidwell, Wayne Young, Nina Maude Minner, Willistene McCann, and Fairris and her brother Jody Wiggins and others started coming to Deering central as Little River school only went through the fifth grade. Billy Gene Watson joined in our group in 1939.

The next year Weyman Autry, Elsie Mae Booker, Bobby Sue Bowling, Pascal Nichols, June Tidwell, W. J. Crabtree and Jackie Wiltshire enrolled in Deering central, also transferring from Little River School. It was sometime during this time that Omahlee James also joined our class and I don't remember exactly where she came from.

Perhaps it was the joining together of friends from Little River school that formed our closeness, but notwithstanding, we were firmly grouped together. The sixth grade was so large, we had two rooms. Miss Grinstead's room was on the north end of the downstairs just across the hall from the boys rest room which always smelled like a zoo. Miss Carters' room was in the southwest corner of the building, back beyond the girls rest room which did not smell much better. The day they divided us into our two classes, Jean Carter and I had it made up that if we got in the room we did not want to be in, we would swap. Sure enough, when we numbered off Jean was designated to be in her mother's room and I was designated to be in Miss Grinstead's room. So when those to be in Mrs. Carters room were told to leave the room, I got up and left and Jean stayed in Miss Grinstead's room. Evidently, nobody ever knew the difference and we were each happy with our choices.

The brick two-story building had a gymnasium for indoor sports. We had steam heat, electric lights, a movie projector, library books and each student had his own desk. There was a water fountain for us to drink water. It also was a quiet building, so quiet in fact, you could always hear the paddles which were administered quite often.

The favorite school bus we ever had was a little black bus which was nicknamed "The Cracker Box." It was the first bus, and after it no longer hauled students around, it was a utility vehicle for the school yard. Reuben Dunn drove it during the early years. It had two rows of seats which faced each other.

One place everyone liked to go in the fall of the year was the county fair at Caruthersville. We would pick cotton all week just so we could go over there and have some fun riding the rides, seeing the carnival shows and watching the horse races.

We were joined by Mary Nell Gunnin, Bonnie Brannum, Margie and Winkie Dye during our grade school years And in junior high Marion and Cytha Mills moved into the Deering school district from Braggadocio. They both had musical instruments and were in the band during its initial formation and on through high school. Miss Emily Lanier was the first band teacher as Miss Cervenka had an orchestra when she was here. Next year, Curt Wilkerson from Kennett came out and taught our band. Later Virginia Mayfield, with her sweet smile and vivacious love for all of us, directed the band. It was always a small band, but we could play pretty well. At least, we thought so.

We were promoted into the seventh grade we finally got to go upstairs in the two-story building. Up until now we were forbidden to even get on the steps leading upstairs. Now we have lockers to keep our books and personal items in, but not for long. They were building the new W.P.A. school house and the lockers were removed and taken over there. So they put planks of wood horizontally along the wall. Teachers would patrol the hall to keep down looting.

It was amazing how they moved the library. They lined up all the 7-12 grade students in a straight row from the old library upstairs to the new library. The librarian had numbered the rows of books and they passed them along the line of students to the new library. The one in charge over there had been instructed how to exactly place them in the shelves. In less than an hour, the library had been moved and was ready for business. James McDonald stated, "I have touched every book in the school library." Well, so have the rest of us.

One of our teachers would put the cover of the Saturday Evening Post on our bulletin board each month on Monday morning, and we had to write a story trying to explain just what Norman Rockwell was depicting in his art work. I cannot remember her name, but she was a good teacher, and she was strict about us using the dictionary for word spellings.

When our class entered the ninth grade, we were joined by those from Pascola;—namely Bill Wood, Francis Cook and others. There were 56 of us enrolled in the ninth grade. Then Jeff Wade moved here from Rector, Arkansas and Mary Lindsey moved in from Bragg City. Both of these were originally from Mississippi.

By this time, Gobler Mercantile Store was in full swing. It was advertised as the largest country store in the south. Virginia Bounds Branch later wrote a little booklet about it.

We all learned our school song and sang it at every basketball game. Deering's basketball teams were also good, and sometimes really excelled.

Home Economics was added to the curriculum when we moved into the new school building. Dorothy Brooks, later Mrs. Nathan Wood, was the first teacher and she taught there for many years. She also taught biology.

The March of Time was shown every month in the gymnasium. The chairs were set up on the gymnasium floor. They were stored on racks under the stage at the north end of the gym. Several high school boys would help the janitors put them in place, but first, a heavy covering was put on the floor so the finish of the wooden planks would not be scarred.

From Bethel or Fairview School we received the Curtis brother and sister, whose first names I cannot recall and, of course, Ouida Bowie joined our group from there.

One of the favorite sports at the school was track. They had so many events that almost everyone could enter into some phase of it. Several of the students were adept in their category. In 1947 we won third in the Pemiscot County track tournament. In 1948 the school was third in boys' softball tournament, second in tennis and third in Kennett Invitational basketball tournament. We also had a trophy for first in another sport in 1948.

It was the World War II years and our school life was changed.

No longer did the school bus go around and pick up the people to bring them to the school for the various events that were held at night, such as basketball games, lyceum programs and school plays. They even quit running the bus to take us to sporting events. Some of the people had extra gasoline and they hauled us in cars to the basketball games. I'll never forget the night Toad Groves was driving a bunch of us girls from Cooter to Deering and he got lost in Holland. It was so foggy you could not tell where you were, and he circled that little village time and again, looking for the main road to lead us out. And we girls were making so much a racket. He's bound to have lost some of his sanity that night.

They formed the Victory Corps for us and taught us how to drill, and we were quite good. The boys had wooden rifles and they drilled quite extensively. We had ration stamps for gasoline, sugar, shoes and probably other things.

The school received word that Doyne Huie who had graduated in 1939 was aboard the "Arizona" when he was sunk in Pearl Harbor. The war had a great impact on our school years.

James McDonald was kicked by a mule and had to be absent from school for several months. He made up his work and rejoined our group and graduated with us.

Jean Ursery, Juanita Phillips, James Gurlen, J. C. Kilburn, and Carlene Rudkin joined our group during this time. In the eleventh grade a brother and sister from Selmer, Tennessee, named John and Carrie Jordan moved into our district, and Bryan Parnell was added to the list. Neal Gibbons was in the junior class, but he transferred to Senath his senior year. But then Nola Treece transferred in during her senior year. We were an agricultural school, so all during our thirteen years we had students always coming in and going out.

During the war years, it was hard to secure teachers as so many of them had gone into military service and others had moved to the cities to take war jobs. J. R. Corbin, who was 4-F served as high school principal, math teacher, school bus driver, boy scout leader, basketball coach, mayor, and just about ran everything.

Mr. Corbin died several years ago from cancer which he only knew he was crippled with it for five weeks.

Mrs. Mills taught us during those years. We all remember Minnie Gay who was a history teacher but switched to the commercial department, even though she did not know how to type. She earned her 30 wpm while teaching us. Fern Rice was living in California when she received word her fiancee was coming home. She flew back to Missouri. He reported back to duty after their marriage and she taught in our school system. We all loved Fern Rice. She was a smooth easygoing teacher.

Miss McCormick and Miss Johnson were there in 1946 and they directed the Junior-Senior play. In the summer of 1946 when we enrolled we were greeted by Mr. Roy Ashabranner, Mr. & Mrs. McKinney, Miss Mayfield and Mrs. Mayfield. The Jonakins returned to Deering for the second time. We had good teachers.

Graduation for the class of 1947 was on May 14 and for the class of 1948 on May 12. John Jordan and Sue Brewer had to sever their ties and so did Jeff Wade and Ophelia Richardson, because one of each was in the other grade. But for several couples in the class of 1947 it meant marriage in the next eight months. Betty Mangold and Carlene Rudkin had already married, and Nola Treece married William Edwards, one of our grade school pals, just as school was out. James McDonald and Juanita Phillips; Bill Wood and Fairris Wiggins; Jack Lewis and Carrie Jordan, all members of the class of '47 married in 1947. Everyone in the class of 1948 has married. From the class of 1947, Marion Mills is the only one that never married. Charline Tidwell waited several years before she married, and she is now a widow.

During our school years we won many trophies, contests and events. Bill Wood, Marion Mills and I won first in a bookkeeping team, and Bill was first individually. Zoetta Clayton excelled in all the secretarial subjects and was instrumental in helping to win many trophies, such as first place in district amateur productive typing and first in district novice shorthand. Individually we were awarded the big blue "D" for our achievements. Roy Ashabranner's algebra team won first in the contest at Cape Girardeau.

We took a Junior-Senior bus trip to Big Springs in 1946, a long extended one to Kentucky in 1947, and a one-day trip to Memphis in 1948. Our Junior-Senior plays were "Here Comes Henry," "There Goes Charlie" and "Take It Easy."

This was the big band era and we collected 78 rpm records of all the bands. We had parties, with chaperons of course. Several of our high school boys worked at Graber's—namely, Bill Watson, Bill Wood, James McDonald and Jeff Wade.

When we graduated from high school, several former Deering students who had served in the armed forces graduated with us with their G.E.D. They were Marvin Crabtree, Billy Grimes, G. C. Grimes, Garvin Holland, Billy Horton, Herman Jennings, Jack Lewis, Norman McCann, Chester Richardson, Billy Bonds and Noel Felker. They did not get to take part in the graduation exercises, but their name was added to our roll. They did not even call their name from the stage. This 50-year error was corrected this past May when I named all of them as I gave out our $2500.00 scholarships. And again, the next year when the next $2500.00 scholarships were presented, the names were repeated again.

These two graduating classes have had joint reunions every five years since graduation. Now that we are in our retirement years, we have chosen to have a reunion every year or so. All of the Deering High School classes have frequent reunions. We were a little country school with love and devotion for each other. In fact, we were so small, that everybody in the high school building knew everybody, no matter what grade they were in.

CHAPTER SEVENTEEN

Dunklin County Land

William Deering, of Evanston, Illinois, purchased 38,126 acres of land in Dunklin County from Cottonwood Lumber Company on 19 August 1899 (Dunklin County Recorder's Office, Book 27, page 131). This was a manufacturing and business corporation of New Madrid, Missouri. David Mann was the president and W. C. Blanvelt the secretary. It was Mr. Deering's plan to build the lumber mill in Dunklin County just west of the county line a few miles southwest of the present town of Gobler. This would have put the mill almost in the middle of the operation. When the equipment got mired in the mud in Pemiscot County, he changed his plans and built the mill in what became the present town of Deering.

This real estate was in T16N R9E, T16N R10E, T17N R9E, T17N R10E, T18N R10E, T16N R10E, T17N R10E, T18N R10E, T17N R11E, T18N R11E, T19N R11E. (T is township, N is north, R is range, E is east.)

In 1904, William Deering and his wife Clara, of Evanston, Cook County, Illinois, deeded this land to Charles Deering, James Deering and Richard F. Howe of Chicago, Cook Co., Illinois, a corporation doing business under the name of Deering Harvester Co. (Book 45 page 49-56)

December 1907, Charles Deering and his wife Marion W., James Deering (a bachelor), and Richard F. Howe (a widower) convey the land to Wisconsin Lumber Company, a corporation which had secured the rights to operate in Missouri in 1906.

Wisconsin Lumber Company was an affiliate of International Harvester Co. (Book 112, pages 544-46). It states: "the Grantee (International Harvester Co.) many years heretofore became the beneficial owner of all of the capital stock of the Grantor (Wisconsin Lumber Co.), consisting of twenty-five hundred (2500) shares authorized, issued and outstanding, and has ever since been the owner, and now owns and controls the same through its nominees; and "WHEREAS, the Directors of the Grantor in a Special Meeting heretofore duly held upon January 27, 1925, in the City of Chicago, Illinois, at which a quorum of the Directors was present, unanimously duly adopted the following resolution, to-wit:

" RESOLVED That all lands owned by the Wisconsin Lumber Company in Pemiscot and Dunklin Counties, Missouri, no longer needed in carrying on its business, shall be sold, and that the President, or any Vice-President, shall have the right at any time to fix and determine the price that shall be charged for any single tract of land . . ."

This quit claim deed clears up the question of who owned everything. International Harvester owned it, but Wisconsin Lumber Company operated it under their name.

Timber was cut and shipped to Deering on the railroad from the Dunklin County land until all that was left on the real estate were the six foot tall tree trunks. They had to stand in boats and cut the trees above the swamp water. Then when the land was drained, this lower portion of the tree became visible and they called them "stumpies." These had to be cleared before it was feasible to farm the land.

The newsletter "Come to The Heel of Missouri Where Diversified Farming Pays Big" sold very little real estate in Dunklin County. International Harvester Company decided to let the land go and not even pay the taxes. The trees had made them money, but the land was not ready to farm and it became a losing proposition.

In the 1930's this land began to change ownership. Some of the deeds were warranty deeds, some were quit claim deeds, and others were sheriff deeds where the land was purchased for the taxes due on it. Sometimes the grantor would be listed as International Harvester. Other times it was Wisconsin Lumber Company listed as the seller. They were one and the same. In checking the records at the courthouse, we found that several of the people did not immediately record their deeds, and in some cases several years elapsed. Several people purchased land more than once. We probably missed a few of the purchasers, but the following were found acquiring this land:

John Abbott, C. M. Abbott, E. Allen, Selma Leny Allenburg, C. Anctill, Walter Anderson, Henry Armour,

T. R. Bain, M. S. Barnett, Rial Bates, T. M. Battles, W. T. Baugher, Ed Beasley, Ed Bensley, Clara F. Bess, James Wesley Bess, Otto Bess, Shelly Bethany, Arnold Birch, L. A. Blankenship, Julia A. Blankenship, Hal Bogle, Perry Booles, Clarice Boone, J. F. Boyland, John H. Bradley, W. O. Branch, A. H. Breckenridge, J. B. Brim, J. H. Brim, Carl T. Brooks, J. F. Brown, B. T. Browning, Mildred D. Brumley, George Buchanan, J. M. Buchanan, Arnold Burch, R. E. Burkett, George Byers, David Byles,

Fred Caney, Martha G. Cannon, Noble Capehart, J. H. Cheek, W. B. Colbert, T. J. Colling, Jr., Aubrey Conway, M. H. Cox, W. E. Craig, Thomas Crawford, Anna B. Cromly, Mrs. A. B. Crowley, Albert Cumb, N. C. Curtis,

John M. Dalton, A. T. Danherty, A. F. Danherty, F. G. Davis, James Defoe, Will Dildine, T. T. Dildine, Joe T. Dollins, A. L. Donaldson, Cass Donaldson, R. L. Donaldson, E.L. Dotson, A. B. Drake,

H. R. Edington, Sam G. Fisher, V. R. Fox Est, V. R. Fox, J. H. Fray, E. A. Frazer, O. E. Frazer, Henry Frison, Millard Gallant, E. B. Gee, J. L. German, S. A. Gibbons, S. R. Gibbons, R. A. Gibbons, L. M. Glover, Ed Gray, F. G. Green, John Green, J. B. Grissom, L. C. Grugett,

J. C. Hankins, E. G. Hankins, William W. Harper, Ruby Harrison, Martha Harrison, Earl C. Hart, Louis Hazeland, Lum Hemphill, Allie May Hockaday, Reo Rex Hockaday, L. F. Hoffman,

Chester Holland, Byron Holly, J. B. Holley, Earl E. Hubbard, Lonzo Hudson, Willie M. Hudson, Roy W. Huffard, Walter C. Huffman, Jr.

E. Jackson, Willard Jackson, George T. Jarrett, W. M. Jefferson, J. B. Jefferson, W. O. Johnson, Ervin Johnson, Rosa Pearl Johnson, R. Irl Jones, Martin Jones, John Jones, Will A. Jones, J. W. Karues, Alonzo J. Keating, Mrs. Ada Kilburn, Elizabeth Lenora Kinder, Nellie R. Kolosick, G. W. Kurtz,

K. M. Larkin, T. E. Larren, Oscar L. Leathers, J. C. Ledford, J. M. Ledford, J. B. Ledford, George M. Lee, Jesse Lentz, Nola A. Lewis, Harne Lewis, Will Lidell, Vanne Lindsey, M. V. Lindsey, Lawrence Little, John H. Love, Sally Lowery,

C. L. Mabrey, Byron Marshall, W. T. Martin, Voyd & Lois Martin, J. E. Martin, C. C. Martin, T. W. Martin, W. A. Massey, Myrtle McAfee, Maude Forbes McAfee, Eva McCanless, W. R. McCann, Ruth McDaniel, J. R. McDaniel, Mary Lou McDaniel, H. G. McDaniel, Hoyt G. McDaniel, Edgar A. McIntosh, J. M. McKee, Richard McNair, David M. Mears, W. H. Meroney, Wesley Miller, John W. Miller, Harvey C. Mills, W. H. Minyard, L. P. Mitchell, Homer Mosely, W. T. Munn

J. W. Nichols, Howard Noble, I. K. Northcutt, Will J. Parker, J. M. Parker, Murdie Parr, Clyde Parr, Melvin Payne, W. E. Petty, Clyde Pharr, Clark Phillips, John Pierson, Roland C. Pike, Jnlins Posey, J. A. Rimpson, Dr. Theo Robb, John T. Robinson, J. T. Robinson, Frank Robinson, Lois Ross, Alice Marie Ross,

Furn Sappington, Leon Schmidt, Ernest Scott, Security Farms, Inc., Leo J. Sellmeyer, F. L. Seratt, W. E. Sexton, R. A. Shands, W. P. Shelton, J. W. Shrader, Tom Smith, George Smith, Lon B. Smith, Mann Smith, Rush Smith, Fred Smith, Ella Smith, George Spence, Dr. E. L. Spence, John Leo Sprangler, C. O. Sprangler, Vaughn Stigler, Norvel Stover,

C. R. Talbert, Robert H. Talbert, Cale Taylor, John T. Taylor, Jr., John F. Taylor, Jr., James E. Taylor, Charles Temkee, H. V. Threet, Will Tiddell, Chester Tinelone, L. N. Tinelone, E. O. Tinker, Roy

Tinkle, R. H. Tinnin, Stanley Tradenburg, Gale Turner, Cleo Turner, R. C. Turner, John Joe Tyler,

    R. J. Umbright, Ernest Vancil, W. T. Vaugher, J. P. Vickrey, L. D. Viemann, Fred G. Walker, Guss Walls, Durham & Una Lee Ward, Mark Welch, J. R. White, J. W. Wilkins, John Williams, Will Willis, Tommy Wilson, W. E. Woolbright, W. E. Woolbright, Gordon Wright, Pink Wright and Fannie Young.

CHAPTER EIGHTEEN

Villages on Highway 84

Mid City

By Woodrow McNutt, February 1970

In 1921 I took livestock up to Yama to Mr. Tom Sissom who did the hauling of logs up there. I was only a kid, but then a child did a man's job. The men who worked at the sawmill slept in tents. When they got up of the morning, they had to break the ice to get the water. Biven Johnson lived back there in a great big house. He was the father of Richard Johnson who lives about two miles east of me.

The old sawmills were operated by A. B. Smith and had no names but went by numbers. This one was number five, I believe, and number two was up north of here. This sawmill had more sawdust piles than just the one pile where the main sawmill set. The big sawmill was on the Miller farm. It was number seven. It had sawdust that was piled up three times higher than any of the others.

The old sawdust piles gradually burned. Every spring when it would get dry, they would set it on fire, and it would burn over, and again they would set them on fire.

This was not a part of the Wisconsin Lumber Company. They had Deering and there was an awfully big mill there. Mr. Smith had a timber right, so much per acre, and when he got that cut out, he would buy some more stumpies.

The logs were cut and sawed back, and the lumber that left here was finished lumber and was hauled all over the world. They used lots of oxen to move the logs with. They kept these oxen in barns and fed them corn and hay that they hauled in. The feed for the mules and horses was also hauled in.

The old sawmill settlement, unnamed as I have said before, was located ½ mile west and one-fourth mile south of where the present Bakerville store building is today. It consisted, of course, of the sawmill with all the machinery needed to operate it.

There was a hotel that sat in a clump of cottonwood trees. The building was painted white, but it had faded away. It was two-story and had about twelve or fifteen rooms. It was on the east side of the road along with about five houses also on the east side.

On the west side of the road was a schoolhouse and about four more residential houses.

The sawmill burned in 1925, and this settlement gradually began to disperse. There had never been a store in the village. In 1927, W. A. Canady opened a general merchandise store on the east side of the tram railroad, south of the main road (known today as Highway 84 - later as 412), and thus took the name of Mid-City. This indicated it was half way between Kennett and Hayti. This store was a long narrow building, and he stocked anything you needed to use on the farm. He ran the store by himself, except for one time he had a niece who helped him. She married Elzie Abbott and he worked there some, too. Orville Lowery lived at Mid-City, and worked at the sawmill. Orville later was the fireman at the cotton gin.

The Baptist Church was built in the fall of 1932 or spring of 1933. The Church of Christ was erected in 1962.

The oldest house of this area was torn down a few years ago. It was just west of the Canady store building and was built by W. E. Petty and he lived there many years.

The house I live in was built by Allen E. Pate which is Mrs. R. M. Tidwell's father. It used to be up at the corner, but when Bert

Richardson built his home up there, he sold the house to me and I moved it down here.

There is a utility pole that runs along the railroad from Bakerville to Bragg City. On one of the poles, which has the railroad whistle board and the mileage number on it, has a cotton stalk sticking right through the pole. The tornado of 1938 did this.

The School House at Mid-City
By Bessie (Huntley) Wright, 1970

Our family lived at Stubtown, west of Caruthersville, when I applied for the job of teaching at this school. Mr. Charles G. Ross was the county superintendent and he hired me. We moved to Bragg City in 1925, and I walked from there to the school, following the same crooks and turns as the railroad did. Carl Looney worked at the sawmill and he had a little hand car that he used to travel to and from work. I learned to try to get up early enough in the morning to ride on his hand car. They paid me $85.00 per month the first year and $80.00 the next year.

The school house was a high-roofed building. When you walked in the front door, there were two rooms and one of these was a cloak room. The narrow hallway then took you back to the two large classrooms. There was a large bell that hung outside and above the building. A rope was attached to it, threaded through a round hole in the wall of the cloak room and hanging in the room. We always had plenty of volunteers to go to the cloak room and ring the bell.

We got our water from the pump at the pump house that had benches on the inside. It was tall and had a top in it, and the sides were done in lattice work. The outhouses were also outside, and were at the back of the building. The school yard was partly cleared, but there were still plenty of trees for it to be shady. It was named Little River School.

The school records were kept in a big book that had leather on the corners to keep it from getting dogeared. The pages were really heavy. We tried to keep the students names in alphabetical order, but with the high student turnover that we had, that was hard to do. We issued report cards with the grading system of "E-S-M-I-F." The children used the rough paper tablets. Some of the desks were individual and some were the kind bolted to wooden runners. The blackboards were the old pasteboard that was painted over. One side of the building was windows. Mosquitoes and snakes were plentiful. Barefooted children attended in July and August, then we dismissed until November. We had to miss a lot of school when the water was high in 1927.

Bill Hancock was the school director. Mr. George Seigler and Carl Mosley also taught there. I taught the 1-2-3 grades, then the 4-5-6 grades were together, and then the 7-8 grades. Arithmetic was taught separately. The school operated until about 1928, then it was sold to Missouri State Life Insurance Company and they moved it to Hillsman-Taylor and made a general store out of it.

The Christmas School Program was the highlight of the year, since we had no eighth grade graduation. It was at night and we used lamps, gas lanterns and oil lanterns to light up the building. Our Christmas tree was cut from the woods, and we would wrap the branches with green crepe paper and use lots of school-made decorations on it. The students would have plays, songs and recitations.

Mangolds Grove—Skinners Place—Seldom Seen

Pemiscot County was settled first along the banks of the Mississippi River and the lands more than five miles westward were seldom seen. Perhaps that is why in 1891 when Captain S. W. Crab of Uniontown, Kentucky considered buying a farm in the backwoods, it was referred to as Seldom Seen, and in all earnestness the name stuck.

To get to Seldom Seen you had to go north of Braggadocio and cross the Eagle Lake Bridge. The old dummy line railroad (sometimes referred to as the tram railroad) ran from Braggadocio through

Seldom Seen, then northeast for three more miles to Pascola. There was a spur line from Seldom Seen then going westward to the Mid City area, circling west of the Canady store building into the Smith sawmill area. In 1920 there were five houses at Seldom Seen. One was a big two-story house. The Oliver family lived in one of the farm houses. The owners of the land were J. J. Garrett and Cap Long.

Later a settlement known as Skinner Place was just a trifle west of Seldom Seen. It took its name from J. A. and Leonard Skinner who owned it. It became known as one of the roughest places in the county. The large building was a grocery store and night club. These two businesses being separated by a double fireplace petition. In the 1930's several killings took place there, one of them being a Mr. Teroy. Sophia Skinner was also killed there, being murdered by her husband. But the reputation of this place still unequaled that of the Bloody Bucket which was just east of it.

In 1937, Clarence Edward Mangold moved his wife and three children - Lois, Earvie and Betty - here from Kennett, originally coming from Mayfield, Kentucky, and bought the store from the Skinners. The large grove of trees south of the store remained intact; thus, the name Mangolds Grove was coined. Gypsies would pitch their tents there, large jamborees would take place, and Fourth of July celebrations became widely known. Such entertainers as Bill Monroe, the Wellburn Family and the Pap Stewart family would perform.

It is undecided if there was ever a school at this place, but there was one at Seldom Seen which joined with Deering C-6. After the schools got organized and school buses came into existence, the school children from Pascola (which only went through the eighth grade) could go to either Wardell or Deering school. Those wishing to attend Deering would dismount from the Pascola bus at Mangolds Grove and then catch the Deering bus.

An old abstract of one of the farms in this area is quite interesting. It reveals that in 1891, Louis Houck bought the land for $1.25 per acre as swampland. He sold it in 1894 to John Franklin, who then sold it to Gilbert Franklin, and he in turn sold it to J. E. Franklin. Charles Harris then became the owner, only to sell it back to J. E. Franklin. Cottonwood Lumber Company then acquired it, and sold it to William Deering and it became part of Wisconsin Lumber Company. From 1930 on the owners then were O. E. Frazer, J. A. Skinner and then the Mangolds. The Pemiscot Southern Railroad Company acquired right-of-way in October 1898.

O'Keena

The first owner of this store was a country peddler. He spent most of his time going around the countryside selling knives, pots and pans, utensils and moonshine liquor. He had a long white beard and the children called him Santa Claus. He was struck and killed by an automobile as he was returning home one day.

To begin with, the store was a four-room residence converted into a store building, eating place, and tavern with drinking and gambling. They were having trouble deciding on a name for it and everything anybody would suggest wasn't agreeable. Finally one of the employees, who had not said much, looked at the can of tomatoes on the shelf, and on the label it had the brand name of "Okeena" standing out in broad letters. The man related that if they were going to choose a ridiculous name like everybody was suggesting, they might as well consider Okeena. By mutual consent, everybody liked the name and that is what it was called.

Charlie Grogan, Terry Grogan, and Parker Morgan owned the business which was west of Mangolds Grove and east of Mid City. The little grocery store and tavern were doing a really good business and they decided to build a dance hall on the back of it. The place got rough, and lots of people talked about getting a petition to close it. The owners decided to change the dance hall into a church building. A few years later, they took this addition from the back of the building and pulled it off to itself and made it exclusively a church building. A woman referred to as "Sister Riley" preached there for years and years.

"The Democrat-Argus" - November 15, 1940, printed this story: O'Keena Community (Highway No. 84)—An unusual thing happened here some time ago. Chas. W. Grogan went to the local minister and told him he was going to open a nite club at O'Keena, but with the understanding if he ever decided to quit he would give the minister the privilege of holding his meetings in his hall. That day came later, and so today the place is conducted exclusively for religious gatherings, and Mr. Grogan reports that more than 100 souls have been brought into the Kingdom of the Lord, and that services are still going strong. A little further down the highway toward Kennett, an ideal baptizing location is maintained at Sandy Beach by Terry Grogan, a brother of the proprietor of O'Keena Community Hall, where Mr. Grogan conducts the O'Keena grocery. A good business is enjoyed not only from the church folk but from the public at large, he reports. He and his wife, Mrs. Tessie Grogan, have no children. Parents: D. H. and Mrs. Olive Grogan, deceased. Parents of Mrs. Grogan: Mr. and Mrs. Albert Permenter, both living. Mr. Grogan is a native of Clay County, Ark. and his wife is a native of Pemiscot County, Missouri. He came to Missouri in 1923, and located here in 1929. Mr. Grogan also operates a service station. The revival meeting at O'Keena Community Hall began in August 1939, and it had resulted in bringing the people closer together, saying nothing for the fact that the O'Keena community is happier and better place in every way, says Mr. Grogan since he changed his place into the Lord's house instead of one where the devil might have crept in more actively. The Lord's blessings upon you, Mr. Grogan and the religious effort at your place, is the wish of everyone.

Hillsman Taylor and Bakerville

By Mrs. Bert (Erma Boswell) Richardson

One of the last settlements in Pemiscot County was Bakerville. It was an outgrowth of the old A. B. Smith Sawmill, and was first named Hillsman Taylor in honor of an official of Missouri State Life Insurance Company which had bought lots of the land in this area. After General American Life Insurance Company merged with Missouri State, the name of the place was changed to Bakerville, in honor of Charles B. Baker who was the field man for the company.

The school house at the Smith Sawmill was moved one-fourth mile north and one-half mile west to a new site and was converted into a grocery and general mercantile store. A room was added on the west side for an office. A cotton gin was built south of the store and several grain storage houses built between them.

Before this time there was no road from Kennett to Caruthersville, and what we now know as Highway 412 (formerly 84) was begun in 1918 and not finished for several years. With its completion, the small settlement at the sawmill dispersed and Bakerville was born.

When the Cottonbelt Railroad opened up its lines, the track ran north and south, crossing the main road with the largest part of Bakerville being on the west side of the tracks. They ran a spur line between the cotton gin platform and the grain houses.

The first cotton gin was built in 1931. The gin stands were downstairs and the press was upstairs and a very large platform accommodated the bales of cotton that waited shipment in the railroad cards. A large steam engine, maintained by Orville Lowery, was the power for the gin, and a water tank was nearby. A small restaurant sat on the gin yard and Claudie Sewell ran it. There were two offices, connected by a roof which covered the scales where the farmer pulled his load of cotton for weighing before ginning. A covered pavilion was north of these offices and the farmer sat on his wagon with a team of mules and waited his turn to be ginned. When Cecil Campbell owned the business, this outdated cotton gin was dismantled and a modern structure built, complete with new office.

Residential houses were built in a row, facing northward toward the main road and extending westward from the store. These were for the store manager, store employees, gin manager and other company workers. Later a large mule barn was built behind this row of houses.

Around 1936, the old Presbyterian church building in Kennett was moved to Bakerville to provide a community church. It was remodeled and classrooms added to it. The citizens of the area used it for church, community affairs and youth meetings.

In 1942, the General American Life Insurance company gave the people of the Church of Christ land for them to build their first building. It was erected a short distance south of the gin. They sold this building in 1963 and built a brick church building north of where the Smith Sawmill used to be, and east of the old Canady store building.

In 1946, General American sold their land holdings, the store, gin, etc. to individual owners. The rich farming land that had once been in the rein by the "Company" was now in the hands of individual owners.

The oldest house, built in 1928, burned in the 1950's when the A. T. Earls family lived there. Its first resident was the Tate family, followed by the Bert Richardson family who occupied it from 1930 to 1946, and then the Earls family moved into it. There used to be six houses in a row, extending westward from the store building, but only three of them remain.

The Richard M. Tidwell family was one of the first families of the area, coming in 1927. Their house was east of the railroad tracks. They originally had lived near Stubtown, but were natives of Tennessee. The A. A. Owen family was another early arriver. Members of these pioneer families still live here today.

The history of the Presbyterian Church, the Church of Christ and the Missouri Mercantile Store have been compiled, and the

Pemiscot County Historical Society has a copy of them. The history of the store was published in the "Daily Dunklin Democrat," February 12, 1969.

CHAPTER NINETEEN

"AUNT PAUL",
Deering Negress and Former Slave,

Dies at 111 of Grief Over Death of Baby Son, 80

The Democrat Argus, Friday, January 12, 1940

A life story that began in Lake County, Tennessee, before that State's favorite son, Andrew "Old Hickory" Jackson, was ushered into the White House amid muddy boots on plush chairs, ended in Deering, Missouri last month with the death of Pauline Rice, colored, who was overcome by the death of her "baby" son who was 80 years old.

Pauline Rice, a former slave, affectionately known as "Aunt Paul", died at the age of 111. Her son, Joe Israel, died on Thursday afternoon December 14, after a short siege of pneumonia.

Aunt Paul, who up to that time had gone about her daily tasks, tending to her chickens, piecing quilts, and enjoying an occasional afternoon of fishing, went to a neighbor's house where, grief-stricken, she went to bed within an hour. The next day she passed into a coma and, without gaining consciousness, died Monday afternoon.

She was born in Lake County, near Tiptonville, Tennessee in 1828. She did not know the day or month she was born, but Pemiscot County Social Security Commission officials, after questioning her as to her age at the time of certain events years ago, felt

This company store served the town from 1910 until it burned in 1962. The first International Harvester red equipment was displayed on the stairway side of the building. To the right is a small view of part of the Wisconsin Company office which burned in 1975.

certain she was born in the year Andrew Jackson was elected president. She received an old age pension in Missouri for three years.

The aged Negress retained all her facilities until her death. She often appeared on assembly programs at the Deering High School and told of her life as a slave. She was a field hand, hoeing, plowing, splitting rails and digging ditches on the land of five masters she served.

An extremely large woman, standing well over six feet tall and at one time weighing 300 pounds, she did not experience the process, but often told of her fellow slaves being confined to barracks for fattening before being sold on the block. She herself was sold four times. Her last master was named Israel, after whom her "baby" boy was named.

She talked much of Lincoln and often recounted her experiences during the Civil War. During the war she slipped through the lines on several occasions to carry food which her aged grandmother had cooked for the Union soldiers. One of her few treasured possessions at the time she died was a canteen used by soldiers during the conflict.

She married Frank Rice and was the mother of three children, two of them dying while young. Joe was her youngest child.

After the war and the gaining of freedom the family moved to Hickman, Kentucky where her husband worked in a rock quarry.

In 1904, when a large lumber company was clearing the swampy west end of Pemiscot County, Frank Rice came to Missouri to work and the next year Pauline joined him there. Joe, meanwhile after fighting in the Spanish-American War, had gone to northeast Arkansas.

Frank died in 1913 and then Aunt Paul sent for Joe to come and live near her. They lived since that time in two adjoining cabins in the colored section of Deering.

When Joe arrived in Deering, Aunt Paul's neighbors questioned her as to discrepance in names, hers being Rice and the son, now past middle age, giving his name as Joe Israel. Old residents tell how she would brighten up as she explained that Joe was born back in slave days, and, naturally took the name of the master.

Her neighbors marveled at her physical strength and all, both Negroes and whites, told corroborating stories of her exploits. W. A. Hudson, Deering Farm official, who knew her twelve years before she died, tells of seeing her lift a barrel of flour and taking it home.

She, with several other Negroes, was waiting in front of a store for foodstuffs which they received as Christmas presents. The proprietor, pointing to a barrel of flour weighing about 200 pounds, told her she could have it if she could take it home. Hudson said the woman, then more than a hundred years old, shouldered the barrel of flour and carried it across the railroad tracks to a cabin in the Negro quarters.

She never wore glasses, yet did a great deal of sewing, threading her own needles and those of her neighbors who were unable to see as well as she. Last fall she dug a small patch of sweet potatoes she had raised. She enjoyed fishing and even last summer made regular excursions to the drainage ditches with her pole and line.

When she died, she was tall and straight, though she had become slender. She enjoyed good health until her son died, and grief over his death is the one cause her friends can give as the reason for her last illness.

Aunt Paul, who had acquired a reputation as the first to pick up little bits of news—which Hudson says were always accurate—fulfilled her own prophecy in her death. Often she told her neighbor, Mrs. L. H. Gibson, teacher at the colored school in Deering, that she would die in Mrs. Gibson's home. And there she went after Joe died and grieved over her son until she passed into the coma from which she never aroused.

The aged Negress was active in social affairs in the Negro community and attended the Caruthersville May Day celebrations in Caruthersville until last year. This was the first such affair she had missed in ten years.

She voted the straight Republican ticket at every opportunity except one. That time she voted Democratic when she "won the election" for a Caruthersville man who had been her friend for twenty years.

She smoked a pipe all her life and her friends say she liked an occasional drink of "bottoms up," as she called it.

CHAPTER TWENTY

Gobler on the County Line Road

Gobler's Black Heritage

By Frances Starks

In 1930, the first black people to come to Gobler were led by the Reverend James Carruthers and his wife, Carrie Carruthers. He was appointed as the leader of the black people when they arrived in what is now Gobler. A section (640 acres) of land was cleared by the blacks and sold for not less than $0.25, nor more than $1.00 per acre. Most people bought land in plots of 20 to 80 acres.

Most of the black people who settled here were originally from Arkansas and Mississippi. Their homes and most of their furniture were built from timber that had been cleared from the land.

Transportation into the area was by covered wagons. There was only one dirt road into Gobler. After the people were settled, their means of transportation was by walking on the railroad tracks back and forth to Deering. The first automobile, a 'Model A' Ford truck, was owned by Jim Jones.

Jim Jones also started the first blacksmith shop and operated it. He brought movies and other entertainment into Gobler. He owned the biggest plots of land, which consisted of 160 acres. In 1940, his brother was convicted of murdering a white man. Jim spent more than fifty thousand dollars trying to save his brother's life, but to no avail. Soon after his brother's death, Jim and his family moved to Michigan. Many of the people followed his lead and moved to different northern states.

There were two churches built in Gobler (both were Baptist.) The church that stood beside the railroad tracks was New Bethlehem Baptist Church. It got its name from the New Bethlehem Brush Arbors, where church was first held. The church burned in 1944, but was soon built back, although it was not located on the railroad; it was built further back. New Bethlehem Baptist Church is still in use today, but it is now called United Baptist Church. The spot where the first church stood became Gobler's first cemetery, which Jim Jones also started.

The second church stood in the middle of the community. Its name was St. John's, and it was first pastured by the Reverend Becton. This church stood until 1960, when it was torn down. Its location is now the spot for Gobler's new cemetery, called St. John's Cemetery.

In 1934, Gobler's population began to grow. Many of the black families moved to Gobler from Deering, after the Kinsall murder.

Gobler got its name from the turkeys which gobbled all night. At first there were so many, but they were soon killed off, and only the name of their sound has remained.

History of Gobler Elementary School

By Jackson Conley, Jr.

The first school was in a one-room frame building. The teachers were: Miss Blanch Gibson, Mrs. Solom Gilmore Nelson, Mrs. Mercy Howard Jones and Thelma Bolden.

The school burned and was moved to the Baptist Church. The new Gobler Elementary School opened its doors July 5, 1948 with an enrollment near two hundred, with Mr. J. F. Taylor, Superintendent. There were eighty pupils in the first grade with Mrs. Regina Clifford Conley as teacher. Mrs. Lillian Gibson, who had taught in the black Elementary School at Deering for more than twenty-five years, entered the new Gobler Elementary School. She taught grades two, three and four for one year. Jackson Conley, Jr. was hired as teaching principal and taught grades five, six, seven and eight.

The new building was very modern with gas furnaces and indoor toilets. It was one of the first to introduce supervised physical education. We followed closely the course of studies provided by the Missouri State Department of Education.

We were active in 4-H programs. We took many interesting field trips to places such as the Memphis Zoo and to Wycliff, Kentucky on a study of ancient Indian Civilizations. We visited Big Springs in the Ozark section of Missouri and Big Oak Park in New Madrid, Mo.

Mrs. Earlene Mullens, an accomplished musician, replaced Mrs. Gibson after her health failed. Mrs. Kathleen W. Conley replaced Mrs. Mullens in 1950. Mrs. Mullens resigned due to a family increase.

After Superintendent J. F. Taylor and S. H. Marcellus resigned, the Board employed Floyd Wilson as superintendent. The Board and Superintendent found overcrowded conditions. They added another classroom, new textbooks and supplies, and employed two more teachers, Mrs. H. Hermon and Mrs. Erma Jackson.

In the early fifties a hot meal program was initiated. Kitchen equipment was purchased by a very active P.T.A. and Mrs. Rebecca Thompson was employed as the cook. She was a very efficient person for the job. When her health failed, she was replaced by Mrs. Odessa Cunningham.

By 1963, with the exception of a few minor incidents, the Deering High School was desecrated with the Junior High and Elementary. By 1965, the entire school was integrated, including the staff at that time.

The Town and Post Office of Gobler

By Paul Harrison Burns and his wife Irene (Neel) Burns, April 14, 1976

We are the oldest white residents of the town of Gobler, having moved here the 23rd of April 1939 from Deering. Paul was originally from Hornersville and Irene grew up in the crossroads community near Senath. Paul opened the post office on May 1st of that year and we continued in this work until he retired 31 May 1971 and she retired 29 February 1976. We were in the post office for thirty-seven years.

The original Gobler was about one-half mile south of where it is today. There was a single sign with the name 'Gobler' on it and a hunter's log cabin, and this was in Dunklin County, on the old Jim Jones farm on the Rives-Gobler road.

In 1937 when Burtig and Sellmeyer came here to build their gin, they didn't like that site, so they built their cotton gin north of the Cotton Belt Railroad tracks (which had been laid many years earlier) and also called it Gobler. Dennye Mitchell built the Gobler Mercantile Company then on the north side of the gin, so this site officially became the town of Gobler.

Leo Sellmeyer was a son-in-law of Mr. Bertig, but Leo sold his interest in the store to Buck Sellmeyer and he became partners with Dennye Mitchell who was from Leachville, Arkansas, and they built one of the largest mercantile stores this area has ever known. The Sellmeyer house is the oldest here in Gobler, and it is still standing and is where Freda Ragin lives today.

It has been said that one of the largest turkey roosts ever found was at this area, and that is where the name was derived. Another story is that the train stopped here and they had to have a name for the place, so Gobler Elliott, and official of the train, named it for himself.

Gobler is located six miles south of Highway 84 and is situated basically on the east side of County Line "NN" Road in

Pemiscot County. It was incorporated as a fourth class town in 1948, the area being one and one-half miles north and south, and one-half mile east and west. Paul Burns was the first mayor and police judge and Willie Stallings the first Marshall. Other mayors were L. V. Elliott, 1949-1950; Hubert E. Garrett, 1951-1952; and Frank Simmons, 1953-1954. When the town was at its peak, the population was 163 people in this small area.

The Gobler Baptist church was established September 1944 and met at our house until 1945 when a pole and cypress building was built on the Elbert Ford property. Today we have a nice brick building located behind the post office. George Walker was the first pastor and T. J. Richardson from Blytheville now preaches for us. The black people have a United Baptist Church, and there is a Church of God a short distance north of town.

The largest business concern in this town was the Gobler Mercantile Store where you could purchase anything you needed. The store was started in 1937 and by 1939 his stock was worth about a thousand dollars. Dennye Mitchell was the clerk in his own store. As he made money he invested back into his store, and his brother Stanley assisted him. Eventually it covered approximately five acres and for several years he did a little more than two million dollars of business per year. He had twenty-three trailer trucks that cost $30,000 each and these trucks brought in his merchandise from everywhere.

He stocked groceries, housewares, appliances, furniture, lumber, medical supplies, barb wire, ammunition, clothing, and later added television sets with his own TV repairman on call every day. He sold cottonseed, animal feed, and practically anything the farmer needed. The store burned March 31, 1956 and the town began declining and has never recovered to its once famous glory. The post office, however, kept growing and business did not slow down at all.

Other places of business were the Elmer Jones poolroom, the Paul Burns cafe, Melvin Russell's barbershop, the Bugs Bunny, and Gerald Burkes had a service station-blacksmith shop-poolroom-grocery store.

Gerald Burke also had the B & B Club, located a little south of town. The major attraction on two different occasions was Elvis Presley. The first time he appeared at the club, he was just getting his start in show business and his fee was something like $50.00. His second appearance, just a short time afterward, was $2,000.00 and he didn't want to come at all, but had promised he would. Gerald sold tickets for $20 each in order to cover this "outrageous" price. The popularity of Elvis had skyrocketed in that short time, and the seats were all sold, there was no standing room left in the building, and there was as many people outside as there were inside.

Today the Ragins and Bounds operate the town businesses of grocery stores, service stations and recreation rooms. There is also the "Soul Shack" just south of the railroad tracks.

Some of the older settlers of this area were the Tom Taylor family and the Blankenship family, and the colored families of Berry Wells and Fanny Kennedy.

The railroad was built before 1910, the exact year I do not know. It runs in a northeast-southwest direction. There are six roads by which people can travel to Gobler, thus enabling anyone in Pemiscot or Dunklin County to have easy access to this town.

The post office is now operated by Mrs. Ann Crain. She is the assistant postmaster at Braggadocio, but is working here until an appointment can be made.

Gobler Mercantile Company

By Virginia (Bounds) Branch

(The following are extracts from Virginia's sixteen page booklet that she published in 1980, which she has given permission to be included in this history. Originally, Deering was supposed to have been a little southwest of the present town of Gobler, but when the mill got mired in the mud, they left it where it was, and created the little town of Deering. The land where Gobler sprang up was part of the 60,000 acres that Wisconsin Lumber Company owned. The timber was cut from it and it was cleared for farming. It is very much a part of this history. Virginia lived in a little white house near the furniture department of this store building. Here is part of her story, as she wrote it.)

Gobler Mercantile Company, "Missouri's Largest Country Store," came into existence sometime in the year 1937. Located in Pemiscot County on the Pemiscot-Dunklin County line in the "boot-heel" of Southeast Missouri, this famous "farmer's market" became a legend in its brief lifetime.

Situated beside a railroad track, Gobler is said to have been named for Gobler Elliott, a railroad man of Caruthersville, Missouri. Attempts to verify this have been less than successful, and we may be forced to turn to a story related by many old-timers who insist the community derived its name from the fact that in the early days a vast number of wild turkeys inhabited the area. This story may be valid as Gobler, even as late as the mid-thirties, was little more than a heavily wooded, frontier-type settlement, populated mostly by blacks who were its original colonists. By 1935 a few whites had filtered in and the wilderness was gradually giving way to civilization. Small farms appeared with cotton and soybeans as the main money crops. The muddy dirt roads were later graveled and finally blacktopped, which made the community more accessible to the outside world.

In 1937 the Sellmeyer brothers of Knoble, Arkansas, took the giant step which propelled Gobler into motion. Once started, growth was spurred by the general economic upswing which came with World War II. The Sellmeyers bought land and started farming operations near Gobler. They then built three modern homes and a big store. In partnership with Joe Bertig of Paragould, Arkansas, they also built a cotton gin. This gin was under the management of Carl "Buck" Sellmeyer, and the store was the responsibility of Dennye Mitchell.

The Sellmeyers had known Mitchell at Leachville, Arkansas, which was his hometown. He was well known as a first-rate salesman. The Sellmeyers had a cotton gin at Leachville, and the two families had become close friends. When the need arose at Gobler for a manager for the new store, he was the natural choice, and a better selection would not have been possible. The story of the Gobler Mercantile Company from the beginning was the story of Dennye Mitchell. In return for his services as proprietor, Dennye was to be a partner in the store. The measure of his success is one of the best known stories in Southeast Missouri, and he was probably the best known businessman in the entire area. Scarcely ever addressed as Mr. Mitchell, he was on a first-name basis with one and all. To Dennye, at one time or another, came practically everyone in the area with some problem.

Most of the local farmers traded with him and many depended on "credit" to get their families through the long summers. Crops were usually "laid by" on or near July 4th, and the meager earnings from cotton chopping was their last spendable income until harvesting began, usually in early September. The onset of cotton-picking time was the signal for an accelerated pace in the community's life style. "Paying off Dennye" was the first order of the day for nearly everyone. Business in the fall of the year was booming from early morning until late at night.

The cotton gin was located nearby and farmers bringing in their cotton always had business at the store. Saturdays were especially busy as most farm work was suspended on this day. Entire families went to Gobler to spend their money and enjoy a day of rest from their labors. Visiting and socializing intermingled with the transaction of business. It was the golden age of country music and thumbing through the memories of those years. One remembered the sounds of the jukebox as Ernest Tubb and Roy Acuff, followed in a few years by Eddy Arnold and Hank Williams, sang the day's favorite songs. Gobler on a Saturday afternoon was not just busy. It was loud, colorful, and hectic.

In the beginning Dennye stocked mostly groceries, housewares, farm implements, hoes, sacks for picking cotton, and other basic essentials required by the farmers who were his chief patrons. He also purchased their excess products such as chickens, eggs, butter, and firewood. In the nineteen years of its life, Gobler was constantly changing. In the beginning there was a simple 30' x 60' building or corrugated tin containing approximately nine hundred dollars worth of merchandise. Through the years as Dennye added departments and new lines of merchandise, buildings would be attached to provide needed space. The growth and expansion of this small country store and the part if played in its community and throughout the Midsouth is still amazing, even to those who were there through it all.

Regardless of any individuals' personal like or dislike of Gobler as a place to live, one always had the feeling that here was no ordinary situation. There was a special, homey equality about this overgrown country store that somehow set it apart. "Going to the store" at Gobler was not necessarily something to be done simply because the cupboard was bare. One went quite often simply as a social encounter. There was never any way of knowing who would be there or what would be going on.

Gobler during the war years was incredible. On Saturdays, the crowds reached unbelievable proportions. Just pushing and shoving one's way through the store was a chore in itself, and making a purchase usually required waiting one's turn. By 1944 Gobler had become a trade center to be reckoned with. Parking areas on the store and gin yards became inadequate as money and cars became more plentiful. It was common for cars to be backed up along both sides of the highway almost to the No.8 Ditch about one mile distant on County Line Road NN.

Occasionally Dennye would sponsor special entertainment to attract even greater crowds. These affairs usually consisted of fairly well known country musicians or gospel singers. The Slim Rhodes'

Show was probably the best known group to appear at Gobler. The most consistent method, however, of ensuring a large crowd was the time honored, absolutely fail-proof "drawing," For many years Gobler's citizens planned their Saturdays around the drawing at four o'clock. With each dollar purchase, each customer was given a ticket, the stub of which went into a large can. As time for the drawing drew near the crowd began to congregate in front of the store and promptly at four o'clock one of the employees, usually Winfred "Wimpy" Isaac, would take the can containing all the ticket stubs, climb on a barrel near the front door of the store and select some small child to draw a ticket from the can. There was always an abundance of available candidates for this job as the day's winner of the drawing usually rewarded the youngster who had drawn the ticket.

As years passed the store continued to expand, eventually covering about five acres and containing special departments for all major fields of merchandise. There was a grocery department and meat market, a drug center, dry-goods section, furniture department, housewares section, a hardware department, a restaurant, and eventually a television shop and a lumber yard. The periods of greatest expansion were probably in 1948 and 1949.

In the early days Dennye's methods of advertising had been rather limited. He depended mostly on printed handbills distributed about the countryside by one of his employees driving a pickup truck. This same truck was used to make deliveries to customers who had no transportation. The advertising field, however, received a tremendous boost in the summer of 1947 when a radio station was established at nearby Kennett, Missouri. Gobler Mercantile Company now began to advertise on a much wider scale and people began arriving from greater distances to see this big store they had heard about on the radio. "Old Camp-Meeting Time," a program of gospel music, was sponsored by Dennye for many years and was a great favorite of the church-folk. The format of this show was the standard procedure of the time—listeners were invited to write in "cards and letters" requesting favorite songs and dedications were made. Between songs would be spot advertisements and invitations to visit the "Midwest's Largest Country Store."

Sometime in the early fifties, Dennye had gone into the trucking business, a field known to be very tough and very competitive. At one time he had more than twenty huge tractor-trailer trucks hauling merchandise for his own store and also doing custom hauling.

About 1952 televisions had come to Gobler and each night, out back on the porch of the furniture department, one of these new inventions was displayed for benefit of the general public. It was here that most of Gobler's citizens saw their first television. A good-sized crowd was on hand every night. There was only one channel at the time so no disagreements could arise as to program choices.

Then almost overnight television became the latest addition to every household bringing a new business angle. A short distance behind the store Dennye now built a television repair shop and hired a full-time repairman. This marked the first case of his putting up a separate building to accommodate new business. Always before he had simply added onto what was already there.

As the fifties progressed and business started to decline, a decision was made to seek outside professional help in his all out effort to get things rolling again. Gobler was about to embark upon a new and completely different chapter in its life. In due time the "business promotion experts" arrived and proved to be a husband and wife team of ex-carnival hucksters. Their first move as the installation of a public address system and from early morning until late at night they kept up a running barrage of promotion gimmicks such as can be seen and heard in any small-town carnival anywhere in America. There were popularity contests, talent contests, raffles, auctions, prizes for this and prizes for that. Crowds jammed the place night after night—mostly to be a part of what was going on. The high point of this giant free show was a new car to be given away at a drawing late in November. The night this drawing was held was extremely cold, but the crowd it attracted was probably the largest in Gobler's history. The car was won by a Mr. Burroughs, a gentleman who lived about two miles distant on the county line road.

The fifties moved along and although everyone knew things had changed a bit, there was no real concern. Gobler by now had become a landmark, a legend in its own time, and in such a short time at that. The war years and postwar years were ancient history and the excitement, color, and crowds of those busy Saturday afternoons possibly would not be equaled again. Still no one doubted Gobler would always be there. She might have her ups and downs, but she'd survive. What no one could possibly know was the fact that time was simply running out in an entirely different direction.

When Gobler's big fire came it was not at all as anyone had imagined it would be. It came at midday on a Saturday, the last day of March 1956, a routine business-as-usual day with no premonitions of the changes it was to bring to so many lives. Two teen-aged boys, employees of the store, had been burning cardboard boxes that day and flames somehow spread to a wooden door which served as a side entrance to the grocery department. From the door, fire jumped to overhead rafters and from this point on there were never any doubts as to the ultimate outcomes. Calls for help went out immediately to fire departments of nearby communities and firefighters from Kennett, Hayti and Deering battled the blaze most of that Saturday afternoon with all odds against them. Water for such a huge fire was almost impossible to obtain.

Most families living near the store expected to lose their homes and with help from neighbors, furniture and personal belongings were carried to safety. Actually only one occupied home, that of the Wesley Gaines family, was lost to the fire. Another house, owned by Paul Burns and used as storage, was also burned. The fire raged furiously for several hours with all manners of explosions and projectiles being hurled into the air. By mid-afternoon the worst was over, but small fires continued to burn for several days and tin cans would occasionally explode three weeks after the fire.

One remembers Dennye and his actions at this crucial time in his life when nineteen years of hard work lay in twisted rubble before his eyes. He walked about calmly, maybe partly in shock. He appeared, on the surface, to be accepting the situation more matter-of-fact than many of those who had only emotional interest involved. Several people who owed him money came that day to pay their debts. What was so sad was that Dennye had recently dropped several thousand dollars of fire insurance. Dennye estimated his losses at one-half million dollars, and he was never able to make a comeback from that disaster.

CHAPTER TWENTY ONE

Settlements in Dunklin County

Tinkerville

by Bessie (Huntley) Wright

A great migration of people from the Latter-Day Saints Church in Louisiana bought hundreds of acres of land adjacent over in Dunklin County. The families moved in and cleared up the land and began farming it. Mr. B. L. Tinker had the forty acres just southwest of the school, and he built a grocery store on the northeast corner of his farm. This little settlement then became known as Tinkerville. Mr. Charles B. Baker built a cotton gin next to the store building. He sold it to Massey and Ferguson, and they in turn, sold it to Bert Richardson. This was all original part of the Wisconsin Lumber Company holdings.

    An interesting fact about this group of people is that they had pooled their money and sent one of the head men to purchase the land, for the back taxes, in one large tract. Then it was their intention to divide it after the purchase, because then they would know the exact cost per acre. The man made the transaction, then he died before the land could be divided. Each family had to file with his estate to get their share according to the money they had invested. These farms were laid out so each family could live up near the road, therefore they were narrow and rectangular. They built a large white church building which still stands today, although church services are no longer held there. Mr. Phillips (father, and later the son) both preached there for several years.

The first school at Tinkerville was called Mapleview. Enoch Tolleson was the first principal and it began around 1930. He taught grades one through eight. Later the building was moved to what is known as the Rice Road and was a school in that area for a few years. Then it was converted into a Baptist Church, which was called the Mapleview Missionary Baptist Church. When the congregation disbanded, they sold the building to Michael Wade.

Meanwhile, the old hotel in Deering had been torn down, so they used the good lumber from it, and built a bungalow-type school building. Also, the old school house at Mid-City, which was known as the Little River school, had been dissolved, so they gave this place the name of Little River School, and Mr. Tolleson continued as principal. This was in 1935, and the school was on the east side of County Line "NN" Road, three miles south of Highway 84.

Mr. Jack Clayton was the second principal of the Tinkerville school, and others following were Dwight Whittaker, Jadie Naile, Mr. Myrant, Mrs. Mills and Arthur Davis. School teachers were Mrs. Esther Clayton, Murriel Sellers, Charlene Sellers Mitchell, Ruby Sudduth Turner, Mildred Callis Farr, Clora Cox Speer, Mrs. Barker, Bobbie Sue Bowling Lawson and myself. Willie B. Naile did the substitute teaching for us.

The school disbanded after 1953 and sealed bids were taken for the building, and the buyer tore down the building and moved the lumber away.

Democrat-Argus, Thursday, July 25, 1936

RELIGIOUS GROUP SETTLES IN PEMISCOT AND DUNKLIN COUNTIES; HAVE BOUGHT OVER FIVE THOUSAND ACRES FARM LAND

"Of more than passing interest in the far western part of Pemiscot County, in fact, located on the county line between Dunklin and Pemiscot counties, is a settlement consisting of a number of families with a unified belief. These families came into this section around two years ago from various locations in the U.S., buying about 5,000 acres of cut over land at tax sales.

"At the present time, there are between 60 and 70 families located in this section, with a number yet to come, who have already purchased land.

"The belief of these people is what is known as the Latter-day Saints, with headquarters at Independence, Mo. A meeting beginning last Saturday and continuing on through next week is being held at a tabernacle about four miles west of Deering. In charge of the meeting is Elder W. E. Haden, of Lamoni, Iowa, and assisting him is his son, William Haden; also Elder A. M. Baker, of Thayer, Mo., Elder Samuel Simmons from the Texas and Oklahoma district, and Elder J. L. Gunsolley of Lamoni, Iowa.

"There has been in the past and is at present, a certain amount of misinformation in regard to their religious belief, that would be eliminated if only the truth were known. Elder Haden states that this group of people have certain ideals to maintain and goals to work forward to, until they are attained. As in a number of churches its members believe in tithing. Elder Haden stated that the first purpose of the leaders in this movement in this section was to get a body of land. After getting the land, the next thing was to get together all these people with a unified belief, who were scattered over the country. Then by working together to attain a number of goals set forth, they will make their community and real modern an up-to-date one.

"The leaders in the organization are at present arranging for the purchase of another tract of land similar in size a few miles west of Sikeston. They think southeast Missouri is a wonderful country and that it has great possibilities, however, all the land in their tracts is yet undeveloped.

"In the near future, possibly within the next month they plan to erect a meeting house in the central part of their land, which location will place it about five miles straight west of Deering. For the past two years they have been using a small building, but the time is at hand that a larger building is essential.

"An outstanding feature, in addition to their regular services is the regular Saturday night entertainment put on by the young people in which religious plays, depicting bible characters and scenes are given. On this coming Saturday night an especially good program is being prepared and the public is invited. At a similar occasion held last Saturday night around 600 people were in attendance.

"Ultimately this group of people have in mind the accomplishment of a number of goals, which will come as a result of their working together to attain them. Such goals are the erection of their own cotton gin, the establishment of a bank, and the building their own schools, which will include both grade and high school.

"The fact that the land is divided into small tracts with each family owning from twenty to forty acres is making for the rapid development of this cut over land into valuable farm land. Crops on the majority of this land are as good as those to be found anywhere in this section.

"The public is invited to attend the meeting in progress at the present time and to hear the capable speakers that have come into this community especially for this meeting."

The Settlement of Deerland

By Bessie (Huntley) Wright

The grocery store at this place was owned and operated by a Mr. Vaughn. He stocked all the staples a family needed, and his business was brisk as this area was so remote from trading centers. There were several families who lived in this area. The Deerland School was across the road and each building faced the other. The correct name for this school was "Lee," but since the community was called Deerland, the school became known as the Deerland School. It was named for Lee Hudson, wife of W. A. Hudson, who was Superintendent of Deering School when it was built.

From the Dunklin County courthouse, Deed book 114, page 84, J. P. And Della E. Vickrey and S. V. and Mary Medling of Pemiscot County, deeded one acre of land to School District #6, 19 June 1936, described as one acre in the northwest corner of the northeast quarter of northeast section 31, township 18, range 10 east.

The school was in Dunklin County, approximately four miles southwest (as the crow flies) from Tinkerville. The building was boxed and stripped, with a small front porch and back porch. The children's seats were on runners in order to make them easy to move about. In the winter time the playground was muddy, so we would push the seats to one side so the children would have a play area inside.

It was heated by a large coal stove with a jacket around it. The bookcases were nailed to the wall. The teacher's desk and chair completed the school room furniture. A few textbooks (left over from the Deering Central school) and one set of old World Books, were our reading material.

We taught from first grade through eighth grade, putting 3-4, 5-6, 7-8 on an alternating schedule. We did this in everything except arithmetic and reading. The enrollment was about twenty-five pupils.

Until 1943, everyone walked to school, when the school bus line was extended this far. At times the road was so bad the bus turned at twin bridges just before you go to Deepwater where the Latter-Day Saints Church is. Then everyone had to walk the rest of the way.

Merle Stone taught at Deerland in 1939. She had been having blackout spells, and one day as she rode into the school yard, she fell off her horse. Her brother, Rhea Stone, saw her and helped her. She died in February 1940 from spinal meningitis. Leonard Teaster replaced her and taught until he resigned in 1942.

I began teaching there in 1943 and taught for four years. Mrs. Mary Lindsey Tidwell, Miss Lydia Branch and then Murriel Sellers Wright taught there before it was disbanded and the children began attending Little River school at Tinkerville.

The Community of Fairview

By Mrs. Stanley (Charlene Sellers) Mitchell

This was a one-room frame school house, built with a high-pitched roof, painted white at one time but known more often without any color except for the drabness of old wood. It had a double front door, with windows all along the east side and at the end of the building. On the inside, blackboards lined the entire west wall and also there were some at the front.

This school started between 1934 and 1938 and disbanded in 1951. I was the last teacher there. I can't remember who else taught, except for Mrs. Flo Brewer. Although it had eight grades, there were approximately 30 to 35 pupils, and only one teacher for all grades.

We all walked to school, took our lunches and drank water from the pump outside. A coal stove heated the building in the winter, and the breezes through the windows made it as comfortable as possible in the summer.

We were part of the Deering School District and they kept us well-supplied with books and all things needed in a school room.

The school was located on a dirt road that went adjacent with the railroad tracks, southwestward from Gobler. Uncle Abe Blankenship lived near it. On down the road was the settlement known as Gibbons where there was a grocery store and cotton gin. All of this was in Dunklin County.

Bethel Community

By Mrs. Arvil (Prue West) Bowie

A preacher by the name of Carrington established a Baptist church in this community and named it Bethel Baptist Church. When the school house was built, it was suggested it take the same name, as the community was called Bethel.

Some of the families of this area were the E. B. Bowie, Arvil Bowie, George Brand, Robert Brand, Johnny Coffer, Tom Dollins, Penn Earls, Joe Flowers, Bennie Graves, Henry Griffin, Jack Howard, Lela Kersey, William Phillips, George Sides, Mr. Stone, and Vestal West.

This was one of the last of the settlements of the Deering School District, and unless one is a native of this area, it is hard to describe exactly where it was, as it was more commonly referred to as back down in the lower country. The easiest way to get there is to go south on County Line "NN" for one and one-half miles south of Gobler, and turn west at the Tom Taylor farm. Follow "ZZ" for two miles, then turn north for three-fourth miles. The school was in Section 5, Township 17, Range 10.

George Brand who moved to this area in 1936, and E. B. Bowie who had moved here in 1935, took a school census of the neighborhood. Mr. Brand caught the train and went to Deering to consult them about a school. He was told they had made an appraisal by airplane, and did not feel that there were enough families to warrant a school. Mr. Brand showed them the census that he had taken, and the school board agreed that they should have a school.

The first school house was built by the citizens of the community with the women taking an active part in it. E. B. Bowie owned a sawmill, and he would dress the timber that each family donated. This one-room building, measuring 16 x 20, was built in the summer after the flood of 1937. When it was abandoned, Mr. Penn Earls added a room to it, and made a residence.

Since that school house only served the community for one year, it only had one teacher and that was Jadie Naile. He boarded with the George Brand family.

Since this area was part of Deering Consolidated District # 6, they built the next building. It was built on a little over an acre of land, on the Kinder farm. It was a wood frame building, constructed in 1938. When the school disbanded in 1954, the building was sold by secret ballot. T.M. Battles bought it for $150.00. He moved it to his property and made a farm shed out of it.

The school was a one-teacher organization, with grades one through eight, with an enrollment of fifteen to twenty per year. The teachers who taught, in order, were Jadie Naile, Vernon Kinder, Reel Blaylock, Gladys Dollins and Gladys Phillips.

SECTION THREE

DEERING— INDIVIDUAL OWNERSHIP

When A. T. Earls purchased Deering Farms he was primarily interested in the farm land. For many years, Mr. Earls was one of the most successful real estate agents in the Bootheel. Immediately he began selling the farm land in plots of eighty and one hundred sixty acres to individual farmers. His motto was "The best security on earth, is earth itself."

Mr. Earls sold the store to Hubert French, the lumber shed to E. P. Crow, and the service station to Gene Willis who later sold it to Alvin Skinner.

In 1956, along with Paul Hutchens and Earl Vick he started the Deering Seed and Fertilizer Company. Later, Jimmy Ward, Bud Calhoun and Johnny Calhoun joined the company. That same year he made a deal for Standard Oil to come to Deering for ten years. Leonard Kindred assumed the proprietorship of the bulk plant. He was succeeded by Dennis Green.

Although Mr. Earls was not a member of the Methodist Church, he was a supporter of it.

He was a member of the Modern Woodmen of the World and IOOF.

Mr. Earls and his wife Mary had three children. Their two

sons are Raymond (deceased) and A. J. Earls. The daughter, Opal, married John Atwill and they have two sons, Johnny and Steve Atwill. The Earls household was always open for other kinfolks, among which was David Crossett, their nephew, who lived with them for many years.

The name which Mr. Earls chose for his business was Earls Enterprises. W. M. Green became manager of the town and farmland. Today, the Calhoun family owns the town of Deering that has not been sold to individual ownership.

CHAPTER TWENTY TWO

Alvin Thomas Earls

August 27, 1886 - March 4, 1958

Mr. Earls was undoubtedly the largest real estate broker in Southeast Missouri when he purchased Deering in May 1955. His tremendous energy and his overpowering faith in the Bootheel contributed much to the development of the fine farming land in this area. After coming to this area in 1910, he lived in the Steele and Hayti area. Originally, he was a farmer and a mule dealer. The Earls Brothers Motor Company in Steele was one of the first automobile dealerships in Pemiscot County. Later he turned to real estate which had been his most profitable venture for the past twenty-four years. His motto was "The best security on earth, is earth itself."

He purchased three large tracts of Southeast Missouri farm land for more than one million dollars each. The first of these land sales was in October 1954, when Mr. Earls and the late Claud Stillman of Peach Orchard and Kennett bought 5,275 acres of Pemiscot County farm land west of Wardell from the Landing Lumber Company of Wichita, Kansas. The price was reported as "more than $1 million."

Then one month later, in November 1954, Mr. Earls bought by contract, 2,835 acres of Arizona land north of Bragg City from Hal Bogle of Dexter, New Mexico. Involved in the transaction was the trade of 2,900 acres of Arizona land which Mr. Earls had purchased. This transaction was reported as a "more than $1 ½ million deal."

The Deering plantation, comprising 3,358 acres of land included the town of Deering with the exception of the school and church property. Included in the sale was the Deering Gin and Mercantile Company, composed of a cotton gin, general store, oil business, lumber shed and machine shop. Later Mr. Earls sold some of the farm land, retaining about 1,800 acres.

Besides operating real estate agencies in Hayti and Blytheville, Ark., Mr. Earls was associated with the Campbell Brothers gin at Bakerville, the Earls-Webb Motor Company in Hayti, the Cook-Earls Motor Company in Caruthersville with Sam Guy and Dr. A. G. Shirey in the Pascola gin and with Mr. Guy in the O. C. Clark gin northeast of Wardell.

He had disposed of most of his interests in Stoddard County but still owned at the time of his death, the 600 acres known as the J. B. Buck Hog Ranch or Gabe Rendleman farm just north of Bloomfield and the DeMange rice farm just west of Dexter comprising of about 1000 acres and various other small tracts in Stoddard County, but most of his holdings were in Pemiscot and New Madrid Counties.

He was born August 27, 1886 near Greenfield, Tennessee and died March 4, 1958 of a heart attack in Hayti, Missouri and is buried in Mt. Zion Cemetery at Steele. Mr. Earls was married to Mary Ethel Rose and they have a daughter, Mrs. Opal Atwill, and two sons, Raymond and A. J. The sons continued to carry on his real estate business after his death. He was a member of the Modern Woodmen and IOOF lodges at Steele.

Alvin Thomas Earls, 1886-1958
He was an outstanding real estate dealer, and his involvement with Deering began in 1955 when he purchased the town and 3358 acres of land which he sold to individuals which changed the plantation system that had been prevelent since the little town was established in 1899-1900.

CHAPTER TWENTY THREE

Deering Consolidated C-6 School

Deering school bells began ringing almost as quickly as the lumber mill and town began operating. They found places for the students to learn with their assigned teacher who taught all grades. The first school house doubled as a church meeting place on Sunday. Its location was on the east side of town near what became known as Pondertown. Later a two-room building, which had served as a boarding hotel for lumber mill workers in the northeast corner of town, was converted into a school building. Another room was added to it and it became the famous three-room white school house that practically every Deering student remembers attending. Pemiscot County Courthouse, Book 28 page 227: William Deering and Clara H., his wife, of Evanston, Cook County, Illinois, on November 27, 1903 gave a quit claim deed for one acre of land. The description reads: "Beginning at a point on the line between sections 16 & 17, township 18 north, range 11 east, 800 feet north of a corner to sections 16, 17, 20 & 21, thence west 208.72 feet to a stake, thence north 208.72 to a stake, thence east 208.72 to the section line, and thence south 208.72 feet to the place of beginning. This land to be used only for a school, and if not, to revert back to their heirs."

All grades through the eighth were taught in that school building. If a student wanted an education higher than the eighth grade, they could catch the moose and ride to Caruthersville, spend the day in school, and ride the train back home in the afternoon. Several of them did that.

A school picture of 1907-08 shows an enrollment of twenty-seven with Mrs. Iona (or Aunie) Adams from Caruthersville as teacher. The 1910-11 picture of the students shows forty-nine pupils and Miss Belle Powell as the teacher. Walter E. and wife Effie Odell Palmer Bess from West Plains, Missouri taught the fifty-seven enrolled students in February 1913 when the school picture was made.

From the book "Sixty-Fifth Report of the Public Schools of the State of Missouri," school year ending June 30, 1914, mention is made of Deering School. It was school # 45, W. E. Bess was the teacher, a position he had held for the past 20 months, earning $75.00 per month. There were 100 books in the library, valued at $45.00; the assessed valuation of the district was $200,000; and the estimated value of the school property was $3,000.00.

The total expense for maintaining the school that year was $1,230 broken down thus: library, $11; repairs, $4; fuel, $27; janitor, $36; salary of a female teacher, $540; salary of a male teacher, $585; board of education, $20; with no expense for water, lights, or textbooks. The levy was 65 cents, the estimated value of equipment was $350, the estimated value of school property was $3,250, and the assessed valuation of taxable property was $135,000. Balance on hand for the school on June 30, 1914 was $724.00.

After the two-story brick school house was completed in 1927, grades three through twelve moved into it. This left the primer, first and second for the little three-room school house until it burned December 15, 1939. The building and all its contents were consumed by the fire, but all students escaped without any injury. They had just completed a fire drill that morning. Two of the classes moved upstairs over the company store, and the primer moved upstairs above the doctor's office. They shared the same playground behind the store building.

One thing all students attending the white three-room school house always looked forward to was playing in the little Rhythm Band. In November 1939 the school purchased red and white uniforms for the fifty of them, and this group always put on a program at Christmas, at the end of school, and other times when called upon. The busses would run to transport the parents to school to see their child perform.

Mr. Brashler was principal of the first high school in Deering. The first graduating class was in 1927. Those graduates were Naomi King Ward, Lilly Copple, Bertha Golden Jackson, and Mamie Stover Ledbetter. The class of 1928 was Frances Dawson, Thelma Copple, Clayborne Connor, Idamae Stout, Carolyn Stout and Norma Manton. In 1929 it was Marvin Long, Roy Arnold, Mary McIntosh, Nellie Kolosick, Ollie Lipsey, Willie Huntley, Enoch Tolleson and Hazel Stover.

No story about the Deering School would be complete without mentioning Ned and Kitty Jonakin. She started teaching at the Deering commercial department in 1932, just out of college. She said she chose to come here for several reasons, the first being that they offered her more money than other schools did. They gave her a challenge to make a better commercial department than they had at that time. This was all she needed, because with her enthusiasm for always doing your best, she certainly accomplished this goal while she was teaching here. She took winning typing, shorthand and bookkeeping teams to District and State competition, usually bringing home the trophy. Business people in the nearby towns would call the school each spring and ask for her top students to come work for them.

The town also promised to build her a new house. The Jonakins lived two houses east of the two-story brick school building. Her husband, Ned Jonakin, lacked eight weeks finishing college, so she came alone, with him joining her a few months later.

Both of them were employed, she as commercial teacher and him as high school principal. Then he was drafted in World War II, and she served as principal for one year, then stored her furniture and joined him in Connecticut where he was stationed. He taught aircraft engineering at Yale in New Haven, and she did auditing work with the Army Air Corps. When the war was over, they returned to Deering in the summer of 1946 and remained for ten more years.

Miss Nola Grinstead was another teacher who taught many years in Deering, eventually becoming principal of the grade school. She had a private room at the teacherage. During the months when school was not in session, she made several trips, both in the U.S.A. and overseas. It was her delight to make talks to each class in grade school and tell them about her journeys. She had a habit, just before the closing bell rang, to leave her office and station herself under the big tree next to where the busses parked. When students came running out of the building, she would make them stand by her until everyone else had taken their seats on the bus.

J. F. Taylor held the position of Superintendent longer than any other. He began in 1938 and retired in 1955. He and his wife moved to their farm near Gobler for the rest of their days.

One family of this area compiled an outstanding record of note. The H. L. and Flossie Sudduth family had seven children, and all seven of them graduated from Deering School. They were Ruby 1935, Gordon 1939, Paul 1940, Gaston 1942, Mildred 1944, Peggy 1946 and Ruth 1948. After Ruby and Ruth got their college education, they taught in the Deering School System.

Between 1927 and 1966, twenty-two families had six or more to graduate from Deering. These were not all brothers and sisters, some were cousins, and some weren't even kin. The surnames were Blankenship 9, Bond(s) 10, Bowling 7, Davis 13, Garrett 6, Hawkins 6, Holbrook 7, James 8, Lance 6, Lebo 7, Lipsey 8, McDonald 8, Pace 6, Richardson 17, Riggs 10, Sudduth 8, Taylor 6, Tidwell 7, Turner 8, Williams 8, Wright 11, and Young 11.

The school at Deering was called Deering Central School. Several outlying schools such as Vicksburg, Seldom Seen, Little River and Maple View joined in with them to become Deering Consolidated #6. Vicksburg school went through the fourth grade, and Little River through the fifth grade. Later, there were other elementary schools in Dunklin County, that fed students into Deering Central such as Deerland, Fairview, and Bethel.

This being an agricultural area, the turnover of students was enormous. Families moved in and out constantly. This was due to crop failures, dissatisfaction, looking for something better, and unable to get along with their relatives and neighbors. Several of the people rented their farms, or else worked for other farmers on a sharecropper basis.

A school lunch room program was started in the late 1930's and Nancy Huie was the first supervisor, later succeeded by Mary Putman Williams. They only operated from November until May, as it was too hot to heat up the cook stove in the summertime. In December 1939, they acquired an electric cook stove, and the year round lunch program began. In the winter, a warm glass of chocolate milk accompanied each meal. The price of a ticket for five weekly meals was nominal, but for those who could not afford it, jobs would be provided for them so they could earn their lunch.

At one time, Deering C-6 had one of the largest bus systems to transport the students in the United States. In 1941 it transported more children than any other school district in Missouri. It took a big family to maintain a forty-acre farm, so the student body was very large. The busses would be overcrowded with three larger students sitting in the seats and three youngsters standing in front of them. By the time the bus got to the school house, the aisle would also be full. But the students started dropping out when they became large enough to do some full days work on the farm. The number of graduates each year never exceeded forty.

As mechanized equipment came into existence, this large man power was not needed, and the families began moving from the farm. The school attendance decreased. Eventually, the Deering C-6 and Braggadocio C-7 schools merged and became Delta C-7. Later the Gobler Colored School integrated with them. The school enrollment today is less than five hundred.

Braggadocio had a two-story brick high school building and the first class graduated in 1923, the last one in 1966. It was then converted into a junior high school as part of the Delta C-7 School System. A modern cafeteria was built on the central campus after the schools combined. The outlying elementary schools of Davis, Speer and Midway sent their students to the Braggadocio school for their junior high and senior high schooling.

An incomplete list of personnel of Deering Consolidated School C-6, taken from school annuals, newspapers, and memory, for school teachers, secretaries, school board members, bus drivers, custodians, and cooks up to 1965 include:

Miss Aunie Adams (all), Miss Louise Ade (second) Jennie M. Allen (all), Miss Alley, Roy Ashabranner (athletic director), Ruth Sudduth Baker (elementary), Miss Baker (home economics), Bonnie Bates (elementary), Miss Bell (primary), Inez Bentley (art), Walter E. Bess (principal and all junior high), Effie Odell Bess (all), Diane Bibb (business), Levi Bingenheimer (all), Nellie S. Bird (primer), Miss Blaylock (elementary), Reel Blaylock (all), Harold Blocker (math and science), Clifford Boatright (math), Thelma Bolden (colored), Wayne Bond (agriculture), Otto Bond (school board), Miss Margaret Bowman, Lydia Branche (all), Henry E. Brashler (principal), Flo Brewer (elementary), Mrs. Gordon Brooks (elementary), Miss Rose Bryant (all), Broadside, Mrs. Kittie Byrd (fifth), Porter Bullock (all), Jane Bynum (home economics),

Mrs. Caldwell (elementary), Floyd Callaway (business), Clarence E. Carnell (primary), Mary E. Carnell (primary), Earlie Carter (history), Maude Carter (elementary), Luke Cassidy (math), Mr. Cassiday (history), Miss Lillian Cervenka (music), Cheatham, Jack Clayton (grade school principal), Esther Clayton (elementary), Lloyd Cleveland, Harlice Coats (elementary), Mrs. R. H. "Ruby" Collier, Sonja Collier (secretary), Jackson Conley (colored principal), Regina Clifford Conley (colored elementary), Mrs. Kathleen Conley (colored elementary), Rev. Everett M. Cook (Mexicans), Miss Cooper, Alvin Cope (elementary), J. R. Corbin (math and high school principal), Miss Croft (elementary), Oliveen Crow (elementary), Lavada Dunnivant Crowe (primary), Mary Crowe (elementary), Lois Cunningham (bus driver), Mrs. Odessa Cunningham (colored cook), Edith Hatley Curtis (all),

Mary Frances Darby (secretary), Miss Davidson (business), Betty Davis (home economics), Claude E. Day (social studies & coach), Camilla Carter Day (third), Sherry Depriest (primary), M. G. Dietenback (all), Gladys Dollins (all), Mr. Duke, Mrs. Duke, Dan Duyer (math), Gladys Dye (elementary), Miss Eaker (English), R. R. Eddleman (elementary principal), Mrs. Eddleman (elementary), Lenard Elder (history), Merry Jim Russ Elder (primary), Tom Elliott, Ernest England,

Mildred Callis Farr (first), C. D. Faulkner (English and speech), Mitchell Fisher (coach), Mrs. Mitchell Fisher (elementary), Larry French (agriculture), Ann Green French (elementary), Ken Garner (bus driver), Nettie Gather (all), Miss Minnie Gaye (social studies), Mr. Clyde Gettings (social studies), Mrs. Gettings (elementary), Blanche Gibson (colored), Lillian Haze Gibson (colored), Mrs. Solom Gilmore Nelson (colored), Mrs. Melvin Goodman (elementary), Talmadge Graham (custodian), Pearl Grimes Graham (cook), W. L. Green (school board), Ben T. Griffin (superintendent), Lillie Hall Grimes (secretary), Miss Nola Grinstead (elementary principal),

Oren L. Hall (social studies & coach), Mariedeth Hamlett (primary), Miss Harlan (commerical), Houston Hankins (custodian), Lela Hankins (cook), Miss Harlan (commercial), John Hawkins (special education), Mrs. H. Hermon (colored), Nelson Holbert (school board), Mrs. Holzworth, Rev. Winifred House (history), Mrs. Margaret House (English), Miss Hubbard (elementary), W. A. Hudson (superintendent), Beulah Huffman (all), Nancy Huie (cook), Paul B. Hutchens (school board)

Harold Jackson (school board), Betty Boone Jackson (primary), Mrs. Erma Jackson (colored), Mrs. Virginia Jameson (music), Arvel Jarrett (custodian), Ruple Jarrett (cook), Curtis Jenkins, Miss Johannaber (high school), Bonnie Johns (primary), Aline Johnson (business), Helen Johnson (elementary), J. J. Johnston (all), C. A. Jolliff (school board), Mr. Jonakin (high school principal), Mrs.

Kitty Jonakin (business), Mrs. Mercy Howard Jones (colored), Montie Juden (all), Ruby Kelley (all), Vivian Kendrick (primary), John Kimmer (principal), Vernon Kinder (all), Leonard Kindred (school board), Miss Kirkendall (elementary), George Klinkhardt, Herbert Kropf, Dr. Lambert (music), Emily Lanier (music), Mamie Stover Ledbetter (elementary) Judith Leist (chorus), Loren Lincoln (fourth), Nell Long (all),

Ada Marberry (all), S. H. Marcellus (superintendent), Lila Marcellus (business), Agnes Alexander Marshall (elementary), Thelma Minner Martin (librarian), Pauline Condit Masters (second & music), Mrs. Alma Mayfield (history), Miss Virginia Mayfield (junior high), Bill McCord, Miss Geraldine McCormick (English), Venita McGraw (chorus), Sarah Boone McGraw (elementary), Marvin McKinney (math), Mrs. McKinney (English), Frank Metzer (bus driver), Allen Mickel (music), Mrs. Marjorie Mickel (elementary music), Mary Shrader Mills (English), Bobby Mitchell (math and science), Martha Mitchell (elementary), Charlene Sellers Mitchell (all), Miss Clarine Moore (elementary), Jay B. Morgan (junior high), Earlene Mullens (colored), Christine Myers (elementary), Pauline Myers (elementary),

Jadie C. Naile (elementary principal), Willie B. Groves Naile (elementary), Rev. Marvin Niblock (fourth), Joe Norton (elementary), Joan Norton (secretary), Cloe Null (junior high), Leila Rice Oldsen (elementary), Miss Virginia Orton, Joe Parks (coach), "Bub" Patterson (custodian), Tim Pearman (math), Mary Pelts (librarian), Miss Mildred Perkins, Miss Florence Peyton (high school), Gladys Phillips (all), Paul Plunkett (school board), Miss Belle Powell (all), Miss Juanita Presson, Opal Light Pulliam (primary), Clara Putman (cook), Cytha Mills Qualls (home economics),

Billy Earl Ramsey (business), James Ratliff (school board), Mr. Joe Redwine (fifth), Elizabeth Reed (cook), Eunice Reynolds (elementary), Tom Richardson (science) Bert Richardson (school board), Bill Richardson (school board), W. B. Richardson (school board), Elmer Richardson (school board), Cooter Riddick (bus driver), Mary Riddick (cook), Miss Ronney (elementary), Miss

Rose (elementary), Mrs. James Rounsaville (English), Vurnie Russell,

Gutherie Scaggs (third), Marjorie Scott (English), Mrs. Pearl Shaw (elementary), Mrs. Lois Shy (music), Mrs. Marie Sigler (elementary), Gladys Sikes (all), Mrs. Simpson (elem), Josephine Skupa (primary), Miss Smith (elementary), Mrs. George Sparling (English), Clora Cox Speer (elementary), Lena Frazelle Speer, Ruby Spears (librarian), Miss Stallcup (elementary), Irene Stewart (colored), R. E. Stokes (principal), Rhea Stone (school board), Merle Stone (all), Miss Stout, Mr. Sweeney (history), Mrs. Sweeney (English), Jim Swink (coach),

J. F. Taylor (superintendent), Betty Mangold Taylor (guidance), Lindell Taylor, Leonard Teaster (all), Mrs. Rebecca Thompson (colored cook), R. M. Tidwell (school board), Joe Tidwell (school board), Mary Lindsey Tidwell (all), Enoch Tolleson, Almyra Johnson Tolleson (art), Paul Townley (custodian), Flossie Townley (cook), Ruby Sudduth Turner (English), Donald Vancil (social science), J. P. Vickrey (all),

Miss Wachter (music), Jeff Wade (school board), Jimmy C. Wahl (math), Miss Wallis (primary), Jim Ward (science), Betty Lindsey Ward (elementary), Fred Warren (coach), Miss Wehling (music), Miss Welch (music), D.L. Whitaker (principal), Mrs. Whitney (fifth), Mr. Curt Wilkerson (music), William Wilkerson (coach), Ruth Wilkerson (primary), Burl Williams (custodian), Mary Putman Williams (cook), Ruby Williams (all), Floyd Wilson (superintendent), Amy Wilson (secretariy), Mrs. Jack Wimp (music), Dorothy Brooks Wood (home economics), Rev. Fred Woods, Mrs. Ruth Woods (English), Bessie Huntley Wright (elementary), Murriel Sellers Wright (all), Mr. Yandell (bus driver), Mrs. J. L. Young.

Deering school was always known as a good learning center. It was a common occurance for incoming students to be put back a grade when they enrolled at Deering. A diploma from Deering school was a coveted possession.

In 1976, the senior class of Delta C-7 chose as their bicentennial project the publication of a little book entitled *History of Delta C-7 School District.* It is 96 pages and lists the faculty, graduates and history of both Deering, Braggadocio and Gobler. It also has several old school pictures in it, along with pictures of the school buildings and residences of the area.

CHAPTER TWENTY FOUR

Deering Post Office

According to the first account we have, the mail was brought to Deering from Pascola by Mr. Miles Miller, who lived in the northeast part of town. The post office was in the general store, as was the custom at that time. Ben Hill served as the rural mail carrier in 1910.

After Mr. Roy Day closed his barber shop in the 1930's and moved to Kennett, the little building was moved to Front Street between the Deering Store and the Deering Office and converted into a post office. Later a modern post office was built, and the abandoned building became a beauty shop. Today, it sits idle where it has been for the past sixty years. Charles E. Ross was the town barber before Mr. Day.

When application was made for a post office, they submitted the name "Deering Sawmill." When the approval came from Washington, D.C., the word "sawmill" was deleted and the name established was "Deering." This was in honor of William Deering, the founder of the town.

The post masters who have served Deering were: John G. Zollman, 3 July 1902; Wilmer W. Proper, September 1902; Peter A. Derks, October 1904; Berl E. Metcalf, February 1905; Adam Lindgren, October 1906; William F. Fleming, December 1907; Sidney H. Stichal/Skichal, May 1909; Andrew V. Christianson, March 1910; William R. Stogsdill, June 1912; Raymond H. Collier, January 1914; John C. Clark, October 1914; Henry E. Braschler, April 1925; Jennie Bensinger, November 1926; Mrs.

This building was a barber shop, a post office, and then a beauty shop. The house in the background is where Johnny Calhoun lives. The Wisconsin Lumber Company business office was between these two, and a portion of the vault is visible as it has not been destroyed.

Frances Ann Brown, November 1940; Ms. Mildred K. Brown, June 1962; and Peggy McDonald, January 1979.

Deering does not have a rural route, but serves the public by post office boxes only. In 1946 it served 200 patrons, but today only 86 families get their mail at the Deering post office.

CHAPTER TWENTY FIVE

Deering Methodist Church

By Thelma (Minner) Martin and Bobby Sue (Bowling) Lawson

The first school building in Deering is now the Deering United Methodist Church. It sat on the west side of what is known as the Neel Road. Before the building was remodeled and converted into a church building in 1909, services were held in homes or in a large room above the Company Store or the schoolhouse which was north of the present church location.

The Methodist Episcopal Church, South was organized in April 1909, by Rev. T. P. Fallin. Other ministers that followed were: S. W. Young, S. A. Bennett, A. Ellis Barrett, J. W. Williams, E. L. Wolverton, J. A. Scamahorn, W. A. Edmundson, Charles T. Young, Everett M. Cook, Harvey E. Stone, O. P. Swope, P. L. Pritchard, Fred Woods, Utley, E. I. Webber, Bill House 1942, C. O. Hall, George S. Sparling, Jr. 1944, J. C. Montgomery, Jr. Henry McDowell, E. M. Coates, J. L. Estep, Andrew Fowler, Jim Wingo, Carl Brandt, Terry Norman, Ron Unser, Jim Powell, Don Enright 1971-78, Charles E. Miller 1978-1980, John R. Ray 1980-83, Virgil Bunch 1984-85, Wesley J. M. Harmon 1985-87, R. L. Hester 1988, Remel G. Grey 1988-95, Ray Hartbarger 1995-97 and Steven L. Turner, the present minister since 1997.

The first records of members in September 28, 1919 by Reverend J. W. Williams was these: Mrs. Sallie Allstum, L. S. Bell,

Mrs. L. S. Bell, H. E. Braschler, O. J. Connor, Myrtle Copple, Lily Copple, Eli Curtis, Mrs. Eli Curtis, Doris Derrick, Guy Fullwood,

Sam Gattis, Mrs. Sam "Mary" Gattis, Lillian Gathis, Mrs. W. L. Grenade, Fred Kinsall, Mrs. W. W. " Mattie" Kinsall, Charles King, Mrs. Charles King, Eva Miller, F. H. Manton, Flora Manton, J. E. Meyers, Mrs. J. E. Meyers, Mrs. Robert "Cora" Ownsby, J. C. Putman, Mrs. J. C. "Vida" Putman,

Frank Shennings, Mrs. Frank "Margaret" Shennings, Eleene Shennings, H. J. Schwartz, Lime S. Sullivan, Mrs. George "Ida" Sands, Herbert Sands, Ruth Tipton, T. E. White, Gladie Manton Wright, and Mary Putman Williams.

In the boom days of the "big lumber mill" Deering was a station, and the preacher served only the Deering congregation. The church died down after the mill left, and then it became a circuit with one preacher serving here and also working with other congregations. Farming became the main occupation in 1932-33 and a minister was again assigned by the Conference to Deering and the church was reorganized by Rev. Fred Woods. There was preaching on the second and fourth Sundays. The church was on the circuit with Bragg City and Braggadocio. The total membership in 1933-35 was 47. Church school enrollment was 118. In January 1935, W. A. Hudson, Superintendent of Deering Schools, was elected Sunday School Superintendent. At this time there were thirty-five young people in The League.

In a Sunday School census, taken in March 1935, it was found that there were 180 white people in Deering. Fifty-five of them attended Sunday School and one hundred twenty-five did not attend any church.

An earlier Methodist minister, Rev. Cook, taught the Mexicans who were brought in to clear the land after the timber had been cut.

After the Negro Population declined, their church building was abandoned and the Deering Lumber Company, under the supervision of E. P. Crow, moved and attached it at the back, to the east side of the Methodist Church and remodeled it into a fellowship hall. It contains classrooms, kitchen and restrooms. Later central heating and cooling were added.

In the spring of 1976, the church interior was redecorated and carpeting was installed in the sanctuary, pastor's study and kindergarten room. A three-foot brass cross was hung upon a beautiful red cotton and rayon dossal curtain at the back of the altar. The Christian flag and the United State Flag sit on each side of the curtain. Floors in the fellowship hall, kitchen, restrooms and hallway were covered with a vinyl tile and a new roof was put on the main building. The outside covering of the entire church was repainted.

The last remodeling to the church took place in 1981. At that time, with $31,000 in donations, new siding, a concrete foundation, stain-glass windows, new carpeting and ceiling fans and fixtures were added.

Due to the decline in membership, the Braggadocio Methodist Church closed its doors in 1970, and five or six members transferred to Deering. The Bragg City United Methodist Church was closed in July 1974, and about fourteen members transferred their membership to the Deering Church. The lights in the Deering sanctuary at the present time were brought from the Bragg City Church.

Total membership in October 1978 was sixty-six. Active membership was about twenty-five. Church school attendance was down. Ten or twelve adults participated in a class taught by Joe Tidwell. Mrs. Betty Calhoun was the Primary teacher and Mrs. Thelma Martin was in charge of the Junior High.

In 1978 the Church School Superintendent was Ben Griffin; the trustees were J. T. Martin, Joe Tidwell and Ray Oldsen. Chairman of the Administrative Board was J. T. Martin, Financial Secretary and Treasurer was Paul Hutchens, Lay Leader was Ray Oldsen and the Lay Leader to annual conference was John Calhoun.

Chairman of Pastor-Parish Relations was Thelma Martin, Enlistment Secretary was Oliveen Crow Colling, Ecumenical Affairs was Grace Thompson, Education was Louise Tidwell, Evangelism was Tommie Tidwell, Missions was Mildred Brown, Social Concerns was Tennie Johnson, Stewardship was Mrs. W. M. Greene, Adult Ministries was Leila Oldsen, Children's Ministries was Thelma Martin and Family Ministries was Mrs. L. E. Bingenheimer.

Chairman of Youth Ministries was Raymond Oldsen, District Mission and Church Extension Representative was Don Tidwell, Honorary Board Member was Mrs. John Wallace, Committee on Nominations was Betty Calhoun and J. T. Martin, Records and History were Ruby Spears and Mrs. W. M. "Roberta" Greene, Communion Steward was Ruby Spear and Church Pianists were Cathy Oldsen and John Calhoun.

Members at Large were Mrs. John Young, Mrs. Carl Pulley, Mrs. Bessie Wright, Chester Jones, Mr. and Mrs. M. M. Anderson and L. E. Bingenheimer.

Over the years several beautiful memorials have been given to the church. The brass cross is in memory of Mrs. Ann Brown, mother of Mildred and T. A. Brown. The Dossal curtains are in memory of Mr. E. P. Crow, husband of Oliveen Crow Colling, father of Brenda Crow Isaacs and grandfather of Tammy Crow. The pulpit is in memory of Elbert C. Minner, father of Thelma Martin. The Hall light fixture is in memory of Phillip Rice, brother of Leila Oldsen.

One chair on the altar is in memory of Mrs. Almena P. Rice, mother of Leila Oldsen and the other chair on the altar is in memory of R. M. Tidwell, father of Joe Tidwell. The carpeting is in memory of W. M. Greene, husband of Mrs. W. M. "Roberta" Greene, father of Betty Calhoun and grandfather of John Calhoun.

Mr. W. M. "Mack" Greene bought new pews for the church around 1970 before carpeting was put on the floors. He gave the congregation the option to pay for one pew or more pews if they so chose. Virginia Bowling Watson chose the second pew on the right side as her mother, Bessie Bowling, always sat there. She put it in memory of Johnny J. Watson, her late husband and father of Bowling Keith Watson. The Otto Bond family also chose to pay for one of the pews. It is not known whether others paid for more pews or not.

The Christian Flag and U. S. Flag and pew Bibles are in memory of Orville Bowling and Virginia Bowling Watson, given by Mrs. Orville "Bess" Bowling, Billy Lawson, Bobby Sue Bowling Lawson, and Bowling Keith Watson.

The communion table is in memory of F. W. Johnson, husband of Tennie Johnson. The altar cross, altar vases, baptismal dish (font), collection plates and candlesticks are in memory of Bill Richardson. They were given by Mrs. Bill "Bertha" Richardson and her son Pat Richardson, his wife Dot, and their two oldest children, Patti and Ricki, grandchildren of Mr. and Mrs. Bill Richardson.

The piano light, was given in memory of Mr. R. M. Tidwell, by the Tidwell family. The Bible bookmark, the pulpit scarf, and communion table runner were bought with memorials given to the church in memory of Mrs. C. A. "Edna" Joliff at the request of her daughter, Scottie Joliff Earls.

In 1941, the Orville and Bessie Bowling family lived on the south end of the Rice Road near their next neighbors to the north, Bill, Bertha and their son, Pat Richardson. That Mr. Orville and Mr. Bill were farmers, they took many sightseeing rides over roads and turn roads to evaluate their crops just as farmers still do today. It was during these field rides that Mr. Bill repeatedly invited Mr. Orville to take his family, Mrs. Bessie and daughters, Bobby Sue and Virginia Ann to church at Deering. After numerous invitations, Mr. Orville took his family to the Deering Church where it still stands today. From his first session with the men's class, which was conducted in the Deering Office at that time under the teachings of Mr. W. A. Hudson, Mr. Orville enjoyed what Mr. Hudson had to say so much, he didn't want to miss a one of his classes.

Now, fifty-eight years later the only survivor of the four that Mr. Bill Richardson encouraged to go to the little white church in Deering is the older daughter, Bobby Sue Bowling Lawson, who still attends that same church. In the remaining portion of this story, Bobby Sue is sharing some of her church memories. She remembers the church sanctuary being a full house in the 40's and early 50's. Most of the attenders were school people. Mrs. Clanton had many single teacher occupants in the teacherage. My, how they loved her good home-cooked meals! There were many husband and wife school people. In the early years teachers in the Deering School System were encouraged to attend church here.

A very vivid memory is hearing Mr. R. M. Tidwell's enthusiastic singing anytime "Love Lifted Me' was selected for a church service. That was his song on which to really turn up his volume to its loudest. His rendition revived the whole congregation. Whatever his reasons for singing then, he'd have more reasons for singing today if he could know his granddaughter, Cathy Jo, and her husband, Randy Bradford, were married in the Deering Methodist Church, May 24, 1974. A Memorial Service was had in this church in honor of his son Lennie L. "Buddy" Tidwell, May 18, 1994. His youngest son, Joe, is a Sunday School teacher in the church where he once sang so vibrantly, so melodiously. He'd also be glad to know his daughter-in-law, Tommie, keeps the congregation and other community folks supplied with her delicious home baked bread. Joe and Tommie not only give of their time, talents and service to the church—but to the community and surrounding area as well.

When Mr. and Mrs. W. M. "Mack" and Roberta Greene moved to Deering in 1956 where Mr. Greene worked in the A. T. Earls' Business Office, right away Mrs. Greene filled her place on the pianist's bench at the Deering Methodist Church. She was a picture of beauty for the congregation to behold as she sat at the piano with her soft white hair so perfectly done. Her manner was that of a genuine lady. She was a staunch believer in everybody going to church. Mr. Green taught the adult Sunday School Class. He moved with such calmness and assurance, yet, his special stories and sense of humor kept his class listening. Mr. "Mack" and Mrs. Roberta Greene earned praises to be sung to them for their dedicated participation and support through their years in the

Deering Church. They would be very proud to know their daughter, Betty Calhoun, and her son, John Calhoun, have followed in their footsteps with their continued service and support in the D. U. M. C. Both Betty and John have filled any and all positions in the church that need leadership. They have kept the church alive and going.

Besides John's cleaning the church, mowing the church yard, turning on heat and air to everyone's comfort and filling his Grandmother Greene's seat as church pianist, when flowers are in bloom, he keeps a beautiful fresh bouquet on the piano for all to enjoy. Along with his full-time teaching job with Special Education students in the Deering School System, John tries to go to every visitation and/or funeral service possible in the community. He is always so good to care for the elderly. John certainly deserves a "Good Citizenship Award" many times over.

J. F. "Bud" and Betty Calhoun, daughter of Mr. and Mrs. W. M. Greene, moved to Deering in 1956 where Betty helped her father in the A. T. Earls' Business Office. Bud and Betty have two sons, Fred and John. Fred and his wife, Paula, live in Kennett where Fred works for Kennett National Bank. Fred and Paula have two daughters, Alesia and Melissa. This family honored their parents and grandparents, Bud and Betty Calhoun, with a 50th Anniversary Celebration in the church fellowship hall October 27, 1991. Later granddaughter, Alesia, and Keith Gammill were married in the church June 4, 1994. Alesia and Keith now have a little son, Tyler, who takes everybody's eye when he comes to church with Grandmother Betty and Uncle John. The other granddaughter, Melissa, and Jeffery Deniston were wed in the church July 25, 1998. Both daughters of Fred and Paula Calhoun, granddaughters of J. F. "Bud" and Betty Calhoun, great granddaughters of W. M. and Roberta Greene, nieces of John Calhoun, were beautiful brides in their lovely weddings in the Deering United Methodist Church, the church of their family's dedicated support and labors since their Grandfather and Grandmother Greene's coming to Deering forty-four years ago. The Calhoun family bought the town of Deering from the A. T. Earls' heirs in 1984.

Of course, there are children of the church who remain in memories. In the late 50's and early 60's there were two little "Buster Brown" boys who walked the aisles of the church for candle lighting. Keith Watson, son of Virginia Bowling Watson, and Michael Tidwell, son of Joe and Tommie Tidwell were so cute dressed in their Buster Brown brand clothes for little boys of that age. They looked like they had been hand picked for Buster Brown's advertisements of kids' clothes of that age and time.

In July of 1957 when J. E. Wingo was pasturing the Deering Church, there was a big tent revival on the block behind Main Street. The tent was packed. The church would not have been big enough for the crowd.

In May 1973, during Don Enright's years as pastor of the Methodist Church in Deering, he rendered a service that no previous pastors had ever done in the history of the church. Virginia Bowling Watson, younger daughter of Orville and Bessie Bowling was diagnosed with terminal cancer in the Armed Service Hospital in Belleville, Illinois. Doctors there decided to send her to a service hospital in Texas for chemo treatments. Virginia and her mother were specially flown—just the two of them, on a big, big six-engine jet to Willford Hall Medical Center in San Antonio, Texas. As they were flying, they discussed and shared the beauty of the day that surrounded them. The fourth day after Virginia's admittance to Willford Hall, she had her first and only chemo treatment. Her mother was alone with her daughter many, many miles from home to be returned somehow along with her deceased daughter's body.

Right away Kenneth McDonald, son of J. B. and Louise McDonald from Deering appeared from somewhere out of the blue for Mrs. Bowling and Virginia. He remained with Mrs. Bowling until she and her deceased daughter was picked up for their return home. Kenneth's presence was greatly appreciated.

It had not been previously known by the Bowling family that their pastor, Don Enright, was a licensed pilot. He, himself,

Deering Methodist Church erected in 1906. To the right is the little house where the gate lived. Note the portion of fence connecting to the house. This fence was all around the town of Deering.

volunteered to fly out and bring Mrs. Bowling and Virginia's body back to the Kennett Municipal Airport where McDaniel's Funeral Service would take the body from there. Don knew where to lease a plane in Memphis, Tennessee for the trip. What a volunteered service to humankind!

Another unusual, unexpected, unfortunate happening during Don Enright's tenure at Deering was the death in 1974 of the Summer Youth Director, Jim Wisner. Jim's work for his assignment had come to a close and he was returning to his home in Mississippi when his car was hit by a train as he was crossing the railroad track in Holland, Missouri. All who knew Jim were greatly saddened by the tragic accident. It has been learned that Don flew Jim's body home, also.

Around 1957, Ray and Leila Oldsen transferred their membership from First Methodist in Kennett to Deering United Methodist. Their children, Cheri, Raymond, Kathryn and Phillip, grew up in the Deering Church. During their days of growing up in the late 60's there was a very active M.Y.F. group for young people. A few to be remembered in that group and time were Raymond Oldsen, Kathryn Oldsen, Larry Patterson, Donald Danley, Doyle Privett and Connie Riggs. M. Y. F. groups and Women's Missionary Society groups have been known to be very active in the Deering Church since early 40's.

Ray and Leila Oldsen's children honored them with a reception for their Fiftieth Wedding Anniversary in the fellowship hall at Deering U.M.C., March 16, 1994. It was a beautiful affair. The response from this area and surrounding areas was tremendous. The Oldsen Family has been an outstanding family not only in the Methodist Church, but to the town of Deering and its surrounding communities.

Ray and Leila's daughter, Kathryn, and her late husband, Steven Wright, from Cape Girardeau had their wedding in the Deering Church, Jan. 5, 1974. Unfortunately, Steven's life recently ended at the young age of 48 in a tragic accident caused so unnecessarily by an eighteen wheeler as he, his wife Kathryn and son, Scott, were on their way to spend Easter with their son, Cory, who was stationed in South Carolina. The accident occurred April 1, 1999. This is not only a tremendous loss to the Oldsen and Wright families, but to the many, many people who knew and loved Steven Wright.

When Ben Griffin was Sunday School Superintendent in the 70's, he believed in activities. There were lots of Halloween and Christmas parties in his period of being S.S. Superintendent. Baskets and toys were distributed at Christmas. Ben was Superintendent of the Deering School System during his attendance period in the Methodist Church while there.

When the Bragg City Methodist Church closed in 1974, about fourteen of its members chose to transfer their membership to Deering United Methodist Church. J. T. and Thelma Martin was some of the transferred ones. What assets they have been to the Deering Church! J. T. has served as Lay Leader and Liturgist. Thelma served on the Pastor Parish Relations Committee and both have served in other positions when needed. J. T.'s knowledge of the workings of the Methodist Church work from top level to bottom level, which he has gained through his many years of Methodism, is unbelievable. He and Thelma were honored by their immediate family and church family with cake, punch, coffee and colas in the church fellowship hall on Sunday, September 27, 1998 in recognition of their Sixtieth Wedding Anniversary.

Others who transferred from Bragg City Church's closure in 1974 were Tennie Johnson, Nettie Crum, Chester Jones, Roberta Jones, Rodney Jones, Janett Jones, Evalene Young, Sam Reed, Vonita Reed, Harry Reed, Polly Reed Newsom, and Mavis Williams. No doubt there were others who are not thought of at this time. Polly Newsom and her daughter, Juliannis are still active members of the Deering Church today. Juliannis is one of the church's prized young people. She has a beautiful voice for singing. She loves to go to summer church camps. Polly's twin sister, Penny, lives in Nashville. She comes to church with Polly and Juliannis when she returns home for visits.

After Braggadocio's Church closure in 1970, some of those who transferred to Deering were Levi and Mable Bingenheimer, Myrtle Pulley, Grace Thompson, Mrs. John "Bertie Bell" Wallace and Learline Smith. Myrtle Pulley's sister, Dorothy Bennett, from Hayti, heard her sister, Myrtle, talk about the comfort and congeniality of the Deering church; so she decided to come and seek the church as her sister, Myrtle, had so often described to her. She, too, found her place of comfort and satisfaction just as her sister had. "Miss Dorothy" makes her drive from Hayti to worship in Deering every Sunday morning that health and weather conditions permit. She has generously shared her crochet skills with the congregation by making each family an afghan and a pillow. So as not to leave the fellows wanting, she has supplied them with ties.

Mr. Edward "Ed" and Elvie Lynn transferred their church membership to the Deering Church from Union Chapel, Alabama in the 70's after they transplanted their family to this area many years earlier. Their youngest daughter, Vickie, and her husband, Tom Lebo was married in the church Dec. 12, 1970. Mr. and Mrs. Lynn's great grandson, Drew Watkins, son of Jeff and Regina Watkins was christened in the church in 1988.

Tom and Vickie Lebo have remained active in their church and community. Vickie operates her own home-based beauty shop just south of the "crossroads" and Tom works for Green Oil Company. They are neighbors to Paul and Pansy Hutchens who have been longtime members of the Deering Church where Paul served as treasurer from 1955-1993 (38) years. Tom, Vickie and their son, Bob, are very helpful to Mr. Paul and Mrs. Pansy, as Pansy's health has become very disabled to the two of them in past years. Mr. Paul, Mrs. Pansy, and their daughter, Paula, are greatly missed in the Deering Methodist Church after their many years of faithful attendance and dedicated service rendered there. Mr. Paul died suddenly at his home near Deering, April 30, 1999.

Mr. and Mrs. Edward Lynn were honored on their 50th Wedding Anniversary, May 22, 1977 with a reception in the fellowship hall of the Deering United Methodist Church. Hosting the party were their daughters, Mrs. Earl (Nettie Lou) Jarrett of Blytheville, Mrs. Buck (Sue Nell) Bonds of West Memphis, Mrs. Jimmy (Wynema) George of Steele, Mrs. Shearl (Betty) Faulkner of St. Charles, Mo., Mrs. Bobby (Jane) Bailey of Deering and Mrs. Tom (Vickie) Lebo of Bragg City and their son, Charles Lynn, of Humboldt, Tennessee. The Rev. Don Enright, pastor, officiated as the couple again pledged the marriage vows.

Attending was sixteen of the couple's eighteen grandchildren, including Mrs. Clay (Brenda) Pritchett and Mrs. Richard (Sandra) Lowery of Blytheville, and Bobby Lynn Bailey of Deering who served, and Mrs. Dennis (Regina) Gray and Yvette Bailey of Deering who assisted with gifts. Also, present were two of the couple's three great grandchildren.

"Ed" Lynn is remembered as one of E.P. Crow's carpenters from his Deering Lumber Company. In later years, Ed and H. C.

"Cleasy" Mays formed a painting team of their own. Mrs. Bessie Bowling, for one, thought they were "the best" painters around.

In June 1993, carpeting was replaced in the sanctuary. Presently the carpeting is red with red pew and altar cushions. At this time of carpet replacement, Bud, Betty and John Calhoun paid for commercial carpeting to be put in the fellowship hall of the church.

A memorable event of honor took place in the Deering U.M.C. March 5, 1995. Mrs. Bessie Bowling, the oldest and longest attending of the congregation at the time with her 85 years of age and 54-year attendance record was diagnosed with terminal colon cancer in September 1994. As her birthday, March 6, was nearing, John Calhoun asked her daughter, Bobby Sue, if she would be able for a birthday honor at the church. After careful thought and consideration of Mrs. Bowling's health condition, it was decided and hoped she would be able for such honor at the church. Plans for a reception began to progress for the Sunday afternoon of March 5, 1995. It was a beautiful time of love, friendship and fellowship shared by family and friends from neighboring churches and community. The crowd was a good mixture of people from the Bakerville Church of Christ, Oak Grove Baptist Church, Vicksburg Church of God, Braggadocio Baptist Church, Gobler Baptist Church, Hayti Methodist Church, Sumach Methodist Church, Emerson Street Church of God and from Kennett, Sikeston and Blytheville areas. Fortunately, Mrs. Bowling was able to enjoy her honor to the fullest. Later that evening after she and her daughter had returned home, these were her words so sweetly, so humbly, so appreciatively spoken, "This is the best birthday I ever had!" Soon afterward, Mrs. Bowling was called to her place of eternal rest, May 29, 1995.

The response to this memorable occasion not only spoke for Mrs. Bowling and her family's years in the Deering area since January 1931, but it showed that the Deering United Methodist Church has been a participating church of the community and surrounding area through all of its years. Thanks to the many dedicated, faithful, steadfast people who have helped it survive the toils and tolls of time.

Nedra Irvin has served as secretary for both the Hayti and Deering churches for eleven years. She has done an outstanding service with her abilities. The two churches have been so fortunate to have had her help through these years. She, her husband, Doug, and son Trey, are active participants in both churches' services and activities. They are a bonded threesome who adds joy and gladness to any and all church affiliated occasions or events. Trey is a volunteered greeter to every Sunday morning worship service as he so freely gives a big smile, hug, and handshake to each and everyone present. Much to everyone's regret, Nedra will be resigning as church secretary from both churches May 31, 1999. How her "good works" will be missed!

Steven Turner, the present pastor of the Deering and Hayti churches, along with his wife, Gwen, and young sons, Christopher 8 and Matthew 6, came to this area from Wayland, Missouri where he previously pastored three churches. Wayland is in the northeastern part of Missouri. The Deering Church has been so fortunate to have had so many good, qualified, educated pastors through the years. Some of them and/or their wives have worked in the Deering School System.

Misfortune has befallen Steven, Gwen and their families since they've been serving the Hayti and Deering Churches. Gwen's parents, Dennis and Mary Madill, who lived in Dryden, Michigan was involved in an automobile accident which took both of their lives. It was a broadside collision at an intersection. Gwen's father was the pastor of the Dryden and Attica Methodist Churches in Michigan. This family has experienced painful trauma and great, great loss as they've tried to serve their people in the two churches this past year. Both of Steve's parents are ministers as well.

Steve has said the most impressive event he has experienced since his tenure in Deering has been the christening of the Ramsey twins, Sterling and Christian, sons of James and April Ramsey, grandsons of Chris and Cheri Oldsen Ramsey, great grandsons of

Ray and Leila Oldsen. The christening ceremony was performed with only family members present. Steve says the christening of twins doesn't happen very often.

Deering United Methodist Church Members in 1999 are: Jane Bailey, Melissa Dawn Bailey, Kris Bailey, Charles Barnett, Phyllis Barnett, Angie Gray Bowen, Cecil Boyd, Loretta Lebo Boyd, Denise Yvette Bailey Berry, Dorothy Bennett, Kathy Bush Clark, John Calhoun, Betty Calhoun, Freddie J. Calhoun, Jonell Spears Crawford, Lenard Elder, Merry Jim Elder, Wynema George, Connie Riggs Holt, Paul Hutchens (deceased 30 April 1999), Pansy Hutchens, John D. "Trey" Irvin, Roberta Jones, Bobby Sue Lawson, Vickie Lebo, J. T. Martin, Thelma Martin, Polly Reed Newsom, Juliannis Newson, Shirley Ann Naile McManigal, Ray Oldsen, Leila Oldsen, Larry Patterson, Harry Reed, Ashley H. Spears, Phillip R. Spears, Billy Q. Spears, Joe Tidwell, Tommie Tidwell, Mavis Williams, David Wright, Jeff Watkins, and Regina Watkins. Out of this list of forty-three recorded members, only fifteen are presently active members.

Though Don and Louise Tidwell are not recorded as members of the Deering Church, Don is an attender and supporter of the church when his health permits. In earlier years, Louise served the church well with her being responsible for ordering the church's literature. The church appreciates Don and Louise Tidwell.

As of April 14, 1999, the pastor is Steven Turner; secretary, Nedra Irvin; Administrative Board of Trustees, Betty Calhoun, Joe Tidwell, J. T. Martin, Bobby Sue Lawson, John Calhoun, Ray Oldsen; Recording Secretary, Leila Oldsen; Pastor Parish Relations Committee, Joe Tidwell, John Calhoun, Bobby Sue Lawson; Treasurer, Betty Calhoun; Liturgist, J. T. Martin and Pianist, John Calhoun.

Church Activities are Weekly Worship Service, Weekly Sunday School, Monthly Communion Service, Bible Study, Monthly Fellowship Eat-Out, Yearly Neighborhood Revival, Easter Sunrise Services and Clean Sing.

Betty Calhoun is Communion Steward and the altar is always open to anyone who desires to partake of holy communion. The

Braggadocio Baptist Church hosts the yearly revival with neighbor-pastors helping to conduct the nightly services for the week. Easter sunrise services are rotated with the Vicksburg Church of God and the Oak Grove Baptist Church. Each pastor of the three participating churches takes turns each year conducting the services. The Clean Sing is a fifth Sunday community singing using as much local talent as possible.

Since the Deering Church is on the same charge as the Hayti Church, one pastor serves both churches. Deering has Worship Service each Sunday morning at 9:30 with Sunday School afterward so the pastor can return to Hayti for an 11:00 Worship Service. The church parsonage is in Hayti.

On October 13, 1998, Deering United Methodist Church was incorporated by Rebecca McDowell Cook, Secretary of State of the State of Missouri. Joe Tidwell, J. T. Martin and Ray Oldsen served and signed as incorporators. The first officers of the corporation were Joe Tidwell, Chairman of Administrative Counsel; Leila Oldsen, Recording secretary; and Betty Calhoun, Treasurer. For the records, the church in Deering is now Deering United Methodist Church, Incorporated.

CHAPTER TWENTY SIX

Eating Establishments in Deering

Hotel Deering was located east of the big grocery store and merchandise building. A dining room in the hotel was located on the ground floor. The hotel was heated in the wintertime with a big coal stove downstairs in the big lobby. Upstairs there was a big veranda that ran the entire width of the hotel. Customers included school teachers, boarders who were working at the lumber mill and/or the railroad and away from their families, men from the main office in Chicago, and other dignitaries. Lela Gibbs worked several years in this establishment as the main cook and waitress.

Ed and Mollie Williams kept about thirty lodgers at their establishment around 1910. In 1920, John and Daisy Blue ran a boarding house. There were probably others, and it can be assumed that meals were served at these places.

Early accounts of a restaurant in Deering refer to Mrs. Book, who had a little eating place in an abandoned railroad car. Her husband, Charlie Book, had a blacksmith shop. She had at least four children which were named Eugene, Aubrey, Lorene and Wanda. The family moved back to Chicago in July 1942.

After the high school began operation in the 1920's, more teachers were needed, so a large two-story house, a block off Main Street, became a place where they could board. Delicious meals were served to them at this establishment. Mrs. Mullins was the cook at one time. When Mrs. Clanton was the cook and manager, she would let each teacher name a selection of food they would like prepared each week. Dorothy Brooks boarded there until she married Nathan Wood, and since she was the high school home economics teacher, she made out the menus for them.

Around 1938, a school lunchroom was built on the campus and began operation, but it was for school children only. In the beginning it operated from November through May, as it was too hot to cook in the summertime, and also they had no way of keeping the food refrigerated. After they acquired an electric stove and refrigeration, it became a nine-month lunch room for school children and teachers only. The price of the meal was nominal, it was nutritious food, and several children were allowed to do small jobs in exchange for their lunch. In the winter, a glass of warm chocolate milk was provided with each meal. Several of the students still preferred to carry their peanut butter sandwich to school each day. Mrs. Nancy Huie was the manager until she moved to Gideon, then Mrs. Mary Williams became manager for many years. Grade school art and health classes were taught in this building by Inez Bentley and Almira Tolleson.

From the very beginning, a person could purchase a bologna sandwich from Horace Renfold, the butcher, in the big grocery store. When Haskell Fairless was the butcher, a lunch counter with stools was added, but not nearly enough for the noonday group of school students. Sometimes pickle loaf, liver cheese or spiced ham was available. This, with a drink and a candy bar, was a noon day lunch for twenty-five cents.

Later a little cafe was attached on the northwest corner of the two-story grocery store. They served a limited short order menu. Someone gave it the nickname of "The Green Fly." Eva Green operated it until about 1960 when she became ill. Ethel Lee Green ran it a year or so until it burned when the store building was destroyed by fire on Friday, April 27, 1962. Mr. Hubert French owned the grocery store. His wife, Cora Etta, with Ethel Lee Green and Albert Miller, the store's butcher, managed to save the firm's records and money from the cash registers. The store building was 50-by-120 feet and was built in 1910 by the Wisconsin Lumber

Company, of native timber, cut in the area and hauled to Deering where it was planed.

From fifty to seventy school children that did not want to eat in the school lunch room, would frequent this cafe each day at noon break. Hamburgers were always the main food item. The students could also purchase school supplies of all kinds in the cafe. It opened early in the morning, and served a delicious breakfast. Two steady customers were Johnny and Steve Atwill. Howard Spears, who worked at the lumber shed across the street, had a cup of coffee there every day, as did several other men.

The new grocery store building was built back in the same location, with Loy and Rosa Cox as the first owners then Lenard and Merry Jim Elder owned it. Again a restaurant was built at the northwest corner. They named it the Deering Cafe. Clyde Fortner opened this eating place in June 1962 with Marie Riggs as manager. Bud Calhoun frequently opened the cafe and made coffee for the early morning crowd. In December 1975, Marie Riggs purchased the Deering Cafe from Mr. Fortner. She ran it until March 1998 when she sold it to her daughter, Connie Riggs Holt. It is still noted for its big, juicy hamburgers.

CHAPTER TWENTY SEVEN

Delta Ruritan Club

By Joe W. Tidwell

Ruritan is a civic organization whose objective is to bring a closer social union between the farmers and the business and professional men in a community in order to make it a better place in which to live. It is patterned after the service organizations of the cities, but changed to meet the needs of rural people and rural communities.

Founded in 1928 in Holland, Virginia, Ruritan has grown from the Tidewater Area of Virginia to the Midwest; from the Great Lakes to the Gulf of Mexico and, in doing so, has become the largest rural civic organization in America.

Meetings of the club are held once a month for a hour and a half in the evening. Delta Ruritan meets the first Thursday evening of each month in the Deering school cafeteria. Attendance at a Ruritan meeting is not compulsory, yet any member who misses four consecutive meetings without an adequate excuse is considered no longer interested in the organization and is dropped from the rolls.

In general, the chief aim of Ruritan is to create better understanding between people, communities and business; to aid in charitable work; to promote industrial and agricultural growth and to encourage the right type of education. It is the Ruritan idea to cooperate harmoniously with those organizations and institutions which help to improve the social and economic conditions in all walks of life and in all sections of the nation in which it is organized.

The object of Ruritan is to make the rural community a better place in which to live. In order to carry out this objective, it endeavors to bring together farmers, business and professional men into one body for the purpose of organizing public spirited and progressive leadership from the various occupations represented in the community and town, that their combined influence may be systematized and utilized for the welfare and up building of the community.

The Walcott, Arkansas Ruritan Club sponsored the Delta Ruritan Club during its organization and were present at the October meeting to get it started. At this time Glen Layer was elected temporary president; Ray Oldsen, temporary vice-president; Joe Tidwell, temporary secretary; and Howard Noble, temporary treasurer.

The first official meeting of the club was November 7, 1967 with twenty men present. The name accepted for our club was Delta Ruritan Club. All the temporary officers were elected to their offices for the 1968 year. Other officers and offices for 1968 were three year director, Ben Griffin; Two year director, Vic Downing; One year director, L. E. Kindred; Chaplain, Alvin Reeves; Song Leader, W. B. Richardson; Reporter, George Byers and Sgt.-At-Arms, Don Tidwell.

Charter members were George Byers, Jackson Conley, Loy Cox, Joe Crain, E. P. Crow, Vic Downing, Lenard Elder, Mitchell Fisher, W. L. Green, Ben Griffin, G. C. Grimes, W. O. Harper, Pat Harris, Harold Jackson, James Jones, Mervill Jones, Leonard Kindred, Glen Layer, R. L. Ledbetter, Jadie Naile, Howard Noble, Ray Oldsen, Woodrow Parish, Alvin Reeves, W. B. Richardson, Gene Samford, Don Tidwell, Joe Tidwell, Jim Ward, Dave Wilkerson, Chester Williams and Jerry Wright

Our club has had many special projects. Each Christmas season, the club gives Christmas baskets to approximately thirty-five families in the area. Last year we sponsored a Christmas party in the school cafeteria for children in the district. All the guests, preschool through fifth grade, were presented with a gift. Refreshments were served and games played.

We cleaned up a community park called the Oakville Park. Picnic tables and trash barrels were donated by our club and we wired the park with electric lights.

In cooperation with the State Highway Department, we were instrumental in getting them to paint the white lines along our paved roads in the area.

We called a special meeting of the people in the area, so they could present to the telephone company a possible arrangement for better telephone service. This simply was to try to connect Deering exchange with Caruthersville, Hayti and Kennett. The telephone company took the suggestion under advisement, and this project is now complete.

One of the high school boys is able to go to Boys State Convention each summer under our sponsorship.

In conjunction with the Lions Club in Caruthersville, we helped some young people obtain eyeglasses.

Our club presents an academic award to the outstanding senior of each years graduating class.

The Little League basketball games each spring are sponsored by us, and we operate the concession stands at these games.

A welfare fund has been set up by us, thereby affording quick help to people in the community who suffer from unforeseen disasters.

We have a fund-raising basketball game each year. The Ruritan men play the Faculty men for the most points to the bitter end. The wives act as cheerleaders for this event.

About three miles from Deering, alongside the four paved roads leading to Deering, we have erected metal signs advertising our Delta Ruritan Club.

In the mid 1980's the Ruritan Club started with the Delta Fair at Kennett with a concession stand. Not only has it been a good money maker but it has been a good public relations program.

Ruritan has a turkey shoot each year on the Saturday following Thanksgiving Day. This was started in the mid 80's also. It has been really successful with over thirty shoot-offs the last two years.

We now have a scholarship fund for all graduates who has a parent in Ruritan. We also give a scholarship to a graduating senior at the Pemiscot County Vocational School.

Each year, one meeting is designated as Ladies Night. All the wives are invited, and this is the meeting when we have almost perfect attendance. We have had box suppers, catfish suppers, and Bar-B-Q suppers, and we have gone to the dinner theater in Memphis, Tenn.

We also have a family meeting each year. One year it was a Labor Day celebration with games and concessions, charging a small token for the youngsters. There was also an Air Show put on that day by Dick Rice. One year we had a potluck barbeque supper with around one hundred in attendance. All the men faculty teachers and their families were our special guests that night.

Some member or members of the club always attend the Area Convention. This is when the local awards are given, and proudly justified, our club always receives its share. Joe Tidwell, of this club, has served as Area Zone Governor. We have also had representatives to the National Convention, usually with the wives also attending.

When the idea of this centennial celebration was presented to us, we jumped at the chance to sponsor it. We had been looking for a project, and the entire club felt this would be a most worthy event. The historical sign became our first priority, and as soon as we came to a decision on the size, color, and wording, progress was just a matter of time. Everything seemed to click into place, and all members were eager to make suggestions and do the work. We have enjoyed working with the International Harvester Collectors Club in this project.

Our officers for the year of 1999 are: president, Mark Ward;

vice president, David Wilkerson; secretary, Joe A. Crain; treasurer, Joe Bryant.

Delta Ruritan members are Jacob Adair, Charles Barnett, Dwight Blankenship, Mike Blankenship, Randy Bradford, Barry Braswell, Joe Bryant, Mark Bryant, Jackie Callis, Larry Chastain, Earl Crain, Joe Crain, Henry Fields, Larry Gatewood, Kenny Grisham, Dennis Hayes,

Doug James, Robert Lewis, Brad Luce, Mark Luna, Noble Nelson, Ray Oldsen, Raymond Oldsen, Coy Owens, Bub Patterson, Gary Riddick, Roger Sawyer, David Smith, Tom Taylor, Don Tidwell, Joe Tidwell, Mike Tidwell, John Tilmon, Mike Tomlinson, Jimmy Turpin, Max Wallace, Jr. Keith Ward, Mark Ward, David Wilkerson, Jerry Young and Ron Young.

No one can deny that we have not been active. The list of our accomplishments justly point to this. Our activities clearly show that we are living up to our aim and our objective. Our farmers, our business and professional men, our youth, and our school has all benefitted because Delta Ruritan Club was organized. We are looking forward to still more work that will make our community a still better place in which to live.

CHAPTER TWENTY EIGHT

My, How Deering Has Changed!

Folks of Deering seldom bother glancing one way or the other when they saunter across their main street. Traffic just isn't that heavy. The town attracts trade from ten miles around, and the establishments draw a good agricultural business.

Deering is located in the south central section of the "heel of the boot" as this chunk of land jutting into Arkansas is called. Several Missourians refer to the boot heel as "swamp east Missouri." That is what it was before 1899 when Wisconsin Lumber Company came in and cut and milled the lumber. The workers stood in boats and cut the trees level with the water, leaving stumpies approximately six feet tall. Throughout the region as late as 1900, muscular cypress, oak and gun trees wrestled each other for a place in the sun. Their limbs intertwined so tightly that they shrouded the region in perpetual gloom.

One hundred years brings many changes to any town, church, family, or school and Deering has been no exception. It was created because it had something to offer. This was the abundance of oak, ash, elm, hickory, cottonwood, cypress, gum, hackberry and maple trees in the swamp lands. These trees disappeared the first thirty years of Deering's existence.

The cottonwood trees that emit cotton fuzz that blew all over the town and shaded the yards and streets of Deering have been supplemented with ornamental trees. The tall, wide boardwalks have been replaced by concrete sidewalks. The plantation system has been discarded and today there is individual ownership, both in residences and businesses.

William McKinley "Mac" Greene, 1894-1974, manager and later trustee manager of Deering for Earls Enterprises, with his wife of over fifty years, Roberta (Lane) Greene, 1892-1980. They moved from Lilbourn, Missouri to Deering in 1955.

On April 22, 1974, the senior class of Delta C-7 took a census of the ones living in Deering and Pondertown. They did this primarily for their book *History of Delta C-7 School*. These are the households they made note of:

Bobby Bailey, Willie Baxter, Arthur Berry, Harold Blocker, J. O. Bond, Inez Bowling, Mildred and Ann Brown, J. F. Calhoun, S. G. Cleveland, Marvin Collier, Luella Cook, Loy Cox, Dale Crockett, E. P. Crow, Lenard Elder, Edward Finney, Leila Gibbs, Talmadge Graham, Garvis Green, W. M. Green, Ben Griffin, G. D. Grimes,

Alene Hensley, Cramer Jackson, Edward Lynn, Clint Masterson, Alton McDonald, Ron Murphy, J. W. Parker, Bub Patterson, John Patterson, Mattie Patterson, Malcolm Privett, Opal Pulliam, Charlie Putman, Dan Reed, James Riddick, D. H.

Riddick, Marie Riggs, Fred Self, Alvin Skinner, Howard Spears, Henry L. Sudduth, L. L. Tidwell, Margaret Via, Bill Walker and William Walker.

Deering establishments and the owner/operator in 1974 was a gas station, Alvin Skinner; a grocery store, Lenard & Merry Jim Elder; a cafe, Marie Riggs; a chemical plant, Jerry Wright; a public school, Ben T. Griffin, Superintendent; a Methodist Church, Don Enright, minister; a United States Post Office, Mildred Brown, postmaster; a business office, W. M. Green, manager; a Standard gasoline dealership, Dennis and Garvis Green; and a beauty shop, Shirley Bush Skinner.

Twenty-five years later, the fourth grade Delta C-7 Elementary class, taught by April McNew, has made a new inventory of the town of Deering. They found a total count of 122 persons, broken down in the following age categories: 50 and up, 24 males and 23 females; 21 to 49, 12 males and 16 females; 5 to 20, 19 males and 19 females; less than 5 years of age, 2 males, and 3 females.

' The heads of the households in 1999 and number of people living in the household are: Bob Bailey 3, Delphia Barnett 3, Yvette Berry 3, Bob Bush 3, John (Bud) Calhoun Sr. 2, John Calhoun Jr. l, Billy Carlton 4, Mary Ann Carlton 3, Otha Cates 2, Dean Cole 3, Misty Cooksey 3, Russell Cooksey 3, Dale Crockett 1,

Lenard Elder 3, David Ellis 3, Jerry Eveland 4, Henry Fields 5, Matt Fowler 3, Talmadge A. Graham 2, Betty Hale 4, Steve Hogan 3, T. J. Hogan 2, T. L. Hogan 2, Connie Holt 3, Doug James 2, Tom Kean 2, Janice Keys 2,

Darrell Malone 3, Harold McDaniel 3, Alton McDonald 2, Sheila McDonald 2, Marcus McNew 3, Lee Meeks 4, Ruby Miller 3, John (Bub) Patterson 2, John Quick 4, Katherine Rensel 2, Pam Riddick 2, Larry Riggs 2, Roger Sawyers 4, Marco Trawick 4, Valentine Vela 3, Tooter Walker 1, Jerry Watson 3, Mr. Wilson 2.

In June 1999, Deering still has the school, although small in number of students. It is called Delta C-7 and it is a consolidation of Deering, Braggadocio and Gobler schools, with Russell Gilmore as the Superintendent. The campus consists of three buildings—the 1925 two-story brick building, the 1942 WPA building and a primary building with a cafeteria. The Methodist Church continues with regular Sunday services in the original building of 1906 which they keep in good repair, with Steven Turner as minister. The post office, with the United States flag flying in front, and also a mail drop box out front, is more modern than ever with Peggy McDonald as the postmaster. The days of a barber shop and beauty shop in Deering are gone, even though Vickie Lebo has a beauty shop a mile out of town. There is no grocery store and no business office. The old cotton gin building has been converted into a storage business.

Deering Seed and Fertilizer Company, Inc.

By Johnny Calhoun

A. T. Earls, Paul B. Hutchens and Earl Vick started the business in January 1956, soon after Mr. Earls purchased Deering. After Mr. Earls' death in 1958, the two partners purchased his part of the enterprise. They operated the business for seven years. This was one of the first individual operations in the little village of Deering.

In 1965, J. E. "Jim" Ward and J. F. "Bud" Calhoun purchased the business from Paul Hutchens and Earl Vick. Jim and Bud added chemicals, farm equipment, parts, and tires to their stock so they could give better service to the farmers. Betty Calhoun was their bookkeeper.

In 1973, Ward and Calhoun sold the fertilizer, seed and chemical part of the business to Deering Fertilizer Company and moved the equipment, parts and tire business across Highway J in the old warehouse building. Jim Ward sold his share of the business to the Calhouns in the fall of 1973, and they became the sole owner. When the office building burned December 19, 1975, all the records were saved and moved to an empty house on main Street.

In 1981 the business was moved into the empty brick store

building where it remains today. In 1990 Bud Calhoun semi-retired and John Calhoun kept the business going. In 1995, Bud Calhoun retired due to ill health. John runs the business when not teaching school, so the business has survived all these years with loyal customers and we have them to thank.

Deering Fertilizer Company

By Jerry Wright

Deering Fertilizer Company has been in existence for forty-four years. It was created and owned by A. T. Earls in 1956 and is still in operation in 1999. Today it is owned and operated by ADI, which is a whole owned subsidiary of Tennessee Farmers Co-op, which is based in LaVergne, Tennessee. ADI is based in Nashville, Tennessee.

Deering Fertilizer Company sold only liquid fertilizer in the beginning. Liquid fertilizer was a totally new concept in fertilizer at this time. Allied Chemical Corporation had pioneered the liquid fertilizer business in the 1940's with the introduction of a liquid 32% nitrogen solution, which they called Uran. Uran was a liquid mixture of ammonia nitrate and urea. In the 1950's fertilizer dealers began to add phosphate and potash to the Uran and we had a complete liquid fertilizer. This was a completely new concept in the fertilizer business.

Indian Point Farm Supply was one of the innovators in the liquid fertilizer. They sold liquid fertilizer to farmers in Athens, Illinois. This company also constructed liquid fertilizer plants. They had constructed the first liquid fertilizer plant in the Missouri Bootheel in 1954 for Pennell Capehart at Holland, Missouri. In 1954, Indian Point and A. T. Earls got together and in 1956 and Deering Fertilizer Company came into existence. A. T. Earls, who was a great innovator in farmland real estate, was now an innovator in the liquid fertilizer business.

Johnny, Freddie, Bettie (Greene) and J.F. "Bud" Calhoun. They moved to Deering in 1955 from Painton, Missouri. Betty was secretary for Earls Enterprises and "Bud" was the gin manager. Today, Johnny takes care of the affairs of the town of Deering which is owned by the Calhoun family.

In 1958 Deering Fertilizer Company was sold to Earl Vick and Paul Hutchens. Paul Hutchens was the father of the cottonseed variety called Paula. Liquid fertilizer was a success because of its easiness of handling. Their motto was "Nothing to lift but the end of the hose." At that time dry fertilizer only came in 100-pound bags. The placement of liquid fertilizer next to the crop was also another factor in the popularity of liquid fertilizer. Also you could get liquid fertilizer custom applied by Otto Bonds who worked with Deering Fertilizer Company.

Bud Calhoun and Jimmy Ward bought the Deering Fertilizer Company in 1964. The farmer begins to see that using fertilizer was a paying proposition. At that time it would cost a big fertilizer user about $10.00 per acre. Today the same amount of fertilizer would cost the farmer $40.00 per acre. The irony is that the farmer is still getting about the same price for wheat, soybeans and corn. Calhoun and Ward added farm chemicals to the business. The farmer was increasing dependency on chemicals more and more. This increased the dollar sales of the company. They also bought the Deering Lumber Company building for farm chemical storage.

In 1973, Deering Fertilizer Company was sold to Wallace Cupples, Richard Simcoke, Dean Cole, Harold Jackson and Jerry Wright. They named it Kennett Liquid Fertilizer Company and an establishment was built in Kennett. Dean Cole was the manager of the Deering branch and the buying of grain was added to that operation. The old Deering Lumber Shed was torn down and a new office and chemical storage building was added.

Deering Fertilizer Company was sold again in 1996 to ADI. The Kennett group decided to get out the fertilizer business due to the interference of state and federal government. New environmental laws made it too expensive to remain in business. ADI has completed all of the environmental requirements. They have built a new office and storage building for the seed and farm chemicals. They have discontinued the purchase of grain. We wish ADI the best of luck at Deering Fertilizer Company.

Green Oil Company, Incorporated

By Dennis and Sandra (Jordan) Green

Deering Farms built a bulk plant and service station in 1946 to service the town and farms of the area. Deering attracts trade from ten miles around. The bulk plant services 112 square miles of farmland that has good yields of cotton, soybeans, wheat, milo and rice. On the farms within Deering's trade territory are more than 900 tractors, 350 automobiles and 377 trucks according to statistics taken in March 1956 by Standard Oil Company.

Another chapter was written into Deering's history when A. T. Earls, farmer and real estate dealer of nearby Hayti, bought 3500 acres of land, including the town of Deering from Deering Farms, Inc. "I bought the farm land," Earls said, "The town was incidental."

Not interested in operating the bulk plant and service station himself, Earls wanted someone reliable to handle the business. He had been a long time customer of Standard Oil and thought it only natural to lease the business to them. They leased the plant and station for ten years in 1956 with an option to renew another ten years.

Leonard Kindred moved his wife, Elizabeth, and children Mike and Martha Jane, to Deering and became the operator of the bulk plant. He continued in this position until 1968. Kindred's father had been associated with Standard Oil in Caruthersville for many years, and Leonard had worked with him. Garvis Green and W. L. Green worked for Leonard. Gene Willis ran the service station, followed by Alvin Skinner.

Green Oil Company was established in 1968 when Dennis Green was hired as a commissioned Agent for Standard Oil Company's western region of Chicago, Illinois. Dennis and his wife Sandra purchased delivery trucks and farm equipment (furnished on the farm) from Standard Oil Company.

Dennis Green hired his father, Garvis to work for him. Garvis had worked for the former agent and was familiar with all customers and locations. He continued working for Dennis until 1981 when he succumbed from a long time illness of cancer. For several years the business had three employees. At this time all agents of Standard Oil had their own territory to service. Green Oil had a limited area to service as Kennett, Hornersville, Steele, Portageville and Caruthersville all had agents.

In 1975, all agents were terminated but given the opportunity to become a jobber operation. As a jobber, Green Oil Company received a contract to buy fuel from Standard Oil. Also the property at Deering, owned by Standard Oil, was purchased by Green Oil Co.

In the early 1980's, Green Oil Incorporated, changed the name from Standard Oil to Amoco in compliance with their supplier. In the late 1980's, Green Oil purchased the petroleum business from Stewart Oil Company of Caruthersville. In 1989, Green Oil purchased a portion of Prance Oil in Kennett, consisting of a warehouse on Fourth Street with bulk storage tanks. In both purchases they got the bulk plant equipment, delivery trucks and farm tanks and equipment furnished to customers.

In 1994 the property at 400 Fourth Street in Kennett was purchased from Burlington Northern Railroad and a branch office was built. W. L. Green, uncle of Dennis, was manager of the Kennett operation from 1989 until he retired in 1997. Brad Green, son of the owners, joined the organization in 1984 and became the manager of the Kennett office.

Green Oil Incorporated, thirty-one years later, has nine employees and services customers with bob truck and transport deliveries of diesel, gasoline, and propane in Dunklin and Pemiscot Counties.

Forrest Warehouse

By Kevin Forrest

This is the newest business added to Deering, as it only started operations a few months ago. It is located in the abandoned cotton gin building. The first cotton gin was built in Deering by the Wisconsin Lumber Company in 1929. It was replaced by a modern gin around 1946 which operated until the 1970's. Bud Calhoun was gin manager from 1956 until then. The gin was purchased by John Atwill and operated a few years.

Nucor Yomato Steel at Barfield, which is just east of Blytheville, needed more places to store its finished products. My wife Karen and I purchased this building in early 1999 and began this warehouse business. I had previously worked for this company and realized the value of its merchandise. At this time our only employees are my father, William Forrest, and myself.

APPENDIX

1900 DEERING FEDERAL CENSUS IN BRAGGADOCIO TOWNSHIP PEMISCOT COUNTY, MISSOURI

272, Enochs, Robt, head, m, Nov 1871, 28, md 2 yrs, TN TN TN, mill
    Jinnie, wife, f, May 1882, 18, md 2yrs, 1-1, TN TN TN
    Bob J., son, m, Dec 1898, 1, MO TN TN
273, Gleaves, J. M., head, m, May 1851, 48, md 23 yrs, TN TN TN, mill
    Tennessee, wife, f, June 1854, 45, md 23 yrs, 6-4, TN TN TN
    James M., son, m, Nov 1877, 23, TN TN TN, mill
    Willie, son, m, May 1885, 15, TN TN TN, mill
McMeans, R.E., boarder, m, Feb 1868, 32, TN TN TN, mill
Noblin, Oscar, boarder, m, Nov 1881, IL IL IL, mill
Worden, Mc, boarder, m, July 1881, 18, TN TN TN - mill
McCann, M, boarder, m, Dec 1855, 44, md, Cheshire England, mill
274, Thompson, G. F. head, m, Nov 1869, 30, md 10yrs, OH OH OH, sawyer
    Mollie, wife, f, June 1867, 32, md 10yrs, 1-1, TN TN TN
    Vernal, son, m, Mar 1891, 9, TN TN TN
    Allie M., dau f, Jan 1895, 5, TN TN TN
Dorr, Monra, stepson, m, July 1892, 6, TN TN TN
    Addidean, stepdau, f, Mar 1885, 15, KY TN TN
    Lillie, stepdau, f, Feb 1889, 11, KY TN TN
275, Faris, James, head, m, Jan 1869, 31, md 7yrs, MO MO IL, farmer

Lelia, wife, f, Feb 1876, 24, md 7yrs, 2-2, KY KY KY
Thomas, son, m, Mar 1894, 6, MO KY MO
Bennie, son, m, May 1896, 4, MO KY MO
Albright, James, boarder, m, June 1869, 30, MO AR AR, mill
Adams, Neal, boarder, m, Aug 1879, 20, MO MO MO, teamster
Haborn, Henry, boarder, m, Aug 1874, 26, KY KY KY, sawyer
Charles, boarder, m, Feb 1883, 17, KY KY KY, mill
276, Skinner, T, head, m, Aug 1861, 38, md 17yrs, KY KY KY, boalt cutting
Mettie, wife, f, June 1850, 49, md 17yrs, 11-8, MO AL AL
Bertha, dau, f, June 1889, 10, MO KY MO
277, (Laborn?), C. B., head, m, Apr 1853, 47, md 9yrs, KY KY MO, mill
Sallie, wife, f, Mar 1870, 30, md 9yrs, 6-5, KY KY KY
Ida, dau, f, Dec 1887, 12, KY KY KY
Jess, son, m, Sept 1892, 8, KY KY KY
James, son, m, Mar 1893, 7, KY KY KY
Lene, dau, f, July 1894, 5, MO KY KY
Rena, dau, f, Feb 1898, 1, MO KY KY
Ollie, son, f, May 1900, 3/12, MO KY KY
278, Welch, James, head, m, Nov. 1858, 41, md 6yrs, KY KY KY, farmer
Mary, wife, f, May 1877, 23, md 6yrs, 3-3, MO TN TN
Minnie, dau, f, Feb 1890, 10, MO MO KY
Nora B., dau, f, Oct 1895, 4, MO MO KY
Jessie R., son, m, Nov 1899, 2, MO MO KY
Clarcy L., dau, f, Jan 1900, 9/12, MO MO KY
Hunt, Jess, boarder, m, Dec 1850, 49, md 28yrs, TN TN TN, farmer
279, Sanders, Jess, head, m, July 1874, 25, md 5yrs, KY KY IL, farmer
Rosie, wife, f, Feb 1880, 20, md 1yr, AR AR AR
Killgore, Lillie, mother, f, Jan 1855, 45, md 20yrs, 5-5, AR AR AR
Effie, dau, f, June 1888, 11, AR AR AR

John, son, m, Nov 1891, 8, AR AR AR
Willie, son, m, Nov 1891, 8, AR AR AR
280, Clayton, John, head, m, Feb 1869, 31, md 11yrs, KY KY KY, farming
Almeda, wife, f, Nov 1873, 26, md 11yrs, 5-3, KY KY KY
James L., son, m, May 1894, 6, MO KY KY
Jessee C., son, m, Feb 1897, 3, MO KY KY
281, Coleman, W.M., head, m, Oct 1856, 43, md 13yrs, VA NC NC, farmer
Mary S., wife, f, Oct 1855, 44, md 13yrs, 0-0, TN TN TN
Clayton, Starling, boarder, m, May 1835, 65, wd, KY KY AL

The above are the last households in the Braggadocio Township 1900 census.
It is believed they are the small town of Deering beginning to be settled.
Month and year of birth is given, along with length of marriage.
3-2 is number of children born to her and number of children now living.)

1910 DEERING
in BRAGGADOCIO TOWNSHIP, PEMISCOT COUNTY, MISSOURI, FEDERAL CENSUS

Alonzo Kersey was the enumerator of this 1910 census and he did not make notations at the top of each page exactly where he was in the township. Perhaps by making mention of some of the history I know about this area, it can help in figuring where the people lived. It seems to me that he began his enumeration of near Deering at about household 105-106. James Robertson was enrolled in the Deering school in 1907, as were the Kinnamon children in 106-107 and the Springer children in 108-109.

109-110 household of Jake Murphy was in Deering, as Mary Putman (who married Burl Williams) was living with them. They lived on the west side of Deering where the WPA high school building is today. She is the one who supplied me with pictures and data about early Deering, as she was only nine years old when she came here with her brother Charlie. She supplied data for one of the essays in this book.

In the census, it gives the number of times they had married just to the right of "md", following by how many years that couple had been married. 7-5 means the mother had given birth seven times and five children are still living. Census were, and still are, taken every ten years. In the 1920 census, Deering is also at the end of the enumeration. The 1920 census is also reprinted in this book.

106 Robertson, Charles, head, m, w, 26, md, 6 yrs, TN TN TN-farmer
    Vick, wife, f, w, 24, md. 6 yrs, 3-3, TN TN TN
    Youma, son, m, w, 5, TN TN TN
    Roy, son, m, w, 4, TN TN TN
    Archie, son, m, w, 2 TN TN TN
Robertson, James, hired man, m, w, 15, s, TN US US-farm labor

107 Kinnamon, James, head, m, w, 33, md2, 10 yrs, KY TN TN-farmer
    Lela, wife, f, w, 30, md2, 10 yrs, 4-4, KY KY KY
    Ruth, daughter, f, w, 9, KY KY KY
    Leda, daughter, f, w, 6, KY KY KY
    Lucile, daughter, f, w, 4, KY KY KY
    Clarise, daughter, f, w, 1, MO KY KY
108 Mills, Frank, head, m, w, 32, md1, 12 yrs, IND IND IND-odd jobs
    Ina, wife, f, w, 28, md1 12 yrs, 3—2 IND IND Kansas
    Genet E. daughter, f, w, 4, IND IND IND
    Alice L., daughter, f, w, 1,ARK IND IND
Echols, William, father in law, m, w, 52, widow, IND IND IND
Mills, Clarence B. nephew, m, w, 18, s, IN IN IN-photographer
109 Springer, Virgie, head, m, w, 34, md1 9 yrs. KY KY KY-farm labor
    Mattie, wife, f, w. 26, md1, 9 yrs, 4-3, KY KY KY
    Stella, daughter, f, w, 8, KY KY KY
    Beulah, daughter, f, w, 6, KY KY KY
    Samuel, son, m, w, 2, KY KY KY
110 Murphy, Jake, head, m, w, 49, md2, 2 yrs, IL OH VA-farmer
    Rosie M. wife, f, w, 28, md1, 2 yrs, 1-1, IL IL OH
    Russell, son, m, w, 2, MO ILL ILL
Putman, Mary, f, w, 10, ILL ILL ILL
111 Sexton, Timothy, head, m, w, 52, md1, 20 yrs, AR NC NC-farmer
    Martha, wife, f, w, 50, md2, 20 yrs, 2-2, TN US US
Friend, Lathy, hired man, m, w, 21, md1, 3 yrs,VA US US-farm labor
    Annie, f, w, 19, md1, 3 yrs, 1-1, ARK TN MS
    William B., m, w, 1, ARK MO ARK
Murray, Ed, lodger, m, w, 36, single, MO Ireland VA-odd jobs
112 Oliver, Boyce, head, m, w, 30, md1, 9 yrs, KY KY KY-farmer
    Beulah, wife, f, w, 27, md1, 9 yrs, 3-1, TN TN KY
    Clyde, son, m, w, 5, MO KY TN

Hayes, Erwin, cousin, , m, w, 19, single, TN TN KY-laborer
113 Waldrop, Tom, head, m, w, 42, md, 20 yrs, MO MS MO-farmer
  Rosie, wife, f, w, 36, md, 20 yrs, 6-3,TN TN TN
  Wisey, daughter, f, w, 13, MO MO TN
  Levi, son, m, w, 11,MO MO TN
  Beulah M.daughter, f, w, 7, MO MO TN
  Wilce, son, m, w, 24, single, MO MO TN-farmer
Acuff, John, nephew, m, w, 21,single, MO MO MO
114 Curtner, Tom, head, m, w, 49, md2, 13 yrs,MO US US-farmer
  Lily, wife, f, w, 32, md1, 13 yrs, 4-3, MO TN AL
  Luther, son, m, w, 11, MO MO MO
  Connie, daughter, f, w, 7, MO MO MO
  Carrie, daughter, f, w, 3, MO MO MO
Clayton, Hiram A., hired man, m, w, 20, s, MO KY KY-laborer
115 Hopper, Thomas, head, m, w, 45, md 17 yrs, KY KY KY-farmer
  Annie E., wife, f, w, 36, md 17 yrs, 0-0, KY KY KY
Curron, Frank, hired man, m, b, 27, single, TN TN TN-laborer
Patterson, Charles, hired man, m, b, 20, s, MO US US-laborer
Johnson, Floyd, hired man, m, w, 25, s,MO US US-laborer
116 Swan, Ed, head, m, w, 27, md 07/12, MO US US-sawmill
  Jessie, wife, f, w, 20, md 07/12- 0-0, IND TN ARK-
Smith, Rood, lodger, m, w, 30, widow, KY US US-sawmill
117 Turner, Alfred, head, m, w, 42, md1, 15 yrs, AR US US- tie maker
  Dollie, wife, f, w, 32, md1, 15 yrs, ARK US US
Hicks, Louise, servant, f, w, 14, single, MO KY KY-servant
Simmons, Evert, m, w, 12, MO US US
Walker, Mira, f, w, 3, ARK US US
White, Sam, lodger, m, w, 19, single, KY US US-sawmill
Dye, James, lodger, m, w, 17, single, MO MO MO-sawmill
118 Charlton, Will, head, m, w, 50, md1, 19 yrs, Eng Eng Eng-sawmill

Annie, wife, f, w, 39, md1, 19 yrs, 8-3, IND IND IND
George, son, m, w, 17, single, MO England IND- clerk
Ida, daughter, f, w, 15, MO England IND
Henry, son, m, w, 8, MO England IND
119 Pemberton, Will, head, m, w, 51, md, 30 yrs, IND VA KY-sawmill
Louisa, wife, f, w, 50, md1, 30 yrs, 8-6, IND IND IND
Stella, daughter, f, w, 28,—, IND IND IND
Ora, daughter, f, w, 23, single, IND IND IND-sawmill
Opha, daughter, f, 1-, single, MO IND IND
McCalister, James, lodger, m, w, 68, widow, MO US US-sawmill
Stephens, Walter, lodger, m, w, 27, md, IND OHIO IND-sawmill
120 Gaines, Edward, head, m, w, 23, md1, 5 yrs, KY KY KY-sawmill
Florence, wife, f, w, 21, md, 5 yrs, 2-2, IND IND IND
Edward, son, m, w, 4, IND KY IND
Francis, daughter, f, w, 1, MO KY IND
Allie, mother, f, w, 56, widow, KY England KY
121 Gaines, Frank, head, m, w, 21, md1,2 yrs, KY KY KY-sawmill
Minnie, wife, f, w, 18, md1, 2 yrs, 1-0, KY KY KY
122 Wilson, E. head, m, w, 22, md 1yr, MO MO ARK-sawmill
Bessie, wife, f, w, 18, md 1yr, 0-0, ILL OHIO ILL
Cash, Bob, lodger, m, w, 31, widow, KY US US-sawmill
123 Garrett, Jonas, head, m, w, 28, md1, 8 yrs, KY KY KY-sawmill
-illey, wife, f, w, 26, md1, 8 yrs, 4-2, MO MO AR
Wilson, son, m, w, 3, MS KY MO
Mary, daughter, f, w, 1 6/12, MS KY MO
124 Stewart John, head, m, w, 50, md2, 24 yrs, KY NY KY-electrician
Martha, wife, f, w, 45, md1, 24 yrs 7-5, ILL ILL TN
Avaie, daughter, f, w, 16, MO KY ILL
Worthey, daughter, f, w, 13, MO KY ILL

Irma, daughter, f, w, 7, MO KY ILL
Benson, son, m, w, 1, MO KY ILL
125 Durham, John, head, m, w, 21, md1, 1 yr, KY KY KY-sawmill
Gertie, wife, f, w, 28, md1, 1 yr 0-0, MO KY ILL
126 Williams, Ed, head, m, w, 49, md1, 20 yrs, IND ILL ILL—
Mollie, wife, f, w, 39, md1, 20 yrs, 5-4, MO Ger MO—
Charles, son, m, w, 19, MO IND MO-clerk
Claude, son, m, w, 16, MO IND MO-clearing ground
Gatewood, Omes, lodger, m, w, 30, single, KY KY KY-sawyer
Gibbs, Claude, lodger, m, w, 27, single. KY KY KY-sawmill
Wells, Charley, lodger, m, w, 56, single, MO MO MO-doctor
Mose, Charley, lodger, m, w, 34, widow, ARK TN ARK-sawmill
Dunning, Charley, lodger, m, w, 21, single, ILL ILL ILL- fireman RR
Perkins, J. W. lodger, m, w, 40, md, ARK US US-superintendent
McDavis, Frank, lodger, m, w, 37, single, VA VA VA-sawmill
Lewis, Charles, lodger, m, w, 23, single, IND IND IND-sawmill
Jenkins, George, lodger, m, w, 46, single, KY KY KY-sawmill
Mellory, Charley, lodger, m, w, 21, single, ARK ARK VA-sawmill
Byrd, J. M. lodger, m, w, 52, md1, 23 yrs, ILL ILL ILL-carpenter
Ray, Ben W. lodger, m, w, 35, md1, 4 yrs, Ireland Ire Ire-bookkeeper
Dobbs, Frank, lodger, m, w, 25, md 3 yrs, Wisconsin, NY VT-carpenter
Acors, John, lodger, m, w, 33, single, TN US US-sawmill
Hicks, Tom, lodger, m, w, 22, single, MO ILL ILL-sawmill
Ross, Dave, lodger, m, w, 39, md 13 yrs, TN TN TN-sawmill
Byrd, Ed, lodger, m, w, 20, single. TN ILL TN-sawmill
Marberry, Ada, lodger, f, w, 22, single, ILL ILL ILL- teaching
Robertson, P. W. lodger, m, w, 34, single. TN NC TN-contractor
Lancaster, Oscar, lodger, m, w, 26, md 6 yrs, TN TN TN-sawmill
Anderson, Robert, lodger, m, w, 20, s, IL Norway, MO-bookkeper WLC
Christianson, Dick, lodger, m, w, 21, s, IN Sweden IN-bookkeper WLC

Jones, Gola, servant, m, b, 29, md 1 yr. TN TN TN-servant hotel
   Selma, f, b, 26, m2, 1 yr, 2-2, TN TN TN-servant hotel
Ross, Ollie, lodger, f, w, 31, m1, 13 yrs, TN TN TN
Lancaster, Bertha, lodger, f, w, 21, md1, 6 yrs, 1-1, TN TN TN
   Clyde, lodger, f, w, 4, TN TN TN
Williams, Louie, son, m, w, 24, single, MO IND MO
Williams, Raymon, son, m, w, 6, MO IND MO
Lynn, Edward, lodger, m, w, 24, widow, ILL KY Germany-laborer
Chriswell, Luther, lodger, m, w, 38, single, ARK US US-sawmill
Hudley, Abe, lodger, m, w, 49, widow, ILL Germany ILL-timber—
127 Reed, Homer, head, m, w, 28, md1, 4 yrs, IND US US-sawmill
   Grace, wife, f, w, 21, md 4 yrs, 2-1, ILL US PA
   William, son, m, w, 2/12, MO IND ILL
   Russell, brother, m, w, 19, single, IND US US-sawmill
128 Murphy, Willis, m, w, 33, md 1 yr, IND US US-sawmill
   Mabel, wife, f, w, 18, md, 1 yr, ILL IOWA IOWA
129 Vanhoosen, Isaac, m, w, 34, md1, 12 yrs, TN TN TN-clearing ground
   Iola, wife, f, w, 28, md1, 12 yrs, 8-3, KY KY KY
   Roy, son, m, w, 10, KY KY KY
   Myrtle, daughter, f, w, 5, MO TN KY
   Otis, son, m, w, 2, MO TN KY
Byrd, Will, brother in law, m, w, 44, wd, KY KY KY-clearing ground
   Nathan, brother in law, m, w, 7, KY KY KY
130 Farris, Monroe, m, w, 60, md2, 9 yrs, TN TN TN-sawmill
   Bell, wife, f, w, 42, md2, 9 yrs, 7-3, Kansas IND IND
   Claude, son, m, w, 8, MO TN TN
Kirk, Monroe, lodger, m, w, 55, widow, KY KY KY-sawmill
Miller, Alexander, lodger, m, w, 74, widow, NC NC PA-odd jobs
131 Fromer, Dave, head, m, w, 72, widow, ILL US US-odd jobs
132 Hill, Ben, head, m, w, 33, md2, 5 yrs, IND US US-rural mailcarrier

Myrtle, wife, f, w, 27, md2, 5 yrs, 5-3, IND US IND
Mabel M, adopted daughter, f, w, 4, TN TN TN
Aleck, brother, m, w, 26, md, 3 yrs, IND US US-odd jobs
Lizzie, sister in law, f, w, 18, md, 3 yrs, 1-1, ILL ILL ILL
Hellen, niece, f, w, 2, MO IND ILL
133 Mewchum, Jesse, head, m, w, 45, md2, 15 yrs, TN TN TN-painter
Zula, wife, f, w, 30, md1, 15 yrs, 4-3, ILL MO MO
Luna, son, m, w, 6, MO TN ILL
Roy, son, m, w, 5, MO TN ILL
J. C. son, m, w, 6/12, MO TN ILL
134 DeBow, Edward, head, m, w, 46, md 22 yrs, TN TN TN-carpenter
Lizzie, wife, f, w, 49, md 22 yrs, 2-2, ILL US US
Intrchen, Katy, daughter, f, w, 21, widow, 3-2, MO US ILL
-larina, nephew, m, w, 2, MO MO MO
Clyde, nephew, m, w, 6, MO MO MO
George, adopted son, m, w, 15, single, MO US US
Range, Eliver, lodger, m, w, 25, single. MS US US-sawmill
135 Smith, Edward, head, w, m, 34, md 6 yrs, IN IN IN-lbr. inspector
Susie, wife, f, w, 37, md 6 yrs, 2-1, KY KY KY
Lenna, daughter, f, w, 17, single, KY IND KY
136 McCain, Walter, head, m, w, 46, md 17 yrs, IND US PA-sawmill
Jessie, wife, f, w, 38, md 17 yrs, 5-5, IND OHIO OHIO
Robert, son, m, w, 14, TN IND IND
Princeton, son, m, w, 12, TN IND IND
Fredie, son, m, w, 8, TN IND IND
Winnifred, daughter, f, w, 5, ARK IND IND
Wayne, son, m, w, 1, MO IND IND
137 Kirby, Albert, head, m, w, 34, md1, 9 yrs, MO TN TN-lbr.inspector
Eve, wife, f, w, 38, md2, 9 yrs, 5-4, ILL MO ILL
Edna, daughter, f, w, 5, OK MO ILL

McCollum, John, stepson, m, w, 17, single, MO MO ILL
138 Jeffers, Price, head,m,w,34, md2, 12 yrs, MO TN MO-lbr. inspector
   Iva, wife, f, w, 2-, md 12 yrs, 3-3, MO ILL MO
   Claude, son, m, w, 9, MO MO MO
   Jessee, daughter, f, w, 4, ARK MO MO
   Sallie, daughter, f, w, 2, MO MO MO
139 Sanders, Dave, head, m, w, 45, md2, 14 yrs, OH OH OH-sawmill
   Nettie, wife, f, w, 30, md 14 yrs, 0-0, ILL ILL TN
   James, son, m, w, 15, single, ILL OHIO ILL-sawmill
140 Fisher, Shelton, head, m, w, 26, md 4 yrs, MO MO MO-sawmill
   Emily, wife, f, w, 18, md1, 4yrs, 1-1, MO MO MO
   Gladys, daughter, f, w, 2, MO MO MO
141 Miller, Miles, head, m,w,34, md1, 9 yrs, MO NC IN-clearing ground
   Cora, wife, f, w, 25, md1, 9 yrs, 5-3, IND IND IND
   Harvey, son, m, w, 8, MO MO IND
   Alvey, son, m, w, 5, MO MO IND
   Reta, daughter, f, w, 3, MO MO IND
142 Harwell, John, head, m, w, 34, md1, 6 yrs, GA GA GA-sawmill
   Alice, wife, f, w, 31, md1, 6 yrs, 2-2, MO ILL KY
   Raymon, son, m, w, 3, MO GA MO
   Gladys, daughter, f, w, 9/12, MO GA MO
143 Holcombe,—, head, m, w, 31, md1, 9 yrs, KY KY KY-sawmill
   Mattie, wife, f, w, 33, md1, 9 yrs, 4-3, TN TN TN
   Halbert, son, m, w, 8. MO KY TN
   Mary, daughter, f, w, 6, KY KY TN
   Mabel, daughter, f, w, 4, KY KY TN
Mooney, Sam, brother in law, m, w, 22, single, TN TN TN-farmlaborer
144 Smith, Robert, head, m, w, 34, md1, 5 yrs, TN TN TN-sawmill

Misscie, wife, f, w, 34, md 5 yrs, 1-1, KY KY KY
Elsie, stepdaughter, f, w, 11, MO KY KY
145 Anderson, Frank, head,m,w,38, md1, 7 yrs, MO MO IL-engineer RR
Clara, wife, f, w, 36, md2, 7 yrs, 6-5, ILL ILL ILL
Chatman, Anne, stepdaughter, f, w, 14, single, MO ILL ILL
146 Durham, James, head, m, w, 49, md2, 4 yrs, KY KY KY-nightwatch
Ellen, wife, f, w, 26, md2, 4 yrs, 3-3, TN TN TN
Edith M. daughter, f, w, 2, MO TN TN
147 Atkinson, Raymon,head,m,w,28 md1,6 yrs, TN TN TN-lbr.inspector
Maude, wife, f, w, 24, md1, 6 yrs, 3-3, TN TN TN
Ruth, daughter, f, w, 4, MO TN TN
Earl, son, m, w, 3, MO TN TN
Sarah, daughter, f, w, 7/12, MO TN TN
Simpler, Mildred, servant, f, w, 19, single, ARK VA ARK-servant
148 Moore, Aaron, head, m, w, 42, md1, 18 yrs, IL KY IL-engineer RR
Lizzie, wife, f, w, 36, m1, 18 yrs, 5-3, ILL ILL ILL
Burr, son, m, w, 16, single, ILL ILL ILL
Ripley, daughter, f, w, 11, MO ILL ILL
Andy, son, m, w, 8, MO ILL ILL
149 Bond, Jay, head, m, w, 28, md1, 1 yr, PA US US-forester
Loivia, wife, f, w, 21, md1, 1 yr, 1-1, OH OH CA
Blanche, daughter, f, w, 9/12, MO PA OHIO
150 Collins, Thomas C. head,m,w,38,md1, 2 yr, OH IN OH-sawmill filer
Josephine, wife, f, w, 25, md1,2 yrs. 1-1, VA VA VA
Fay, son, m, w, 10/12, MO OHIO VA
151 Brown, George, head, m, w, 43, md1, 9/12, IN IN OH-scaler sawmill
Iona, wife, f, w, 30, md1, 9/12, MO KY MO
152 Ellrod, Amos, head, m, **b**, 50, md2, 2 yrs, TN SC TN-sawmill

Jeanette, wife, f, **b**, 26, md1, 2yrs, 4-2, MO 'un' MS
Lilburn, son, m, **b**, 3, single, MO TN MO
Plase, son, m, **b**, 1, single, MO TN MO
153 Crawford, Milton, head, m, **b**, 26, m1, 3 yrs, MS MS MS-sawmill
Julia, wife, f, **b**, 29, md1, 3 yrs, TN TN TN
Smith, Jenny, lodger, m, **b**, 59, md2, 24 yrs, GA GA GA-sawmill
Allen, Dawson,—, m, **b**, 4, TN TN TN
154 Cook, Richard, head, m, **b**, 40, md1, 17 yrs, TN TN TN-railroad
Bettie, wife, f, **b**, 37, md1, 17 yrs, 6-3, TN VA TN
Dean, Georgia, stepdaughter, f, **b**, 23, wd, 1-1, TN TN TN
Bettie, granddaughter, f, **b**, 7, ARK US TN
155 Parker, George, head, m, **b**, 29, m1, 1 yr, TN US US-sawmill
Willie, wife, f, **b**, 24, md1, 1-0, TN US US
Jackson, Joe, lodger, m, **b**, 30, single, TN U US-sawmill
Young, Sam, lodger, m, **b**, 28, single, MO MO MO-sawmill
156 Lawson, Flowers, head, m, **b**, 25, md1,1 yr, TN US US-sawmill
Georgia, wife, f, **b**, 30, md1, 1 yr, TN US US
Kathleen, daughter, f, **b**, 8, "un"
Will D. son, m, **b**, 4, "un" TN TN
Allen, Laura, lodger, f, **b**, 27, widow, TN TN TN
157 Washington, Isiah, head, m, **b**, 29, md1, 5 yrs, TN AR TN-boarding
Hattie, wife, f, **b**, 34, md2, 5 yrs, 1-0, NC NC NC
Mamer, George, lodger, m, **b**, 34, single, TN NC NC-sawmill
Smith, L. W. lodger, m, **b**, 24, single, MS MS MS-sawmill
Dawson, Buster, lodger, m, **b**, 20, single, TN TN TN-sawmill
Mailiss, Dan, lodger, m, **b**, 30, widow, KY US US-sawmill
Thompkins, Nat, lodger, m, **b**, 36, widow, MO MO MO-sawmill
Caustledy, Harrison, lodger, m, **b**, 33, single, 'un', - sawmill
Cosson, Ernest, lodger, m, **b**, 30, single, TN US US-sawmill
Allen, Boyd, lodger, m, **b**, 24, single, ARK US US-sawmill

Hurt, Bud, lodger, m, b, 31, single, TN TN TN-sawmill
Ellis, Otis, lodger, m, b, 26, widow, Neb Neb Neb-sawmill
Sanders, Adolph, lodger, m, b, 19 single, MO TN TN-sawmill
Rogers, Louis, lodger, m, b, 24, widow, ARK US US-sawmill
Taltert, James, lodger, m, b, 24, single, 'un' US US-sawmill
Johnson, Virgie, lodger, m, b, 22, single, TN TN TN-sawmill
Hobtan, Sam, lodger, m, b, 23, single, 'un' -sawmill
Williams, Jerry, lodger, m, b, 23, single, MS MS MS-sawmill
Benson, Will, lodger, m, b, 40, widow, 'un', -sawmill
Mitchel, Henry, lodger, m, b, 35, single, 'un', -sawmill
Wilson, Lon, lodger, m, b, 30, single, TN TN TN-sawmill
Lewis, Will, lodger, m, b, 36, single, US US US-sawmill
158 Rogers, James, head, m, b, 30, widow, TN TN TN-sawmill
Jackson, Nolia, cook, f, b, 33,widow, MS MS MS-hotel cook
159 Lee, Andrew, head, m, b, 34, md1, 2 yrs, AL AL AL-sawmill
    Milly, wife, f, b, 28, md2, 2 yrs 0-0, ARK ARK ARK
Nailin, Will, lodger, m, b, 22, md, KY KY KY-sawmill
Hamilton, Ora, lodger, f, b, 17, single, KY KY KY
160 Walker, Fred, head, m, b, 32, md1, 5 yrs, MS MS MS-sawmill
 Alice, wife, f, b, 38, md1, 5 yrs, 0-0, TN TN TN
161 Isreal, Joe, head, m, b, 35, md2, 5 yrs, TN TN TN-sawmill
    Hannah, wife, f, b, 32, md1, 6 yrs, 0-0, MS MS MS
Rice, Paul, mother in law, f, b, 45, md2, 16 yrs, 3-3, TN US US
162 Currise, Ike, head, m, b, 36, md1,1 yr, TN TN TN-railroad
    Suda, wife, f, b, 26, md1, 1 yr, 0-0, TN TN TN
Gailor, Annie, sister, f, b, 50, md, 1-1, TN TN TN
Kelly, George, lodger, m, b, 37, single, KY KY KY-sawmill
163 Anderson, Henry, head, m, b, 53, md2, 8 yrs, VA VA VA-sawmill
    Mattie, wife, f, b, 50, md2, 8 yrs, 1-0, MO US US
Borrum, Sam, lodger, m, b, 54, widow, MS US US-sawmill
Jones, Walter, lodger, m, b, 56, widow, TN MS NC-woodcutter
Lewes, John, lodger, m, b, 41, md, 2 yrs, MO US MS-barber
164 Harris, Zack, had, m, b, 28, md 5 yr, MO US US-sawmill

Cinda, wife, f, b, 24, md 5 yrs, 4-3, MO MO MO
Manuel, son, m, b, 4, MO MO MO
Andrew, son, m, b, 3, MO MO MO
Zack, son m, b, 1, MO MO MO
165 Terrell, Ed, head, m, b, 30, md, 4/12, US 'un', -sawmill
Rosie, wife, f, b, 19, md1, 4/12, TN TN TN
Lee, Grace, cook, f, b, 18, single, TN TN TN-cook private family
166 David, Will, head, m, b, 27, md1, 2 yrs, US 'un' 'un -sawmill
Jennie, wife, f, b, 24, md, 2 yrs, 0-0, ARK, 'un'
167 Brown, Ike, head, m, b, 25, md, 5 yrs, TN TN TN-sawmill
Jackson, Jim, partner, m, b, 33, single, TN 'un' -sawmill
168 Johnson, Will, head, m, b, 40, widow, US 'un" -sawmill
Tailor, Callie, cook, f, b, 45, widow, 2-2, US 'un' -cook private family
Elbert, lodger, m, b, 18, single, US 'un'
169 Gilbert, Charley, head, m, b, 55, md 4 yrs, MO 'un' -sawmill
Hattie, wife, f, b, 36, md 4 yrs, 1-0, MO MO MO
Lee, Georgia, lodger, f, b, 19, md. 1yr 1-1, TN TN TN
Willie, lodger, m, b, 7/12, MO ARK TN
170 Beizle, Roxie, head, m, b, 27, md 2 yrs, MS MS MS-sawmill
Willie, wife, f, b, 26, md. 2 yrs, 1-1, TN TN TN
Dave, son, m, b, 10, TN TN TN
171 Hall, Charley, head, m, b, 25, md. 4 yrs, TN TN TN-sawmill
Liza, wife, f, b, 23, md. 4 yrs, 3-3, ARK TN KY
Roselle, stepson, m, b, 6, ARK TN ARK
Green, stepdaughter, f, b, 5, ARK TN ARK
Mary, stepdaughter, f, b, 4, ARK TN ARK
Bell, Mary, mother in law, f, b, 36, widow, KY US US
172 Rice, Will, head, m, b, 38, widow, KY US US-sawmill
Jackson, Fannie, cook, f, b, 36, widow, TN TN TN-cook
173 Jenkins, Bud, head, m, b, 33, md, 4/12, OH OH OH-sawmill
Rosie, wife, f, b, 19, m 4/12, TN TN TN
174 Kellenbarger, Martin, head, m, w, 24, md. 3 yrs, OH OH OH -blacksmith

Bertha, wife, f, w, 18, md. 3 yrs, 0-0, MO MO MO
Wilson, Henry, lodger, m, w, 41, widow, MO MO MO-blacksmith
175 Tolle, Buford, head, m, w, 28, m 6/12, KS KY KY-clerk retail store
Martha, wife, f, w, 18, md 6/12, 0-0, MO IND IND
176 Ankton,Charley, head, m, b, 21, md 2 yrs , MS MS MS-sawmill
Lily, wife, f, b, 17, md 2 yrs, 1-0, MS MS MS
177 Lyed, Simson, head, m, b, 30, md. 2 yrs, SC SC SC-sawmill
Morris, Alice, f, b, 26, widow, ARK ARK ARK-cook private family
Williams, Ruth, f, b, 28, md 7 yrs, 7-3, TN US US-cook private family
Murphy, Ernest, lodger, m, b, 12,ARK US TN
James, lodger, m, b, 7,TN US TN
Henry, lodger, m, b, 5, ARK US TN
Crenshaw, Wiley, lodger, m, b, 15, single, ARK US TN
178 Crowe, Louisa, head, f, w, 48, widow, 8-7, TN TN TN
Farris, son, m, w, 15, single, TN TN TN-laborer
Oscar, son, m, w, 13, single, TN TN TN-laborer
Elvie, —, f, w, 10, TN TN TN
179 Morgan, Lula, head, f, w, 73, widow, 10-3, TN TN TN
180 Culp, David H. head,m,w,74, md2, 21 yrs, AR US US-notary public
Mary A. wife, f, w, 70, md2, 21 yrs, 2-1, IL Ger Germany
181 Long, Ernest, head, m, w, 22, md 6/12, MO MO ARK-retail clerk
Jinnie, wife, f, w, 19, md 6/12, 0-0, KY KY KY
182 Endsley, Elizabeth, head, f, w, 57, widow, 4-0, ARK NC TN
183 Long, Will, head, m, w, 50, md1, 30 yrs, TN TN TN-grocer merchant
Tina, wife, f, w, 47, md1, 30 yrs,———, ARK TN TN
Curtice, son, m, w, 27, s, MO TN ARK-grocer merchant
Bonnie, daughter, f, w, 24, MO TN ARK

Ethel, daughter, f, w, 19, MO TN ARK
　　　Emma, daughter, f, w, 17, MO TN ARK
　　　Carl, son, m, w, 12, MO TN ARK
　　　Harvey, son, m, w, 9, MO TN ARK
　　　Joy, daughter, f, w, 4, MO TN ARK
　Lambert, Frank, lodger, m, w, 47, widow, ILL ILL ILL- retail grocer
　184 Darnell, George, head, m, w, 47, md1, 24 yrs, MO TN TN-farmer
　　　Mollie, wife, f, w, 41, md1, 24 yrs, 4-3, MO TN MO
　　　Carey, daughter, f, w, 21, single, MO MO MO
　　　J. A., son, m, w, 19, single, MO MO MO-laborer
　　　Lela, daughter, f, w, 15, MO MO MO
　185 Dale, Baker, head, m, w, 28, md1, 4 yrs, ILL ILL ILL-farmer
　　　Katie, wife, f, w, 24, md2, 4 yrs, 3-3, ILL ILL ILL
　Strode, Willie, stepson, m, w, 7, MO IND ILL
　Dale, Leslie, son, m, w, 3, MO ILL ILL
　　　Lester, son, m, w, 8/12, MO ILL ILL

(These last households are Braggadocio people, and it seems evident after he did the enumeration of Deering, he went back and picked up some that were not at home in Braggadocio when he called on them the first time.)

1920 Federal Census Deering, Missouri in Braggadocio Township
The enumerator was Geo. R. Long
Taken January 19-26, 1920

197 Blue, John E., head, m, w, 40, m, Kentucky, Kentucky, Kentucky, boarding house keeper
   Daisy V., wife, f, w, 39, m, Missouri, Missouri, Tennessee, none
   Johnson, Rufus J., head, m, w, 23, m, Tennessee, Tennessee, Kentucky, Fireman on train
   Willia G., wife, f, w, 18, m, Missouri, Indiana, Missouri, none
   Evelyn, daughter, f, w, 2/12, s, Missouri, Tennessee, Missouri, none
   Wells, Charles A., none, m, w, 43, s, Missouri, Tennessee, Missouri, Doctor of medicine
   Robinson, Jessie R., none, m, w, 70, w, Kentucky, Tennessee, Kentucky, carpenter
   Broadwell J. Richard, none, m, w, 48, m, 1879, France, France, France, Lumber inspector
   Dawill, J. L., none, m, w, 54, m, Kentucky, Kentucky, Kentucky, Car foreman DSW RR
   Dawson, Frank N. none, m, w, 41, m, Illinois, Switzerland, Illinois, Supt. DSW RR
   King, Charles A., none, m, w, 25, m, Tennessee, Ohio, Tennessee, Sawer, Wis Lbr Co
   Arnold, Hoy N., non, m, w, 32, s, Kansas, Kentucky, Indiana, Machinest Hand
   Brown, Virgin, none, m, **b**, 48, w, Tennessee, Mississippi, Mississippi, cook - hotel

I left these lines for people that stayed at the hotel - this was the number told me by Mr. Blue the Hotel Keeper. But as I called at their rooms some had already been enumerated and others said they would be enumerated in other townships. Just my mistake.

198 Ownby, Robert M., head, m, w, 30, m, Arkansas, Tenn, Tenn, brakeman on railroad
   Cora B., wife, f, w, 25, m, Missouri, Missouri, Missouri, none
   Rex, son, m, w, 2 2/12, s, Missouri, Missouri, Missouri, none
   Robert W., son, m, w, 10/12, Missouri, Missouri, Missouri, none
199 Edgerton, Lorenzo D., head, m, w, 45, m, Wyo, N Y, Germany, auditor, Wisconsin Lbr
   Georgia M., wife, f, w, 44, m, Kansas, Ohio, Ohio, none
   Windfield D., son, m, w, 21, s, Kansas, Wyoming, Kansas, high school student
   Gifford D., son, m, w, 16, s, Kansas, Wyoming, Kansas, none
   Lilia M., daughter, f, w, 14, s, Kansas, Wyoming, Kansas, none
   Georgia Orlando, daughter, f, w, 10, s, Arkansas, Wyoming, Kansas, none
   Rennie D., daughter, f, w, 8, s, Arkansas, Wyoming, Kansas, none
200 Myere, John L., head, m, w, 45, m, Mississippi, U. S., U.S., Yard foreman, Wis Lbr Co
   Owxney M., wife, f, w, 35, m, Mississippi, Mississippi, Mississippi, none
   Mary Evelen, daughter, f, w, 4 3/12, s, Mississippi, Miss. Miss., none
201 Clark, J. Clyde, head, m, w, 42, m, Virginia, Va., Va., manager of dry good store

Maude, wife, f, w, 27, m, Kentucky, New York, Virginia, none

Gail, daughter, f, w, 6, s, Kentucky, Virginia, Kentucky, none

Mary C., daughter, f, w, 4 3/12, Missouri, Virginia, Kentucky, none

202 McGinty, Geo, head, m, w, 27, m, La., U. S., U. S., clerk in store

Fay C. wife, f, w, 18, m, Illinois, New York, Ohio, none

203 Garrett, Jonas J., head, m, w, 36, m, Kentucky, U. S., U. S., lumber inspector

Virginia E., wife, f, w, 27, m, Missouri, Missouri, Kentucky, none

204 Bess, Cole C., head, m, w, 63 m, Missouri, Missouri, Missouri, carpenter

Nancey C., wife, f, w, 60, m, Tennessee, Tennessee, Tennessee, none

205 Woodruff, Herbert, head, m, w, 41, m, Kentucky, Kentucky, Kentcuky, carpenter forman

Ada, wife, f, w, 30, m, Arkansas, Arkansas, Arkansas, none

Rice, Ruby M. stepdaughter, f, w, 11, s, Arkansas, Arkansas, Arkansas, none

Thermajean, stepdaughter, f, w, 10, s, Arkansas, Arkansas, Arkansas, none

206 Allatun, William R., head, m, w, 61, m, Kentucky, Kentucky, Kentucky, carpenter

Sarah E., wife, f, w, 61, m, Missouri, Tennessee, Missouri, none

Alphus B., Dr., son, m, w, 41, m, Missouri, Ky, Mo, doctor of medicine

Thelma J., granddaughter, f, w, 9, s, Missouri, Missouri, Indiana, none

Elma M., granddaughter, f, w, 5, s, Missouri, Missouri, Indiana, none

207 Ross, David J., head, m, w, 48, m, Tennessee, Indiana, Tenn,

Public works, sawmill
    Ollie, wife, f, w, 42, m, Tennessee, Tennessee, Tennessee, none

208 Manton, Frank H., head, m, w, 38 m, Illinois, Ill. Ill. cashier of DSW RR
    (Flora?) E. wife, f, w, 38, m, Iowa, New York, Ohio, none
    Glada E., daughter, f, w, 11, s, Illinois, Illinois, Iowa, none
    Doris E., daughter, f, w, 11, Illinois, Illinois, Iowa, none
    Norma J., daughter, f, w, 8, s, Illinois, Illinois, Iowa, none
    James J., son, m, w, 1 4/12, s, Illinois, Illinois, Iowa, none

209 Collier, Raymond H., head, m, w, 33, m, Illinois, U.S., U.S., Shipping clerk Wis Lbr Co.
    Ruby O., wife, f, w, 23, m, Illinois, Illinois, Illinois, none

210 Thomas James Kenneman, head, m, w, 43, m, Ky, Ky, Ky, Section foreman railroad
    Nola E., wife, f, w, 25, m, Tennessee, Tennessee, Tennessee, none
    Kinnamon, Bertha L., daughter, f, w, 15, s, Kentucky, Kentucky, Kentucky, none
    Lucille, daughter, f, w, 13, s, Kentucky, Kentucky, Kentucky, none
    Henry P., son, m, w, 8, s, Missouri, Kentucky, Kentucky, none
    Burnett, Frank, stepson, m, w, 7, s, Missouri, Kentucky, Tennessee, none
    Lonnie, stepson, m, w, 5, s, Missouri, Kentucky, Tennessee, none
    Felix G., stepson, m, w, 1 9/12, Missouri, Kentucky, Tennessee, none

211 Hargrove, Robert N. head, m, w, 31, m, Arkansas, U. S., U.S.,, conductor on railroad

Myrtle G., wife, f, w, 31, m, Missouri, Missouri, Missouri, none

(Garner?), Ada L., stepdaughter, f, w, 16, s, Missouri, Missouri, Missouri, none

Hargrove, (Genoth?), daughter, f, w, 5, s, Missouri, Arkansas, Missouri, none

Emma, daughter, f, w, 10/12, s, Missouri, Arkansas, Missouri, none

212 James W., head, m, w, 26, m, Arkansas, U.S., U. S., brakeman on train

Apalone H., wife, f, w, 17, m, Kentucky, Kentucky, Kentucky, none

213 Gray, Tom, head, m, w, 39, m, U. S., U. S. U. S., public works, saw mill

Jennie, wife, f, w, 28, m, Missouri, Kentucky, Kentucky, none

Turner, Cordia, stepdaughter, f, w, 10, s, Missouri, Kentucky, Missouri, none

Lillie, stepdaughter, f, w, 7, s, Missouri, Kentucky, Missouri, none

William J., son, m, w, 2 8/12, s, Missouri, Kentucky, Missouri, none

214 Schwartz, Huston J., head, m, w, 34, m, Arkansas, Kansas, Arkansas, work on railroad

Ora, wife, f, w, 31, m, Tennessee, Tennessee, Tennessee, none,

Anna M., daughter, f, w, 13, s, Missouri, Arkansas, Tennessee, none

George E., son, m, w, 7, s, Missouri, Arkansas, Tennessee, none

Henry H., son, m, w, 1/12, Missouri, Arkansas, Tennessee, none

215 Bell, Lenord, head, m, w, 40, m, Tennessee, Alabama, Tennessee, laborer on railroad

Tomrie?), wife, f, w, 39, m, Tennessee, Tennessee, Tennessee, none

Granada, Willis, stepson, m, w, 23, m, Tennessee, Ark, Tenn, laborer on railroad

Graham, Jim, bro in law, m, w, 52, s, Tennessee, Tenn, Tenn, laborer on farm

216 Goodman, Frank M., head, m, w, 51, m, Kentucky, , U. S., Tenn, laborer at saw mill

Leler?) M., wife, f, w, 39, m, Kentucky, Kentucky, Tennesse, none

Altha, daughter, f, w, 12, s, Missouri, Kentucky, Kentucky, none

Lee R., son, m, w, 5, s, Missouri, Kentucky, Kentucky, none

Otis, son, m, w, 1 9/12, Missouri, Kentucky, Kentucky, none

217 Raines, Elmer, head, m, w, 25, m, Tennessee, Tenn, Tenn., laborer on lumber mill

Linnie, wife, f, w, 26, m, Missouri, Tennessee, Missouri, none

Agnes, daughter, f, w, 5, s, Missouri, Tennessee, Missouri, none

John E., son, m, w, 2 2/12, s, Missouri, Tennessee, Missouri, none

Stella M., daughter, f, w, 1 3/12, Missouri, Tennessee, Missouri, none

218 Dooeze, Burrel, head, m, w, 32, m, U. S., U. S., U. S., laborer at saw mill

Mamie, wife, f, w, 21, m, Tennessee, Tennessee, Tennessee, none

Essraw, son, m, w, 2 6/12, s, Missouri, U. S. Tennessee, none

Ramond, son, m, w, 1 4/12, Missouri, U. S.,Tennessee, none

219 Simmonds, Arthur, head, m, w, 26, m, Missouri, Mo, Mo, laborer at Machine shop

Elsie, wife, f, w, 27, m, Missouri, Missouri, Missouri, none

Thomas, son, m, w, 1 5/12, s, Missouri, Missouri, Missouri, none

Johnson, Ethel, sister, f, w, 14, s, Missouri, Missouri, Missouri, none

220 Thomas, Robert, head, m, w, 22, m, Missouri, Missouri, Missouri, laborer lumber yard

Bessie, wife, f, w, 15, m, Missouri, Missouri, Missouri, none

221 Robertson, Walter P., head, m, w, 41, m, Tennessee, U. S., U. S., farmer, General Farm

Dollye J., wife, f, w, 34, m, Mississippi, Mississippi, Georgia, none

Walter P., Jr., son, m, w, 6, s, Tennessee, Tennessee, Mississippi, none

222 Parker, Howard G., head, m, w, 58, m, Maine, Maine, Maine, carpenter

Bobbie, wife, f, w, 43, m, Kentucky, Kentucky, Kentucky, none

May, daughter, f, w, 14, s, Nebraska, Maine, Kentucky, none

Georg, son, m, w, 12, s, Tennessee, Maine, Kentucky, none

223 Johnson, Jesse, head, m, w, 33, m, Tennessee, Tenn. Tenn. sawer at saw mill

Maybell, wife, f, w, 23, m, Tennessee, Tennessee, Tennessee, none

Jesse N., son, m, w, 4 2/12, s, Arkansas, Tennessee, Tennessee, none

Damond, son, m, w, 1 7/12, s, Missouri, Tennessee, Tennessee, none

224 Price, Jessie U., head, m, w, 56, m, New York, Eng., Eng., manager mill supply house

Molie/Madie, wife, f, w, 34, m, Missouri, Germany,

Missouri, none

Harvey W., son, m, w, 14, s, Arkansas, N.Y., Mo., clerk in store

Allen M., son, m, w, 13, s, Arkansas, New York, Missouiri, none

225 Allen, Geo. J., head, m, w, 56, m, Indiana, New York, U.S., saw filler

Lula J., wife, f, w, 42, m, Arkansas, Kentucky, Arkansas, none

Jennie M., daughter, f, w, 20, s, Arkansas, Indiana, Ark, school teacher

Geo J., Jr. son, m, w, 18, s, Arkansas, , Ind., Ark. saw filler helper

Mary J., daughter, f, w, 4 10/12, Arkansas, Ind., Ark., none

226 McEwing, John B., head, m, w, 48, m, Tennessee, Tenn. Tenn. night watchman saw mill

Lizzie, wife, f, w, 39, m, Tennessee, North Carolina, Missouri, none

Benita, daughter, f, w, 7, s, Missouri, Tennessee, Tennessee, none

Virginia, daughter, f, w, 5, s, Missouri, Tennessee, Tennesse, none

Robert, son, m, w, 2 10/12, s, Missouri, Tennessee, Tennessee, none

(Craomae?), America, mother in law, f, w, 78, w, Missouri, Virginia, U. S., None

227 Johnson, Corbin E., head, m, w, 29, m, Tennessee, U. S., U. S., fireman on train

Floice, wife, f, w, 28, m, Missouri, Tennessee, Missouri, none

Almaria, daughter, f, w, 7, s, Missouri, Tennessee, Missouri, none

J. R., son, m, w, 5, s, Missouri, Tennessee, Missouri, none

Clarence H., son, m, w, 7/12, s, Missouri, Tennessee, Missouri, none

Cross, Lizzie, sister in law, f, w, 24, w, Missouri, Tenn., Mo., time keeper at mill

228 Gattis, Samuel T., head, m, w, 42, m, Mississippi, Miss. Miss. machinest

Mary S., wife, f, w, 35, m, Mississippi, Miss. Miss. none

Samuel G., son, m, w, 14, s, Mississippi, Miss, Miss. none

Mary L., daughter, f, w, 12, s, Mississipppi, Miss. Miss, none Richard A., son, m, w, 8, s, Mississippi, Miss. Miss. none

229 Eheman?), Charles C., head, m, w, 31, m, Ohio, Germany, Germany, lumber inspector

Florence E., wife, f, w, 31, m, Indiana, Indiana, Indiana, none

230 Yarbro, Early E., head, m, w, 28, m, Alabama, Alabama, Alabama, laborer saw mill

Josey E., wife, f, w, 24, m, Alabama, Georgia, Alabama, none

Viola M. daughter, f, w, 2 2/12, s, Alabama, Alabama, Alabama, none

231 Wright, Silas E., head, m, w, 27, m, Arkansas, U. S., U. S., laborer DSW RR

Alice, wife, f, w, 23, m, Arkansas, Mississippi, Louisiana, none

Waymond, son, m, w, 2 6/12, Arkansas, Arkansas, Arkansas, none

232 Simmons, Everett C., head, m, w, 22, m, Mo, U. S. U. S. laborer railroad bridge gang

Lora/Love, wife, f, w, 20, m, Illinois, Illinois, Illinois, none

White, Tom, bro in law, m, w, 29, m, U. S., U. S., U. S., laborer machine shop

Lizzie, sister in law, f, w, 22, m, Illinois, Illinois, Illinois, none

233 Renfold, Horace, head, m, w, 46, m, Indiana, Ind., Illinois, butcher
    Jessie F., wife, f, w, 45, m, Illinois, Tennessee, Illinois, none
    Hubert G., son, m, w, 11, s, Illinois, Indiana, Illinois, none
    Robert P., son, m, w, 8, s, Illinois, Ind, Illinois, none

234 Black, Jules, head, m, w, 57, m, Missouri, Ill, Ill, laborer section crew railroad
    Mary M., wife, f, w, 50, m, Missouri, Ky, Ky, none
    Wilburn L., son, m, w, 24, s, Missouri, Mo. Mo. none
    Floyd H. son m, w, 18, s, Missouri, Mo, Mo. laborer section crew railroad
    Jonnie L., daughter, f, w, 12, s, Missouri, Mo, Mo, none
    Ham, Amos, none, m, w, 42, w, Tennessee, U.S., U.S., laborer railroad section crew

235 Williams, Burrel F., head, m, w, 27, m, Tennessee, Tenn, Ill, laborer machine shop
    Mary E., wife, f, w, 14, m, Illinois, Illinois, Illinois, none
    Glendol L., son, m, w, 1/12, Missouri, Tenn, Illinois, none

236 Putman, James C., head, m, w, 26, m, Illinois, Ill, Illinois, laborer saw mill
    Vida M., wife, f, w, 20, m, Missouri, Kentucky, Illinois, none

237 Gibson, Willie H., head, m, w, 52, m, Missouri, Tenn. Tenn. laborer saw mill
    Cora F., wife, f, w, 48, m, Missouri, Missouri, Missouri, ,none
    Granvill, son, m, w, 20, s, Missouri, Mo, Mo, laborer saw mill
    Lincoln H., son, m, w, 17, s, Missouri, Missouri, Missouri, none
    Rena M., daughter, f, w, 13, s, Missouri, Missouri, Missouri, none

238   White, John A., head, m, w, 26, m, Tennessee, U.S., Tenn., bridge gang
         Irene Z..., wife, f, w, 26, m, Tennessee, Alabama, Tennesse, none
         James H., son, m, w, 5, s, Missouri, Tenn, Tenn, none
         Georgia C., son, m, w, 4 0/12, s, Missouri, Tenn, Tenn, none
         Janice I., daughter, f, w, 1 3/12, s, Missouri, Tenn, Tenn, none
239   Jackson, Isaac C. head, m, w, 68, m, Indiana, U.S., U.S., laborer saw mill
         Minnie A., wife, f, w, 42, m, Kentucky, U. S., Tenn, none
         Mary L., daughter, f, w, 16, s, Missouri, Ind. Ky, none
240   Day, Roy B., head, m, w, 29, m, Missouri, U. S. U. S., sawyer at mill
         Vera, wife, f, w, 27, m, Arkansas, Tenn, Tenn, none
         Byran D., son, m, w, 7, s, Arkansas, Missouri, Arkansas, none
         Jack B., son, m, w, 5, s, Missouri, Missouri, rkanss, none
         Rollan, son, m, w, 1 2/12, s, Missouri, Missouri, Arkansas, none
241   Schemming, Frank, head, m, w, 36, m, Arkansas, Germany, Ind., stationary engineer
         Margaret, wife, f, w, 30, m, Arkansas, Ireland, Tennessee, none
         Elleen, daughter, f, w, 3 6/12, s, Missouri, Arkansas, Arkansas, none
242   Predmore, Joseph L., head, m, w, 50, m, Ohio, Ohio, Ohio, lumber inspector
         Syra J., wife, f, w, 49, m, Tennessee, Miss., Tenn. none
         Lester E., son, m, w, 8, Arkansas, Ohio, Tenn, none
243   Tipton, Andrew A., head, m, w, 45, m, Tennessee, U. S., U. S., bridge foreman
         Letha, wife, f, w, 34, m, Illinois, Tenn. Illinois, none

Lilah, daughter, f, w, 10, s, Arkansas, Tennessee, Illinois, none

Opal, daughter, f, w, 8, s, Arkansas, Tennessee, Illinois, none

Burrel, son, m, w, 2 0/12, Missouri, Tennessee, Illinois, none

244 Jackson, Charles A., head, m, w, 18, m, Missouri, Ill, Ky., laborer in saw mill

Marie, wife, f, w, 17, m, Kentucky, Kentucky, Illinois, none

Verlin, son, m, w, 9/12, s, Missouri, Missouri, Kentucky, none

Burris, Loyd, none, m, w, 19, m, Missouri, Ill. Ill. laborer railroad brakeman

Neva, none, f, w, 17, m, Illinois, Illinois, Illinois, none

245 Kinsall, Walter, head, m, w, 46, m, Illinois, Illinois, Illinois, millwright

Mattie, wife, f, w, 40, m, Illinois, Illinois, Illinois, none

Fred, son, m, w, 18, s, Illinois,, Illinois, Illinois, none

Claude, son, m, w, 15, s, Illinois, Illinois, Illinois, none

Carrie, daughter, f, w, 13, s, Missouri, Illinois, Illinois, none

Alvin, son, m, w, 1 5/12, Missouri, Illinois, Illinois, none

246 Potter, Clarence P., head, m, w, 33, m, Illinois, Ill. Ill. bookkeeper Wisconsin Lbr Co

Ruby M., wife, f, w, 30, m, Illinois, Tennnessee, Illinois, none

Clarence B. son, m, w, 8, s, Illinois, Illinois, Illinois, none

Samuel R., son, m, w, 6, s, Arkansas, Illinois, Illinois, none

Mary M., daughter, f, w, 2 2/12, s, Arkansas, Illinois, Illinois, none

247 Wallen, Nicholas R. head, m, w, 57, m, Missouri, Mo. Mo. farm laborer

Mittie, wife, f, w, 53, m, Missouri, Kentucky, Misouri, none

248   Alt?), Marie, head, f, w, 23, s, Illinois, Ill. Ill. stenographer DSW RR

248   Moore, Oce O., head, m, w, 47, m, Tennessee, Tenn. Tenn. Supt. of Wisconsin Lbr Co

    Nettie?) P., wife, f, w, 46, m, Tennessee, Tenn. Tenn. none

    Geo W., son, m, w, 24, s, Tennessee, Tenn. Tenn. druggist

    Mary L., daughter, f, w, 21, s, Tennessee, Tenn. Tenn. none

249   Smith, Alfred F., head, m, w, 26, s, Tennessee, Ind. U. S., clerk in office Wis Lbr Co.

    Johansen, Ole H., none, m, w, 39, s, Norway, Norway, Norway, cashier, Wis Lbr Co.

250   Nunnery, Douglas L., head, m, w, 30, m, Miss, Miss. Miss. mechanic machine shop

    Flora M., wife, f, w, 20, m, Missouri, Missouri, Illinois, none

    Williams, J. W., none, m, w, 72, w, U. S., U. S. U. S. preacher

251   Parker, John, head, m, b, 60, m, Mississippi, U. S., Virginia, laborer saw mill

    Mary F., wife, f, b, 45, m, Mississippi, U. S., Virginia, none

    Jones, James, stepson, m, b, 19, s, Mississippi, Miss. Miss. laborer saw mill

    Parker, Maggie L., daughter, f, b, 16, s, Mississippi, Miss. Miss. none

    Margie, daughter, f, b, 14, s, Mississippi, Mississippi, Mississippi, none

252   Reed, Henry, head, m, b, 37, m, U. S., U. S. U. S., laborer at saw mill

    Alice, wife, f, b, 38, m, Tennessee, Tenn. Tenn. none

253   Sanford, John, head, m, b, 58, m, Loisiana, Louisiana, Louisiana, trapper

    Rosa J., wife, f, b, 38, m, Alabama, Georgia, Alabama, none

Luther, son, m, **b**, 23, s, Alabama, Ala. Louisiana, laborer at saw mill

John T., son, m, **b**, 18, s, Alabama, Alabama, Louisiana, none

253 Sanford, Ollie, head, m, **b**, 25, m, Alabama, Alabama, Louisiana, laborer saw mill

Hattie, wife, f, **b**, 27, m, Mississippi, Mississippi, Mississippi, none

Murreail, daughter, f, **b**, 8, s, Mississippi, Alabama, Mississippi, none

Vivian, daughter, f, **b**, 6, s, Mississippi, Alabama, Mississippi, none

254 Robinson, Melvin, head, m, **b**, 37, m, Mississippi, Miss. Miss. hotel keeper

Sarah, wife, f, **b**, 28, m, Mississippi, Miss. Miss. none

Young, Jim, none, m, **b**, 50, w, Tennessee, Tenn. Tenn. laborer railroad

Bradford, Louis, none, m, **b**, 37, m, Tennessee, Ark. U. S., laborer saw mill

Lewis, Harrison, none, m, **b**, 26, s, Tennessee, Tenn. Tenn. laborer saw mill

Harris, Arian, none, m, **b**, 19, s, Tennessee, Tenn, Tenn, laborer saw mill

Davis, Willie, none, m, **b**, 23, s, Louisiana, N. C., N. C., laborer saw mill

Wood, Dossy, none, m, **b**, 27, s, Missouri, U. S., U. S., laborer saw mill

Ross, Commada, none, m, **b**, 17, s, Mississippi, Miss. Miss. laborer saw mill

Reeves, Minnie, none, f, **b**, 24, s, Arkansas, Tenn, Ark, servant hotel

Stewart, Bretia B., none, f, **b**, 1 2/12, s Ark, Ark. Ark., none adopted child of hotel keeper

255 Parker, Coleman, head, m, **b**, 27, m, Mississippi, Miss. Miss. laborer saw mill

Luella, wife, f, **b**, 20, m, Mississippi, Miss. Miss. none

Carrie B., daughter, f, **b**, 1 6/12, s, Missouri, Miss. Miss. none

*256 McFarland, Tom, head, m, **b**, 29, m, Mississippi, Miss. Miss. laborer at saw mill

Pearl, wife, f, **b**, 30, m, Mississippi, Miss. Miss. none

Mary, daughter, f, **b**, 6, s, Mississippi, Miss. Miss. none

Fred, son, m, **b**, 5, s, Mississippi, Miss, Miss. none

Mattie L., daughter, f, **b**, 3 4/12, s, Mississippi, Miss. Miss. none

257 Staten, Sadie, head, f, **b**, 23, w, Arkansas, U. S. U. S. cooking

Elam, Richard, none, m, **b**, 26, s, Georgia, Georgia, Georegia, laborer at saw mill

Johnson, Ike, non, m, **b**, 23, m, Arkansas, U. S., U. S., laborer at saw mill

258 Morris, Will, head, m, **b**, 38, m, Arkansas, U. S., U. S., laborer at saw mill

Pearl, wife, f, **b**, 28, m, Tennessee, Tenn., Missouri, none

Phillips, Love, none, f, **b**, 60, w, Louisiana, Louisiana, Louisiana, none

259 Nailen, Dan, head, m, **b**, 48, m, Kentucky, U. S. U. S., laborer at saw mill

Sophia, wife, f, **b**, 29, m, Mississippi, Miss. Miss. none

260 Reed, S. M. head, m, **b**, 39, m, Tennessee, Tenn, Tenn., preacher

Fesna, wife, f, **b**, 24, m, Arkansas, Miss., Tenn. none

Caldwell, Charley B., stepson, m, **b**, 6, s, Arkansas, Kentucky, Arkansas, none

261 Gray, Willie J., head, m, **b**, 30, m, Mississippi, Miss. Miss. preacher

Mary E., wife, f, **b**, 39, m, Mississippi, Louisiana, Mississippi, none

262 Clark, Geo. head, m, **b**, 52, m, Tennessee, Kentucky, Alabama, laborer saw mill

263 Penny, Henry, head, m, **b**, 30, m, North Carolina, Arka, U. S. laborer saw mill
    Alice, wife, f, **b**, 33, m, Alabama, U. S., Georgia, none
Lylas, Bob, none, m, **b**, 51, m, Mississippi, Miss. Ga, teamster
264 Wilson, John, head, m, **b**, 27, m, Arkansas, Arkansas, Ark, laborer at saw mill
    Mary, wife, f, **b**, 24, m, Louisiana, Louisiana, Mississippi, none
265 Griffen, James, had, m, **b**, 51, w, Arkansas, S. C., S. C., teamster at saw mill
Mitchell, Will, none, m, b, 32, m, Tennessee, U. S., Tenn. laborer saw mill
266 Isreal, Jere/Jas, head, m, **b**, 46, w, Tennessee, U. S., Tenn, laborer saw mill
    Rice, Pauline, mother, f, **b**, 77, w, Tennessee, U. S., U. S., none
267 Thomas, Will, head, m, **b**, 37, m, Tennessee, Tenn. Tenn. laborer saw mill
    Fannie, wife, f, **b**, 34, m, Arkansas, Ark. Ala. none
Pillow, Bettie, mother in law, f, **b**, 77, w, Alabama, Alabama, Alabama, none
268 Long, Henry, head, m, **b**, 25, m, Arkansas, Arkansas, Ark. laborer saw mill
    Katie, wife, f, **b**, 22, m, Louisiana, La. La. none
269 Davis, Eddie, head, m, **b**, un, m, U. S., U. S., U. S., laborer saw mill
    Mary, wire, f, **b**, 39, m, Mississippi, U. S. U. S. laborer saw mill
Jackson, Gladis, neice, f, **b**, 6, s, Mississippi, U. S. U. S. none
270 Brown, Charlie, head, m, **b**, 27, m, Louisiana, Miss. Miss. none
Purdy, Will, none, m, **b**, 25, m, Mississippi, Ark. , La., laborer saw mill

Crump, Ed, none, m, **b**, 28, m, Mississippi, Miss Miss, laborer saw mill

Willi, none, m, **b**, 25, s, Mississippi, Miss. Miss. laborer saw mill

271 Sims, Fred, had, m, **b**, 28, m, Mississipp,U.S. U.S., laborer saw mill

Maudie, wife, f, **b**, 25, m, Mississippi, Miss. Miss. none

271 Jackson, Will, head, m, **b**, 38, m, Louisiana, La., La., laborer at saw mill

Bertha, wife, f, **b**, 20, m, Tennessee, N.C., N.C., none

272 Hart, Beatrice, head, f, **b**, 22, m, Tennessee, Miss., Miss., none

John, son, m, **b** 9, s, Arkansas, Ark., Tenn., none

Brown, Rufus, none, m, **b**, 34, m, Mississippi, Miss. Miss. laborer saw mill

Smith, Napoleon, none, m, **b**, 22, s, Tennessee, Tenn., Tenn., laborer saw mill

Smith, Cora, none, f, **b**, 28, m, Mississippi, Miss. Miss. none

Robinson, Charlie, none, m, **b**, 22, m, Texas, Texas, Texas, laborer saw mill

273 Hunter, Oscar, head, m, **b**, 40, m, Mississippi, U.S., Ga., lumber stacker

Pearl, wife, f, **b**, 25, m, Kentucky, Miss. Miss. none

274 Dean, Richard, head, m, **b**, 38, m, Arkansas, Ark. Ark. laborer saw mill

Georgia L., wife, f, **b**, 26, m, Tennessee, Tenn. Tenn. none

Brown, Lizzie, daughter, f, **b**, 16, m, Arkansas, Ark. Tenn. none

Wilson, Geo. none, m, **b**, 50, m, Missouri, U. S., U.S., laborer lumber yard

275 Cook, Richard, head, m, **b**, 70, m, Tennessee, U.S., U.S., laborer saw mill

Bettie, wife, f, **b**, 57, m, Tennessee, N.C., Tenn., none

Syvand, Lura, none, f, **b**, 24, m, Mississippi, Miss., Miss., cooking.

276 Hunter, Condy, head, m, **b**, 49, m, Mississippi, U. S., U. S., laborer saw mill
   Katie, wife, f, **b**, 35, m, Tennessee, Tenn. Tenn. none
   Steed, Earl, grandson, m, **b**, 4 3/12, Missouri, ga Tenn. none

277 Burkes, Will, head, m, **b**, 46, m, Mississippi, Ky. Miss., laborer saw mill
   Clara, wife, f, **b**, 36, m, Mississippi, Miss. Miss. none

278 Johnson, Media, head, m, **b**, 21, m, Alabama, Okla, Ala. lumber stacker
   Minnie, wife, f, **b**, 18, m, Missouri, Tenn. none
   Freeman, Burden, head, m, **b**, 29, m, Georgia, Ga. Ga. lumber stacker
   Jonnie, wife, f, **b**, 28, m, Louisiana, Virginia, Louisiana, none
   Jeff, son, m, **b**, 10, s, Louisiana, Georgia, Louisiana, none
   Willie, son, m, **b**, 7, s, Arkansas, Georgia, Loisiana, none
   Charlie, son, m, **b**, 4 10/12, s, Arkansas, ,Georgia, Louisiana, none
   Lillie M., daughter, f, **b**, 1 10/12, Missouri, , Georgia, Louisiana, none

280 Harris, Milton, head, m, **b**, 28, m, Louisiana, La., La., lumber stacker
   Bulla, wife, f, **b**, 23, m, Louisiana, Virginia, Louisiana, none
   Lula, daughter, f, **b**, 6, s, Arkansas, , Louisiana, Louisiana, none
   Alfred, son, m, **b**, 1 2/12, s, Louisiana, , Louisiana, Louisiaian, none

281 Jones, Ivan, head, m, **b**, 29, m, Mississippi, U. S. U. S. lumber stacker
   Beckie, wife, f, **b**, 30, m, Alabama, , U. S. U. s. none

282 Nicholson, Willia, head, m, **b**, 23, m, Arkansas, , Illinois, Illinois, laborer saw mill
   Nicholson, Machenry, wife, f, **b**, 21, m, Arkansas,, Geor-

gia, Ala. none

283 Simmonds, Andrew, head, m, **b**, 30, m, U. S., U. S. U. S. laborer at store

Grace, wife, f, **b**, 22, m, Illinois, U. S., , Illinois, Illinois, none

Quentiss T. daughter, f, **b**, 6, s, Missouri, , U. S., Illinois, none

Ethel, daughter, f, **b**, 5, s, Missouri, , U. S., Illinois, none

Bernice C., daughter, f, **b**, 1 6/12, s, Missouri, U. S. Illinois, none

284 Taylor, John, head, m, **b**, 30, m, MississippiMiss. Miss. laborer black state saw mill

Delsecie, wife, f, **b**, 20, Mississippi, Miss. Miss. none

285 Gilbert, Charlie, head, m, **b**, 60, m, Tennessee, Tenn. Tenn. laborer livery stable

Hattie, wife, f, **b**, 46, m, Missouri, Missouri, Missouri, none

Currin, Frank, none, m, **b**, 34, m, Tennessee, Tenn, Tenn. laborer machine shop

286 Torbik, James, head, m, **b**, 32, m, South Carolina, Virginia, S. C., laborer saw mill

Gillespia, Vera, none, f, **b**, 21, s, Arkansas, Tennessee, Tennessee, none

287 Cureen, Barbara, head, f, **b**, 43, m, Illinois, Mississippi, Mississippi, none

288 Grey, Charlie, head, m, **b**, 57, s, Tennessee, U. S., U. S., laborer at store

Wilson, Silles, none, f, **b**, 65, m, Mississippi, Miss. Miss. cook

Dye, Joe, none, m, **b**, 26, m, Mississippi, U. S. U. S. laborer saw mill

Ezell, Bob, none, m, **b**, 40, m, Texas, U. S. U. S. laborer lumber yard

289 Donnel, Willie, head, m, **b**, 22, m, Mississippi, Miss. Miss. laborer lumber

Willie May, wife, f, **b**, 27, m, Mississippi, S. C., West Virginia, none

290 Hobson, Geo W., head, m, **b**, 46, m, Mississippi, Miss. Miss. night watchman

Willie May, wife, f, **b**, 27, m, Mississippi, Miss. Miss. none

291 Sumrall, Frank, head, m, **b**, 23, m, Mississippi, Miss. Miss. laborer saw mill

Susie, wife, f, **b**, 19, m, Mississippi, Miss. Miss. none

292 James, Geo. head, m, **b**, 22, m, Loisiana, Louia, Louis, oiler at saw mill

Virginia J., wife, f, **b**, 28, m, Arkansas, Alabama, Kentucky, none

Moore, Elina, stepdaughter, f, **b**, 10, s, Arkansas, Alabama, Arkansas, None

293 Burrell, Will, head, m, **b**, 34, m, Louisiana, La. La., laborer saw mill

Bomona, wife, f, **b**, 28, m, Louisiana, La. La. none

Benard, son, m, **b**, 8, s, Arkansas, La. La, none

293 Washington, Eliza, head, m, **b**, 34, m, Tennessee, U. S. U. S., laborer lumber yard

Violet, wife, f, **b**, 30, m, Arkansas, Alabama, Alabama, none

294 Reynolds, Elie, head, m, **b**, 29, m, ouisiana, La. La. laborer lumber yard

Maude, wife, f, **b**, 29, m, Georgia, Georgia, Georgia, none

295 Hicks, Morris, had, m, **b**, 31, m, Tennessee, U. s. U S. laborer saw mill

Lula, wife, f, **b**, 31, m, Georgia, Georgia, Georgia, none

Presker, S., son, m, **b**, 11, s, Georgia, Georgia, Georgia, none

Simmonds, Phobe, none, f, **b**, 64, w, Alabama, Kentucky, South Carolina, none

296 Hooder, Berry, head, m, **b**, 27, m, Tennessee, Tenn., Ark.

laborer lumber yard

Johnie, wife, f, **b**, 17, m, Alabama, Ala. Ala. none

296 Prayor, John, head, m, **b**, 37, m, Iowa, Iowa, Georgia, laborer rail road

297 Prayor, Emmabet, wife, f, **b**, 26, m, TennesseeTenn. Tenn. none

Gardner, Simpson, none, m, **b**, 23, s, Mississippi, Texas, Miss., laborer railroad

298 Steward, Henry Y., head, m, **b**, 33, m, Arkansas, Ark. Ark. barber

Irene, wife, f, **b**, 28, m, Louisiana, Ala. La. school teacher

Henry Jr., son,m, **b**, 7, s, Arkansas, Ark. Louisiana, none

Francis C. daughter, f, **b**, 6, Missouri, Arkansas, Louisiana, none

299 Partee, Thomas, head, m, **b**, 45, m, Tennessee, U. S. U. S. laborer lumber yard

Partee, Mary, wife, f, **b**, 25, m, Illinois, U. S. U. s. none

300 Anderson, Henry, head, m, **b**, 50, m, U. S, U. S. U. S. laborer saw mill.

Martha A., wife, f, **b**, 50, m, Mississippi, Georgia, Georgia, none

Jackson, R. W., stepson, m, **b**, 9, s, Missouri, U. S., Mississippi, none

301 Gillbert, Charlie, had, m, **b**, 54, m, Tennessee, N. C., Tenn. feeder of stock

302 Carson, Ernest, head, m, **b**, 37, s, Texas, Georgia, Tenn. laborer lumber yard

Scott, Robert, none, m, **b**, 32, s, Arkansas, Miss. Miss. laborer lumber yard

303 House, Will, had, m, **b**, 40, m, U. S., U. S. U. S. laborer saw mill

Hoskin, Mary, none, f, **b**, 21, m, Mississippi, Miss. Miss. none

304 Shammon, Love, had, m, **b**, 55, m, Tennessee, U. S. U. S. laborer saw mill

Ruthey, wife, f, **b**, 33, m, Mississippi, U. S. Miss., none

Arnold, Annie, mother in law, f, b, un, un, Mississippi, U. S. U. S. none

305 Prater, John, head, m, b, 38, s, Mississippi, Miss. Miss. labor farm, General Farm

Miller, Mary, mother, f, b, 56, w, Mississippi, South Carolina, South Carolina, none

Rodger, half bro, m, b, 13, s, Mississippi, Miss. Miss. none

Caro, half bro, m, b, 11, s, Mississippi, Miss. Miss. none

Cassibell, half bro, m, b, 9, s, Mississippi, Miss. Miss. none

Lurenza, half sister, f, b, 7, s, Mississippi, Miss. Miss. none

306 Thomas, John, head, m, b, 43, m, Mississippi, U. S., U. S., laborer saw mill

Rinca, wife, f, b, 23, m, Mississippi, Miss. Miss. none

Bird Virddie, son, m, b, 6/12, Missouri, Miss. Miss. none

307 Wemer, Geo. P., head, m, w, 28, m, Illinois, Germany, Illinois, agent depot

Leila, wife, f, w, 27, s, Illinois, Illinois, Illinois, none

308 Sands, Geo W. head, m, w, 35, m, Missouri, U. S. U. S., blacksmith

Ida E., wife, f, w, 31, m, Missouri, Missouri, Missouri, none

George H., son, m, w, 11, s, Missouri, Missouri, Missouri, none

Mary L., daughter, f, w, 9, s, Missouri, Missouri, Missouri, none

Vera M., daughter, f, w, 7, Missouri, Missouri, Missouri, none

Myrdle B., daughter, f, w, 4 6/12, s, Missouri, Missouri, Missouri, none

308 Cobbs, Charlie, head, m, b, un, m, Arkansas, U. S. U. S. laborer machine shop

Mattie M., wife, f, **b**, 36, m, Tennessee, Kentucky, Tennessee, none

Grant, Katie, daughter, f, **b**, 20, m, Arkansas, Mississippi, Tennessee, none

309 Curtis, H. M., head, m, w, 33, m, Tennessee, Tenn. Tenn. farm laborer

Media, wife, f, w, 32, m, Tennessee, Tenn. Tenn. none

Lula, daughter, f, w, ll, s, Tennessee, Tenn. Tenn. none

Ailie, daughter, f, w, 9, s, Tennessee, Tenn. Tenn. none

Ellen M., daughter, f, w, 7, s, Missouri, Tenn. Tenn. none

Cordell, Fred, none, m, w, 18, s, U. S., U. S., U. S., orphan boy

310 Alexander, Raniell, head, m, **b**, 49, m, Illinois, U. S. Illinois, farmer, General Farm

Flora, wife, f, **b**, 32, m, Missouri, Arkansas, Arkansas, none

James R., son, m, **b**, 8, s, Missouri, Illinois, Missouir, none

Central, son, m, **b**, 0/12, s, Missouri, Illinois, Missouri, none

Franklin, Janie, none, f, **b**, 49, s, Louisiana, Kentucky, U. S., servant in home

311 Majors, Tom, head, m, w, 38, m, Missouri, Missouri, U. S., farmer, General Farm

Lena, wife, f, w, 32, m, Missouri, Tennessee, Tennessee, none

Alline, daughter, f, w, 10, s, Missourik Missouri, Missouir, none

Emma, daughter, f, w, 8, s, Arkansas, Missouri, Missouri, none

Roy, son, m, w, 5, s, Arkansas, Missouri, Missouri, none

Troy, son, m, w, 2/12, Missouri, Missouri, Missouri, none

312 Barkesdale, Willie, head, m, w, 29, m, Tennessee, Tenn. Tenn. farmer, General Farm

Lulu, wife, f, w, 27, m, Tennessee, Tennessee, Tennessee, none

Horace, son, m, w, 6, s, Missouri, Tennessee, Tennessee, none
Edgar, son, m, w, 5, s, Arkansas, Tennessee, Tennessee, none
Marie, daughter, f, w, 8/12, s, Arkansas, Tennessee, Tennessee, none
Margaret, daughter, f, w, 0/12, s, Missouri, Tennessee, Tennessee, none

313 Oak, Ivory, head, m, w, 33, m, Missouri, Tennessee, Missouri, farm laborer
Hollie E., wife, f, w, 30, m, Missouri, Missouri, Missouri, none
Gordon H., son, m, w, 12, s, Missouri, Missouri, Missouri, none
Nova A., daughter, f, w, 7, s, Missouri, Missouri, Missouri, none
Glenda C.daughter, f, w, 5, s, Missouri, Missouri, Missouri, none
Sherman H., son, m, w, 10/12, s,Missouri, Missouri, Missouri, none

314 Hasting, Flurina B., head, f, w, 44, w, Tennessee, Tenn. Tenn. housekeeper
Bruce, son, m, w, 16, s, Tennessee, Tenn. Tenn. laborer railroad section gang
J. T., son, m, w, 5, s, Missouri, Tenn. Tenn. none

314 Robinson, Albert, none, m, w, 34, s, Kentucky, Kentucky, Kentucky, carpenter

315 Vaughn, Ed, had, m, w, 32, m, Kentucky, Ky, Ky, laborer at saw mill
Izora M., wife, f, w, 38, m, Arkansas, Ark. Ark. none
Vaughn, Aggie, mother, f, w, 58, w, Kentucky, Kentucky, none

316 Gibson, Rodger, head, m, w, 26, m, Missouri, Texas, Missouri, laborer Sec gang RR
Elta, wife, f, w, 20, m, Tennessee, Tenn. Tenn. none

317 Worley, Fred, head, m, w, 25, m, Missouri, Mo, Mo., laborer sec gang RR
Levy, wife, f, w, 17, m, Tennessee, Tenn. Tenn. none
318 Copple, Gather, head, m, w, 41, m, Illinois, Ill. Ill. laborer saw mill
Eva M., wife, f, w, 32, m, Illinois, Illinois, Illinois, none
Lillie M., daughter, f, w, 11, s, Missouri, Illinois, Illinois, none
Thelma I., daughter, f, w, 9, s, Missouri, Illinois, Illinois, none
Lewis A., son, m, w, 8, s, Missouri, Illinois, Illinois, none
Chester A., son, m, w, 6, s, Missouri, Illinois, Illinois, none
Sherman M., son, m, w, 4 0/12, Missouri, Illinois, Illinois, none
319 Johnson, Carl O., head, m, w, 35, m, Kentucky, Ky, Ky, farm laborer
Mamie B., wife, f, w, 22, m, Tennessee, Tennessee, Tennessee, none
Ora V., daughter, f, w, 7, s, Missouri, Kentucky, Tennessee, none
Ethel, daughter, f, w, 2 0/12, s, Missouri, Kentucky, Tennessee, none
*320 Williams, William M., head, m, w, 44, m, Kentucky, Tenn. Germany, merchant
Carlis J., wife, f, w, 27, m, Arkansas, Tenn. Tenn. none
Boyd R., son, m, w, 9, s, Tennessee, Kentucky, Arkansas, none
Robert L., son, m, w, 8, s, Missouri, Kentucky, Arkansas, none
Ruby N, daughter, f, w, 3 10/12, s, Missouri, Kentucky, Arkansas, none
William E., son, m, w, 1 2/12, Missouri, Kentucky, Arkansas, none
Tidwell, Kathryn T., mother in law, f, w, 55, w, Tennessee, Tennessee, Tennessee, none

Ramond E., nephew, m, w, 9, s, Missouri, Arkansas, Missouir, none

Stallings, Floyd J., none, m, w, 24, m, Missouri, U. S., U. S., laborer railroad

Julia E., none, f, w, 20, m, Missouri, Missouri, Missouri, none

Larma B., none, f, w, 3 9/12, s, Missouri, Missouri, Missouri, none

Lillian P., none, f, w, 11/12, s, Missouri, Missouri, Missouri, none

321 Ross, Charlie E., head, m, w, 26, m, Tennessee, Arkansas, Arkansas, barber

Myrtle, wife, f, w, 24, m, Arkansas, Arkansas, Arkansas, none

Robert L., son, m, w, 6, s, Arkansas, Tennessee, Arkansas, none

Lelia B., daughter, f, w, 28, s, Arkansas, Tennessee, Arkansas, None

322 Henning, Larena F., head, m, w, 37, m, Kentucky, Kentucky, Kentucky, carpenter

Mattie J., wife, f, w, 45, m, Missouri, Iowa, Iowa, none

Jenkins, Bornie E., stepson, m, w, 25, w, Arkansas, Missouri, Missouri, laborer saw mill

Henning, Kennith L., son, m, w, 10, s, Missouri, Kentucky, Missouri, none

323 Miller, Miles A., head, m,w, 45, m, Missouri, N. C., Indiana, farm laborer

Cora E., wife, f, w, 35, m, Indiana, Indiana, Kansas, none

Harry A., son, m, w, 18, s, Missouri, Mo. Ind., laborer on farm

Clarence A., son, m, w, 15, s, Missouri, Missouri, Indiana, none

Reta R., daughter, f, w, 13, s, Missouri, Missouri, Indiana, none

William H., son, m, w, 8, s, Missouri, Missouri, Indiana, none

Cora M., daughter, f, w, 1 6/12, s, Missouri, Missouri, Indiana, none

324 Ezell, Francis L., head, m, w, 50, m, Tennessee, Tenn. Tenn. carpenter

Carrie B., wife, f, w, 48, m, Tennessee, Tenn. England, none

Jones, Ernestine C., grandchild, f, w, 8,s, Tennessee, Tennessee, Tennessee, none

325 Murphy, Jacob N., head, m, w, 56, m, Illinois, Ohio, Ohio, farmer, General Farm

Rosa M., wife, f, w, 37, m, Illlinois, Illinois, Illinois, none

Russell N., son, , w, 11, s, Missouri, Illinois, Illinois, none

Douglas F., son, m, w, 3 8/12, s, Missouri, Illinois, Illinois, none

326 Baxter, Isom, head, m, w, 23, m, Kentucky, Tenn. Tenn. laborer lumber yard

Willie E., wife, f, w, 17, m, Kentucky, Kentucky, Kentucky, none

327 Mitchell, Fred, head, m, w, 28, m, Tennessee, Michigan, Tenn. farmer, General Farm

Chloe M., wife, f, w, 23, m, Kentucky, Kentucky, Kentucky, none

Omer F., son, m, w, 5, s, Missouri, Tennessee, Kentucky, none

Plaska E., daughter, f, w, 3 3/12, s, Missouri, Tennessee, Kentucky, none

Burma C., son, m, w, 4/12, s, Missouri, Tennessee, Kentucky, none

328 Robinson, Will, head, m, **b**, 45, m, Missouri, Michigan, Michigan, farmer, General Farm

Leona, wife, f, **b**, 35, m, Michigan, U. S. U. S., none

329 Morgan, Charles E., head, m,w, 27, m, Missouri, Missouri, Missouri, farmer

Ethel L., wife, f, w, 22, m, Arkansas, Indiana, Tennessee, none

330 Baker, Spencer, head, m, **b**, 47, m, Mississippi, Miss. Miss. farmer, General Farm
Oliver, son, m, **b**, 15, s, Mississippi, Miss. Miss. none
Caline, mother, f, **b**, 55 or 65, w, Mississippi, Miss. Miss. none

331 Ash, Elike E., head, m, w, 27, m, Tennessee, Tenn.Tenn. farmer, General Farm
Lillie V., wife, f, w, 29, m, Tennessee, Tenn. Tenn. none
William H., son, m, w, 4 0/12, s, Missouri, Tenn. Tenn, none
Richmond, Sam, none, m, w, 22, w, Arkansas, U. S., Missouri, farm laborer

332 Downs, Walter, head, m, w, 26, m, Missouri, Tenn. Mo. farming laborer
Minnie, wife, f, w, 17, m, Mississippi, Missisippi, Mississippi, none
Minnie, daughter, f, w, 2/12, s, Missouri, Missouri, Mississippi, none

333 Downs, Berry, head, m, w, 67, m, Tennessee, Tenn. Tenn. farmer
Lee, wife, f, w, 49, m, Missouri, Tenn. Georgia, none

334 Downs, Dave, head, m, w, 22, m, Missouri, Tenn. Missouri, farmer
Emma, wife, f, w, 22, m, Alabama, Arkansas, Alabama, none

*335 Connor, Miller H., had, m, w, 47, m, Indiana, Ind. Ind. farmer, General Farm
Mary J., wife, f, w, 39, m, Indiana, Ind. Ind. none
Clayborne M., son, m, w, 9, s, Indiana, Ind. Ind. none
Mosley, John T., father in law, m, w, 71, m, Indiana, Ind. none
Lettitia A., mother in law, f, w, 61, m, Indiana, Ind. Ind. none

336 Moore, Will, head, m, w, 36, Illinois, Ill. Ill. farmer laborer
Beckie Pearl, wife, f, w, 29, m, Missouri, Missouri, Missouri, none
Ralph J., son, m, w, 9, s, Missouri, Illinois, Missouri, none
Sylvia S., daughter, f, w, 6, s, Missouri, Illinois, Missouri, none
William A., son, m, w, 4 6/112, s, Missouri, Illinois, Missouri, none
Alice, daughter, f, w, 2 5/12, s, Missouri, Illinois, Missouri, none
Walker, Earl, none, m, w, 29, s, Missouri, U. S. U. S. farm laborer

337 Davis, Willis, head, m, w, 33, m, Missouri, U. S., U. S., laborer saw mill
Emma, wife, f, w, 25, m, Tennessee, U. S., U. S., none
Clarence E., son, m, w, 8, s, Missouri, Missouri, Tennessee, none
Ray X., son, m, w, 3 3/12, s, Missouri, Missouri, Tennessee, none
Gladis M., daughter, f, w, 11/12, Missouri, Missouri, Tennessee, none
Smith, Ethel M., neice, f, w, 10, s, Missouri, U. S., Tennessee, none

338 Murphy, Finnely L., head, m, w, 32, m, Missouri, Illinois, U. S., farmer, General Farm
Bertha E., wife, f, w, 24, m, Missouri, Missouri, Missouri, none
Gladis M., daughter, f, w, 8, s, Missouri, Missouri, Missouri, none
William L., son, m, w, 1 9/12, s, Missouri, Missouri, Missouri, none

339 Ferrol, Eff, head, m, w, 39, m, Tennessee, U. S. U. S., farmer, General Farm
Bettie F., wife, f, w, 37, m, Missouri, Tennessee, Missouri, none

Willie, son, m, w, 9, s, Missouri, Tennessee, Missouri, none

John, son, m, w, 5, s, Missouri, Tennessee, Missouri, none

Levi, son, m, w, 3/12, s, Missouri, Tennessee, Missouri, none

Wells, Louis, stepson, m, w, 17, un, Missouri, Kentucky, Missouri, none

Sydney, stepson, m, w, 14, s, Missouri, Kentucky, Missouri, none

340 Jackson, Jess, head, m, w, 25, m, Illinois, Ill. Ill. farm laborer

Mary, wife, f, w, 18, m, Missouri, Kentucky, Missouri, none

341 Garrett, Allen W., head, m, w, 45, m, Kentucky, Ky, Ky, farmer, General Farm

Fannie L, wife, f, w, 39, m, Kentucky, Kentucky, Kentucky, none

Coy F., son, m, w, 18, s, Kentucky, Ky, Ky, laborer on farm

Ruby O., daughter, f, w, 14, s, Kentucky, Kentucky, Kentucky, none

Hubbert E., son, m, w, 12, s, Kentucky, Kentucky, Kentucky, none

Ray W., son, m, w, 10, s, Kentucky, Kentucky, Kentucky, none

Barney W., son, m, w, 5, s, Kentucky, Kentucky, Kentucky, none

342 Hayes, Clarence, had, m, w, 29, s, Missouri, Missouri, Missouri, farm laborer

Hurt, James, nephew, m, w, 10, s, Missouri, Missouri, Missouri, none

*343 Waldrop, John T., head, m, w, 51, m, Missouri, Tenn. Missouri, farmer, General Farm

Rosa L, wife, f, w, 46, m, Tennessee, Tennessee, Tennessee, none

Bulla, daughter, f, w, 17, un, Missouri, Missouri, Tennessee, none
Ethel, daughter, f, w, 8, s, Missouri, Missouri, Tennessee, none
Tommie, son, m/f, w, 5, s, Missouri, Missouri, Tennessee, none

344 Waldrop, Edward K., head, m, w, 27, m, Missouri, Mo,Tenn, farmer, General Farm
Edith J., wife, f, w, 16, m, Missouri, Tennessee, Kentucky, none
Muerrel L., son, m, , Missouri, Missouri, Missouri, 11/12, s, none

345 Ward, John B., head, m, b, 41, m, Tennessee, Tenn, Tenn, farmer, General Farm
Viola, wife, f, b, 28, m, Arkansas, Alabama, Virginia, none
Robert, son, m, b, 18, s, Tennessee, Tenn. Tenn. laborer on farm

346 Ward, Ellie, head, m, b, 21, m, Tennessee, Tenn. Tenn. laborer on farm
Agusta, wife, f, b, 21, m, Missouri, U. S., Mo. none

347 Wilburn, Tom, head, m, b, 37, m, Tennessee, U. S. U. S. laborer on farm
Jennie, wife, f, b, 22, m, Tennessee, S. C., Mississippi, none

348 Ray, William J., head, m, w, 33, m, Missouri, Miss. Miss. laborer on farm
Minnie B., wife, f, w, 30, m,Missouri, Miss. Miss. none

349 Crane, Arthur B., head, m, w, 31, m, Tennessee, Tenn. Tenn. laborer on farm
Lessie A., wife, f, w, 28, m, Tennessee, tenn tenn. none
William H., son, m, w, 9, son, Tennessee, Tenn. Tenn. none
Hattie I., daughter, f, w, 7, s, Tennessee, Tenn. Tenn. none

  Marie E., daughter, f, w, 5, s, Tennessee, Tenn. Tenn. none
  Claude A., son, m, w, 2/12, Tennessee, Tenn. Tenn. none
*350 Webb, Geo. W., head, m, w, 61, w, Tennessee, N. C., Tenn. farmer, General Farm
  Fredia F., daughter, f, w, 19, s, Missouri, Tenn. Tenn. none
  Winfield, son, m, w, 16, s, Missouri, Tenn. Tenn. none
  Jewell, daughter, f, w, 14, s, Missouri, Tenn. Tenn. none
  Hazel, daughter, f, w, 6, s, Missouri, Tenn. Tenn. none
351 Myler, Mary M., head, f, w, 67, w, Tennessee, Tenn. Tenn. laborer on farm
  Morgan, Inez G., granddaughter, f, w, 16, s, Mo, Mo, Indiana, laborer on farm

Notes from Ophelia:

The enumerator skipped two pages in his census book when he started the enumerator of the town that is Deering.

201 - Clyde Clark was the postmaster of Deering in 1920.
235 - Mary Williams, nee Putnam, supplied me with pictures and a wealth of information.
239 - This is nee Minnie Turner.
244 - Charles Jackson is son of Isaac Jackson #239.
246 - I double-checked the spelling on this, as I felt his name should be Clarence Ponder.
320 - When the 1936 sixth-grade class was doing their history of Deering, they consulted with William M. Williams.
323 - Miles Miller lived northeast of Deering. The enumerator has now moved out of town of Deering and into the countryside to enumerate the farmers of the area.